Indians of the Southeast: Then and Now

Indians of the Southeast: Then and Now

Jesse Burt
and
Robert B. Ferguson

illustrated with original drawings by
David Wilson and photographs

ABINGDON PRESS   Nashville and New York

Library of Congress Cataloging in Publication Data

Burt, Jesse Clifton, 1921-
Indians of the Southeast.

SUMMARY: Describes the origin, history, and cultures of the Indians
of the southeastern United States from prehistoric times to the present.
Bibliography: p.
1. Indians of North America—Southern States—Juvenile literature.
[1. Indians of North America—Southern States] I. Ferguson, Robert B.,
joint author. II. Wilson, David, 1947-   illus. III. Title.
E78.S65B8   970.4'5   72-4695

ISBN 0-687-18793-1

Quotations from *Jean-Bernard Bossu's Travels in the Interior of North
America, 1751-1762,* translated and edited by Seymour Feiler, copyright
© 1962 by the University of Oklahoma Press, are reprinted by permission.

Dedicated to the memory of Emmett York,
the great Choctaw statesman whose
influence on the contemporary Indian
and non-Indian world is ever present

Foreword

Three years ago at a meeting of the United Southeastern Tribes Intertribal Council, Bob Ferguson announced that he and his friend, Jesse Burt, were writing a book on southeastern Indians of yesterday and today. Although some Indians have blended into modern-day white society, Bob said that he hoped the book would be accurate enough for use in Indian and non-Indian school libraries and that it would help correct a lot of errors in present-day histories.

I think that all of us at that meeting on the Seminole Reservation in Florida, including the late Emmett York of the Mississippi Choctaws, Johnson Catolster of the Cherokees, Betty Mae Jumper and Joe Dan Osceola of the Seminoles, and the present chairman of the Choctaws, Phillip Martin, realized the difficult task of preparing such information and the fact that it could not be perfect; however we believed that Bob and Jesse could do a good job. We know Jesse's background as a historian of the South, and we know of Bob's research and continuing involvement with the southeastern Indians.

We have not been disappointed. I believe their book is an important contribution to the knowledge of our southeastern Indian people and that it will be a valuable source book in years to come.

Most of all I believe it will help our young Indians

understand their own rich heritage better and that it will help other Americans know our problems and the ways we are working to eliminate them.

BUFFALO TIGER, *Chairman*
Miccosukee Indians of Florida

Acknowledgments

The authors and the publisher wish to express their appreciation to Prof. Adolph L. Dial, Department of History, Pembroke State University, Pembroke, North Carolina, Dr. Charles M. Hudson, Department of Anthropology, University of Georgia at Athens, and Dr. Ronald Spores, Department of Sociology and Anthropology, Vanderbilt University, Nashville, Tennessee, who read the manuscript and made helpful comments.

Acknowledgments

The authors and publishers wish to express appreciation to all those who have permitted the use of their photographs to illustrate this book. The source, location, and other pertinent information is given below for many of these.

For photographs courtesy the Smithsonian Institution National Anthropological Archives; the National Collection of Fine Arts, Smithsonian Institution; and the Smithsonian Institution National Anthropological Archives, Bureau of American Ethnology Collection, negative numbers are indicated below in **bold face** type.

The Smithsonian Institution National Anthropological Archives.
By Du Pratz: p. 76, Natchez bison hunt, neg. **45,068-B.** by Le Moyne and de Bry: p. 26, Ceremonies at the death of a chief, neg. **57,580;** p. 42, Timucua village, neg. **57,570;** p. 69, Proceedings in deliberating on important affairs, neg. **57,569;** p. 78, Depositing their crops in the public granary, neg. **57,652.** By John White: a watercolor, p. 97, Indians dancing, neg. **18,724.** De Bry engravings of John White watercolors: p. 50, Town of Secota, neg. **57,539,** and p. 55, Making canoes, neg. **44,479-C.**

Smithsonian Institution National Anthropological Archives, Bureau of American Ethnology Collection.
By Du Pratz: p. 21, Great Sun of the Natchez, neg. **1168-B-2;** p. 31, Natchez man in summer, neg. **1168-B-4;** p. 32, Natchez man in winter, neg. **1168-B-5;** p. 70, Natchez dance, neg. **1168-B-3;** p. 100, Chitimacha ceremony of the calumet, neg. **1168-B-9.** By Le Moyne and de Bry: p. 42, Timucua tilling and planting, neg. **57,561,** and p. 85, Youth at their exercises, neg. **1186-b-13.** By John White: a watercolor, p. 77, Food cooks in an open pot, neg. **867.** By Bernard Romans: p. 41, Chickasaw warrior's head, neg. **1071-B,** and p. 62, Line drawing of Choctaw burials, neg. **1102-D.** Engraving by Isaac Besire: p. 126, Cherokee Indians in London in 1730, neg. **1063-H-2.** Photographer and date not recorded: p. 172, Sho-ni-on. In Jackson *Catalogue,* published in 1877, neg. **1067.** An unidentified Chickasaw man, copied by A. Zeno Shindler, Washington, D.C., 1868, neg. **1071-A.** Painting by Frances Bernard: p. 212, Choctaw settlement, neg. **2860-zz-1.** Catawba chief Sam F. Blue and his family, p. 224, neg. **Swanton V. 1, No. 32-B.** Catawba girls in front of Mormon church, neg. **Swanton, V. 1, no. 30-E.**

The National Collection of Fine Arts, Smithsonian Institution.
Paintings by George Catlin: p. 127, Tchow-ee-put-o-kaw, neg. **1095;** p. 131, Deer Without a Heart, neg. **499-F** and Chee-a-ex-e-co, his daughter, neg. **635-B;** p. 133, Black Coat, neg. **473-B;** p. 139, Seminole woman, neg. **578-G;** p. 151, King Phillip, neg. **639-A;** p. 169, Peter Pitchlyn, Snapping Turtle, neg. **578-D;** p. 176, Ben Perryman, neg. **42095-E;** p. 177, Sam Perryman, neg. **42095-G.**

The woodcuts of Antoine Simon Le Page Du Pratz appeared in *Histoire de la Louisiane,* published in Paris in 1758. The paintings of Jacques le Moyne de Morgues, cartographer and artist for the French Huguenot colony of Fort Caroline in Florida, were engraved on copper by Theodore de Bry for *Brevis Narratio Eorvu Qvae in Florida Americae Provincia,* Frankfurt-am-Main, 1591. John White was artist and cartographer for the Roanoke colony of Sir Walter Raleigh in 1585. A Dutch botanist and surveyor, Bernard Romans came to this country from England in 1755.

Etchings of George Catlin paintings on pages 180, 187, and 189 are from *The North American Indians* by George Catlin published by Leary, Stuart, and Co., Philadelphia, 1913; photographs by Bracey Holt. Photographs of George Catlin art on pages 89 and 90 are made from original lithographs.

Paintings on pages 111, 138, 175, 193, 196, 197, and 198 from *Indian Tribes of North America* by Thomas L. McKenny and James Hall, Philadelphia, 1836-1844, are reproduced through the courtesy of the Tennessee State Library and Archives; photographs by Bracey Holt.

Contents

1   From Out of the West   15

2   "Through the Still Lapse of Ages"   23

3   Peoples on the Southeastern Scene   35

4   How the Peoples Lived   48

5   Religious Beliefs, Rituals, and Ceremonies   63

6   Menus of the Indians   75

7   Games of the Southeast   84

8   Dance and Music   96

9   Indian Childhood   106

10   Traders and Imperial Rivalry   112

11   "Like Little Birds Before the Eagle"   118

12   The Changing Scene   125

13   A Small Gallery of Notable People   140

14 Race to Survive   159

15 The Removal   165

16 The Remnant   209

17 The Long Eclipse   225

18 A Great Day Coming   241

19 It's Happening with
    Southeastern Indian Youth   264

    Appendixes   273

      Notes   273

      Places to See and Experience   276

      Glossary   282

      Selected Bibliography   288

    Index   298

Indians of the Southeast: Then and Now

From Out of the West

Culture historians are fairly well agreed that the first people on the American continents came out of the west from Asia by a land bridge where the present-day Bering Straits separate the territory of Siberia from the state of Alaska. Thousands of years ago, when a much greater portion of the planet was covered by ice, the seas lowered to reveal this bridge of land, which varied in width during different periods, but on occasion extended almost one thousand miles north to south.

Harvard historian Samuel Eliot Morison believes that the first crossing from Asia took place between 25,000 and 12,000 B.C. Archaeology has established 9200 B.C. as a possible date of man's antiquity in this hemisphere, but there is considerable evidence for even earlier occupation.

Curious hunters, who knew about stone tools and the protective warmth of animal skins, wandered from their Asian homeland. They simply drifted eastward, then southward, probably following the long corridors between the glaciers or moving along the ice-free coasts. Thus, of the three great races of man—Caucasoid, Negroid, and Mongoloid—the first people on this continent were Asians, probably derived from the Mongoloid geographical race. Hereditary features common to many east Asian and American Indian peoples include:

1. The epicanthic fold. A fold of skin on the eye-lid, most obvious near the nose, which makes the eye appear deep set, or as a slit.
2. The Mongoloid or sacral spot. A blue or green-ish-colored area near the base of the spine of infants. It may be large or small and is di-minished or absent in adults.
3. Straight black hair and little body hair.
4. Shovel-shaped incisor teeth. An indentation on the back of the incisors gives the teeth the ap-pearance of a small scoop shovel.

These traits (which may be lacking or greatly modified from individual to individual), with a light brown or cop-per skin color, make up what some anthropologists call the "Mongoloid wash." Vanderbilt University anthropolo-gist Ronald Spores points out, however, that Indians and Mongoloids do tend to diverge rather markedly in blood type relative frequencies, a fact not yet explained by anthropologists.

With the gradual melting of the glaciers in the centuries that followed, the seas swelled once again, covering the Bering Straits. Those hunters who had wandered to this continent were isolated—separated from their Asian rela-tives and life-styles. This land became their home. They pushed deeper to the south, feeding themselves by hunting and by collecting roots and plants.

By approximately 7000 B.C., the mastodon and mam-moth, the giant bison, the camel, the great sloth—known to have inhabited the vast reaches of the Americas—were gone.

Giant sloth

Aware of nature's own harvest of plants, roots, nuts, and the eggs of birds, man gradually acquired skills lead-ing to a highly complex transformation in his life-style. These beginnings of agriculture have been the subject of continuing, intensive archaeological study. Archaeologist Richard MacNeish has explained that innovators among early man on the American continents began experiment-ing in ancient times, more than 9,500 to 7,500 years ago,

16

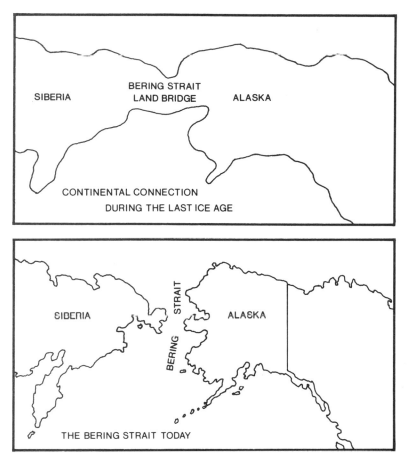

with the cultivation (in present east Mexico) of bottle gourds, pumpkins, peppers, and a sort of runner bean. Though still essentially gatherers of wild plants, and still largely dependent on hunting and trapping to provide a food supply, man's plant cultivation gradually increased.

Of the seeds which man so long gathered the most important was maize, or corn. By 4000 B.C. in central Mexico, man's cultivation of corn had resulted in its developing from a seed pod only a few inches long to the approximate size we know today. Easily stored and adaptable to countless uses from vegetable to bread to nutritious drink, corn became the mainstay in the people's diet.

Unless man cultivates it, corn cannot survive. The seedlings that would grow from one untended ear of corn

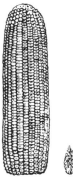

Modern and early corn

17

would be so abundant they would quickly smother them-selves and die. Thus as these first peoples in the Americas transformed their life-styles with their early agriculture, they began to roam less, to build more permanent homes, and to sow and raise corn. Because of corn and other food products such as squash and pumpkins that were being grown, the need to be forever wandering in search of food was gone.

Around the planting, blossoming, and harvesting of corn, ceremonies developed. With increased leisure, there came in time the heightened development of skills and crafts, dance, music, medicine, and clothing. More com-plex cultures evolved.

In the Southeast, too, the dependence on corn and the development of religion and the arts followed the same general pattern. What is the *Southeast?* Broadly speaking, this region stretches from the lands bordering the Missis-sippi River eastward to the Atlantic Ocean, from the Gulf of Mexico to the Ohio River. This book is primarily con-cerned with a more limited area—all or part of the pres-ent states of North and South Carolina, Georgia, Florida, Alabama, Mississippi, Louisiana, and Tennessee.

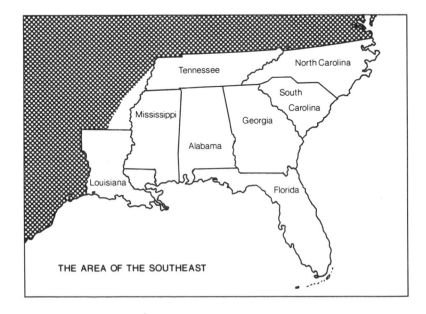

THE AREA OF THE SOUTHEAST

BILL WITSELL

On streams such as this early villages were built.

This limited area measures some four hundred thousand square miles. While the Appalachian Chain reaches into this broad area, it tapers out in present-day north Georgia. The Southeast is often described as predominantly Gulf plains bordered by coastal regions.

The summers are hot. The winters, if not ferociously chill, can be disagreeable. Rainfall is distributed throughout the year, with the climate generally influenced by winds blowing from the Gulf of Mexico.

For a long time, this was forested country that was part of the great eastern woodlands and in which were found live oaks and stately pines and tall cypresses. Artist and ornithologist John James Audubon reported, however, after tramping over a good part of the Southeast in the 1820s, that although trees were abundant in some areas, there were barrens here and there with few trees.

Long before the Roman Empire fell and the dimness of the Dark Ages had settled over many parts of western Europe, the peoples in the Southeast were already constructing with geometric precision high burial mounds, sculpting objects large and small, and engaging in an interregional trade in which they bartered conch shells from the Gulf Coast and other shells from the Atlantic

19

Carved stone pipe of the
Hopewell Culture
Coast, mica from the Appalachians, and carved stone
tobacco pipes for such things as grizzly bear teeth and
obsidian from the present-day Rocky Mountains, copper
and lead from the Great Lakes and upper Mississippi
Valley. And in the trading, ideas and attitudes were also
exchanged.

These people left permanent evidence of their early
civilizations, though no written record is known to exist.
Their burial and temple mounds and some of their crea-
tive handwork in stone, copper, clay, shell, and bone remain to haunt the observer and to tantalize the scholar.

Civilizations had thrived, declined, and disappeared to
be replaced by countless others by the time the Europeans
arrived. To the people who watched the arrival of the
Europeans, *this* was their land. The trees and shrubs,
mountains, valleys, rivers, and lakes were theirs to cherish
and protect.

Who were the people who watched the arrival of the
white man? People with melodious-sounding names like
the Cherokee, Creek, Choctaw, Catawba, Timucua, Chitimacha, Miccosukee, Tuscarora, Natchez, Apalachee,
Chickasaw, their kinsmen, allies, and sometimes enemies.
In historic times they often were similar in life-styles,
though there were differences as among other men.

This was home, or *gala-tsa-di,* to the Cherokees, *tele-*
vea to the Creeks. The fruitful earth, from which some

20

thought they came, was *yakni* to Choctaws. The equally lovely Cherokee word for it was *e-la*.

Most tribes had legends that explained their beginnings. *"Tsoyaha yuchi,"* or "We are children of the sun from far away." That was how one of the most mysterious groups of Indians in the Southeast replied to questions about themselves. Known as the Yuchi, they spoke a language uniquely their own. But other tribes in the Southeast also claimed descent from the sun.

The sun was the source of life and its substance to many of the strong tribal groups in the Southeast. Arrows were not to be shot overhead (the location of the sun) or punishment would come. Fire was evidence on earth of the Supreme Being, and many southeastern peoples kept sacred fires burning in their temples. One of the most notable of all the southeastern tribes, the Natchez, were led by a ruler revered as the "Great Sun." This was the general character of religion when the Europeans arrived around 1530-40 and began to make written records.

The Great Sun of the Natchez being carried on a litter to a harvest festival

Drawing by Le Page Du Pratz from Histoire de La Louisiane, *1758*

Of their tribal beginnings, the Cherokees told of a long journey of many miles from the northwest, led by the Delawares, an Algonkin-speaking people. The Delawares themselves they called grandfathers of all the Indians

SMITHSONIAN INSTITUTION

and they, the Cherokees, uncles of all the Creeks, Choctaws, and Chickasaws. Certain other tribes the Cherokees called brothers, as the Iroquois and the Tuscaroras. (One legend states that in this trek from the northwest the various tribes separated—just before or after crossing "a great body of water"—and some returned to the north. They were the Iroquois, consisting of the Cayuga, Mohawk, Oneida, Ononodaga, and Seneca.)

Some of the members of the band of Choctaw Indians now living on the federal Indian reservation in Mississippi, subscribe to the belief that the Choctaws and the Chickasaws once were one people, and as a united people were migrating eastward on a difficult and protracted journey from the west. Two brothers, *Chatah* and *Chikasah,* were leaders. After unnumbered months of arduous marching, and after many sunrises and much wailing by the tired and sorely burdened youth, who were entrusted with carrying the sacred bones of their ancestors, the migrants came to a wonderfully green land where game was plentiful. There they stopped.

For some reason Chatah and Chikasah fell into sharp disagreement, and their friends began to take sides. Finally, the old men said, "No war!" For the brothers and their respective followers to separate would be good; fighting to compel a union would not be good. As a solution, a game of chance was devised to settle the issue. The Chickasaws lost and as losers they resumed their journey. After a time they found new homes to the north of their brothers, the Choctaws, in present-day Mississippi.

Those who identified themselves as children of the sun, the Yuchis, left present-day east Tennessee and north Georgia soon after 1539, blending their Yuchian (also Uchean) language into the Muskogean spoken by the peoples called Creeks and those who one day would be called Seminoles. Since Creek and Seminole, and many others, thought of themselves as the sun's children the Yuchis were made welcome.

"Through the Still Lapse of Ages"

Man has lived in the lands of the Southeast for thousands of years. He has come and gone leaving traces that he has passed that way.

When the massive mastodon and the saber-toothed tiger stalked the land and the giant beaver thrived, man first entered the Southeast. That was at least ten thousand years ago, or longer, according to achaeological studies of artifacts recovered in Russell Cave, Alabama. The story, as archaeologists have reconstructed it, is one of bands of human beings, probably several families, following the migrating animals. In Russell Cave, projectile

Two early projectile points, a hand ax, and a knife

points, flint knives, scrapers, and the bones of a man who stood only five feet two inches in height have been found.

By approximately 6000 to 5000 B.C., a new era had begun. Although he still made long hunting trips, man lived in settled villages, such as is found in the Eva site in Tennessee. Besides hunting animals, large and small, he fished and gathered wild foods like nuts and berries and roots.

Villages often developed along rivers or coasts where clams and other mollusks were available. Shells and other refuse tossed in heaps downwind from the villages grew over the centuries into large mounds. These heaps received broken tools, broken pottery, animal bones, even

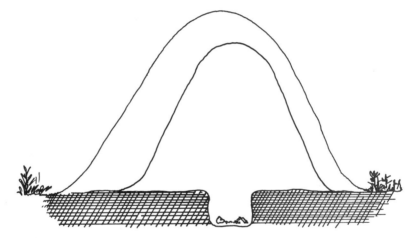

Burial mound

the bodies of the dead. It is from such mounds that the history of these ancient men is being reconstructed.

Although leather from the skins of animals that were hunted was a prime material for garments, some fabrics were woven from plant materials.

Marine shell and copper ornaments have been found in small quantity at the Eva site which suggests trade with distant people, since the shells had come from the Gulf of Mexico and the copper from the Lake Superior region.

Along the streams that flow into the Ohio River a new custom evolved. In large circular areas enclosed by walls of earth, people began to cover their dead with mounds of earth. Burial would follow burial on the cone-shaped mounds, until in time they became quite high.

With the more settled existence made possible by early agriculture and with increased leisure, the arts became increasingly significant. Copper bracelets, beads, gorgets, and rings were made by beating nuggets of copper into thin sheets which were rolled and bent to the desired shape and then decorated. Increasing technical knowledge and artistic ideas found expression in the shaping, decorating, and making of pottery from that great natural plastic, clay. Some of the earliest pottery was "stamped," or imprinted before firing by pressing carved wooden objects on the clay. The stamping technique of some two thousand years ago continued as an artistic tradition in the Southeast until the nineteenth century when it was still practiced by the Catawbas of South Carolina and the Cherokees of east Tennessee, the western Carolinas, and north Georgia. The duck hawk, carrion crow, wolf, cougar, and snake are often pictured on decorated objects.

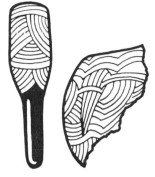

Carved paddle and pottery with stamped design

A spectacular monument is the Serpent Mound near the village of Loudon in southern Ohio. A wall of earth almost a quarter of a mile long, it uncurls in the shape of a striking snake. Excavations into the mound have shown that the builders marked the shape the mound was to take with stones and lumps of clay. Baskets of earth were then dumped over this outline to form the serpent.

The Adena Culture, as this way of life is called, is believed to have lasted from about 1000 B.C. to A.D. 700.

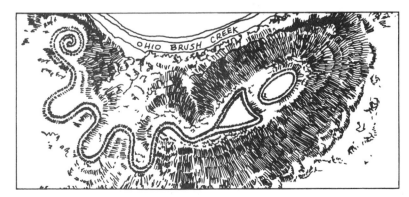

OHIO BRUSH CREEK

The Serpent Mound

Though it was centered in what is now Ohio, Illinois, and West Virginia, peoples with similar customs lived as far away as Florida and southern Louisiana. In southwestern Louisiana near the Gulf of Mexico a mound of clam shells in the shape of an alligator, and believed to be part of the Adena Culture, has been found. Even after a near-by lake had washed part of it away, the mound, showing the body, tail and three legs of an alligator, was 500 feet long.

*Hopewell vessel
with duck design*

Another culture thrived during much of this time with the Adena. Called Hopewell after the name of an Ohio farmer on whose land evidence of the culture was first uncovered, it lasted from about 300 B.C. to A.D. 600.

The Hopewell, too, built tall mounds over their dead, but these were usually round rather than cone-shaped as were the Adena, and they were in circular, octagonal, and square walls of earth. These Hopewell peoples farmed more, raising corn of Mexican origin.

Art was important. Special decorated pottery, different from that used every day, was made for funeral purposes. Smoking pipes, jewelry, and copper collars and pendants

SMITHSONIAN INSTITUTION

Ceremony at the death of a chief. In such a way burial mounds began.

Engraving by de Bry after painting by Le Moyne of Timucuans in Florida

26

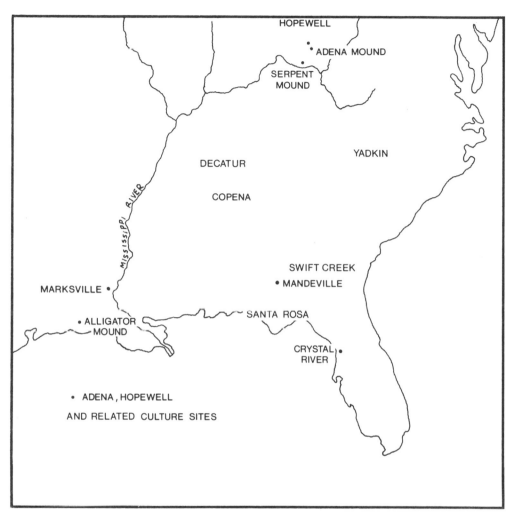

were carved and decorated. Although often geometrical, these decorations were sometimes in animal or even human forms.

Hopewell, though it too was centered in southern Illinois and Ohio, was widespread. Mounds such as those of Marksville in Louisiana, Crystal River in Florida, Mandeville in Georgia, and Copena in northern Alabama all had artifacts similar to those found around the Ohio River.

Objects found in these Hopewell burial mounds reveal how extensive trade networks were. Large conch shells

Hopewell copper breastplate

were brought from the Florida Gulf Coast, copper from Lake Superior, flint from Indiana, galena from Missouri, obsidian from the Yellowstone area in Wisconsin, grizzly bear teeth from the Rocky Mountains, and mica, fossil shark teeth, and quartz crystals from the Appalachian Mountains.

From Adena and Hopewell customs, with possible Mexican influence, a new culture slowly began to develop called the Mississippian because it was strong along the Mississippi River and its streams. The people who followed this way of life were found throughout the Southeast, as well as in present-day Oklahoma, Missouri, southern Illinois, and Ohio.

Life was very different from those earlier cultures. For the first time, the bow and arrow was the major weapon and hunting tool. Farming was all important. Corn was the major crop, but beans, squash, and pumpkins were important, too.

In addition to burial mounds each major center had one or more temple mounds which were surrounded by village dwellings and cornfields. At the top of the main mound was the temple containing the holy fire, which was kept constantly burning. Most mounds were no higher

Mississippian temple mound village

than thirty feet, measuring up to 250 feet around at the base, but some were as high as 75 feet and 600 feet around. Usually temple mounds were set to face each other or the burial mounds across an open plaza that served as a meeting place for ceremonies and games.

Because of the likenesses in art, the identical plants that were grown, and the similar temple mounds with their eternal fires and the nearby open plaza, it is believed that the Mississippian cultures of the Southeast were influenced by those of Mexico and Middle America. This contact could have come by boat across the Gulf of Mexico or by a trail along the shores of the Gulf of Mexico and across eastern Texas into northern Louisiana.

Important Mississippian centers were on the sites of Spiro, Oklahoma; Moundville, Alabama; Etowah, Okmulgee, and Kolomoki, Georgia; Mound Bottom, Tennessee; and Cahokia, Illinois.

Cahokia, across the Mississippi River from present-day St. Louis, was perhaps the largest of all the Mississippian centers. It had more than eighty-five mounds and a village area that extended for six miles along the Illinois River. These mounds, like all the mounds in the Southeast, were constructed without the use of beasts of burden or wheeled vehicles. Because of this feature, culture historians have assumed the presence of an organized, well-functioning society able to enlist a considerable labor force and to build over a long period of time. Some writers speculate that possibly tens of thousands of people may have participated in building the mounds.

A Cahokia mound

The ideas and technological systems of the Mississippian Culture reached their peak from approximately A.D. 1300 to 1600. Agriculture increased as the result of improved strains of corn. Ceramic techniques became more sophisticated, as the variety of shapes of temple-mound pottery suggests. Artistic ideas were expressed in smooth, often highly polished, pottery, sometimes painted in designs of red on a buff background. Freehand design, which is only easy to one who hasn't attempted it, gave a real

Mississippian bottle with freehand design

29

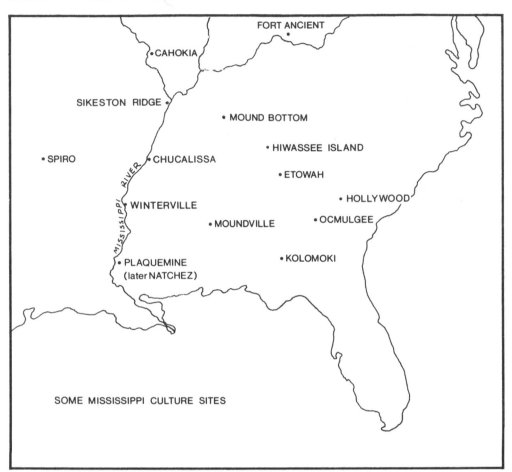

FORT ANCIENT

• CAHOKIA

SIKESTON RIDGE •

• MOUND BOTTOM

• HIWASSEE ISLAND

• SPIRO   • CHUCALISSA

• ETOWAH

• HOLLYWOOD

WINTERVILLE

• OCMULGEE

• MOUNDVILLE

• PLAQUEMINE   • KOLOMOKI
(later NATCHEZ)

MISSISSIPPI RIVER

SOME MISSISSIPPI CULTURE SITES

distinction to shallow bowls, large basins, long-necked bottles, and jars with handles. Since fabrics sometimes were used in decorating pottery, being pressed against the unfired clay to leave an imprint of the weave, some idea of weaving practices can be gained. Fabrics interpreted from pottery vary from materials somewhat like modern burlap, or coarse muslin, to netting and matting. Some anthropologists assume from this evidence that the people wore clothing made of woven materials.

In summary, archaeological evidence indicates that the Mississippian Culture was complex with large populations in many towns, abundant beans and corn, and a richly ceremonial life.

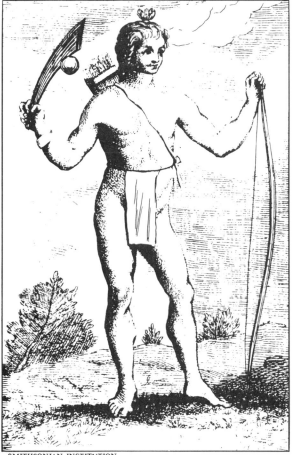

A Natchez man in summer. In his right hand he holds a war club.

Drawing by Le Page Du Pratz from Histoire de La Louisiane, *1758*

SMITHSONIAN INSTITUTION

The Natchez Indians, with an autocratic government head who was both religious and political leader, are said to have been a last remnant of the Mississippian Culture. The largest and strongest tribe on the lower Mississippi when the French founded the colony of Louisiana, their nation was centered at White Apple Village on St. Catherine Creek near the present location of Natchez, Mississippi.

The young French Jesuit, Father Paul Du Ru, was personal chaplain to Sieur Pierre Lemoyne d'Iberville, founder of the Louisiana colony, when he visited the Natchez Indians on March 12, 1700. Father Du Ru wrote in his journal:

*A Natchez man wrapped
in fur robe for winter*

*Drawing by Le Page Du Pratz
from* Histoire de La
Louisiane, *1758*

SMITHSONIAN INSTITUTION

We arrived at the landing place of the Natchez at about
nine o'clock in the morning, and were not there long before
the calumet was brought to us. The chief's brother has come
to lead the French chief [d'Iberville] to the village. He is
accompanied by well-formed men. . . . We set out at two
in the afternoon to climb the hill on which the Great Chief's
cabin is situated. . . . We met him half way there, escorted
by the principal personages of the tribe. The chief's manner
impresses me; he has the air of an ancient emperor, a long
face, sharp eyes, an imperious aquiline nose, a chestnut
complexion, and manners somewhat Spanish. . . . The respect with which the other Savages approach and serve him
is astonishing. If he speaks to one of them, that person
thanks him before answering. They never pass in front of

him if it can be avoided; if they must, it is with elaborate precautions.[1]

Upon arriving in the chief's cabin, Father Du Ru noted that an important item of furniture was "a sort of bed of state, very broad, about three feet from the floor and supported by four large columns which are all painted in different colors." He learned from the Natchez that their principal leader never mounted that bed except when death approached. When he died, some thirty of his chief subordinates customarily were put to death.

The day began in the village when the Great Chief saluted the rising sun as soon as it appeared above the horizon. He raised his hand above his head and turned from the east to the west showing his elder brother, the sun, the direction he must take in his course.

French visitors reported that the Natchez had a temple in which stone or baked clay objects depicting men and women, heads and tails of rattlesnakes, jawbones of large fish, stuffed owls, and pieces of crystal were contained.

The Natchez believed in the immortality of the soul. They explained that when they left the world it was to go live in another world, to be rewarded or punished.

Father Paul Du Ru's report on the Natchez and others he had seen on his mission was made in 1700 to the Seminary of Quebec. "As near as I can make out, their whole cult and religion is limited to the performance of their duties to the dead." [2] The bones of the dead, he explained, were placed in arrangements in the temple, which had places or recesses for them.

Pointing out to his Jesuit superiors that he knew the Natchez were unredeemed spiritually, Father Paul added that he, for one, found them far from primitive in the way they lived in their environment. In fact, it puzzled his admittedly fervent Roman Catholic mind that people he thought unsaved could have so developed a culture.

Other peoples besides the Natchez are believed descended from the influential technological systems of the

Mississippian Culture and from its socio-religious ideas. The Creeks who lived in what is now Georgia and Alabama, the Choctaws and Chickasaws in present-day Mississippi and Alabama, and the Shawnees to the north, for example, all showed relationship to these earlier peoples.

But why did the Mississippian temple-mound life vanish? Probably an important factor was disease brought by the European for which the Indian had no immunity and his medicine, no cures. Small pox often was a calamity, at least in early historic times. Documented proof of recurring epidemics among coastal tribes leaves little doubt that wave after wave of pestilence swept inland from European settlements in Mexico, Canada, and the Atlantic Seaboard.

Just behind the waves of disease was an even more ominous threat to the native cultures. A whole new way of life was transported intact from its European sources to tiny communities that would grow and expand. It would in time require a complete reevaluation of even the most basic ideas of life and death. It would evoke many changes. One of the first of these would be the end of the temple-mound, or Mississippian, way of life.

Peoples on the
Southeastern Scene

When the Europeans entered the Southeast they found a number of Indian groups so populous and well-organized that they called them nations.

It was discovered there wasn't just one universally spoken Indian language among the nations in the region, there were many. Four predominant language families were Algonkin (also Algonquian), Iroquoian, Siouan, and the Muskogean that was heard from present-day south Georgia through the areas now comprising Alabama and Mississippi to the wide river that the explorers learned to call the Mississippi. With the exception of Muskogean, these languages were also spoken by peoples in other regions. These non-southeastern Indians had their own nations, whose total populations were larger (for example, the Algonkin) than the same language group in the Southeast. In prehistoric times the large language-families split so as to produce a kind of dispersion of their members.

Explanation of language distribution among Indians would be as difficult as explaining language distribution among other peoples. Although Muskogean and its dialects is sometimes called the language of the Southeast, the immense Cherokee nation (in historic times the largest Indian tribe in the region), and certain other southeastern groups spoke a form of Iroquoian, the language

LANGUAGE GROUPS IN THE SOUTHEASTERN AREA

Muskogean:

Chakchiuma	Cusabo	Avoyel
Chickasaw	Tangipahoa	Bayogoula
Choctaw	Timucua	Okelousa
Chiaha	Mobile	Quinnipissa
Guale	Houma	Taensa
Tuskegee	Natchez	Miccosukee
Apalachicola	Pascagoula	Yamasee
Alabama	Acolapissa	Seminole
Hitchiti		Koasati
Creek Confederacy (Muskogee)		Calusa

Tunican:

Tunica	Chitimacha
Yazoo	Opelousa
Atakapa	Washa
Chawasha	Koroa

Iroquoian:

Cherokee	Meherrin
Tuscarora	Nottaway

Caddo:

Adai
Eyeish
Natchitoches Confederacy

Algonkian:

Shawnee
Chowanoc
Powhatan Confederacy

Siouan:

Biloxi	Occaneechi	Shakori
Catawba	Saponi	Sissipahaw
Congaree	Tutelo	Woccon
Peedee	Winyaw	Yadkin
Santee	Moneton	Manahoac
Sewee	Cape Fear Indians	Monacan
Sugeree	Cheraw	Nahyssan
Waccamaw	Eno	Quapaw
Wateree	Keyawee	Yuchi
Waxhaw		

(Note: Not all authorities agree on the above language categories, but this listing is representative of the rich language heritage of the southeastern Indians. Interested readers should discover the works of Mary R. Haas.)

commonly associated with northern groups. The European found the Siouan-speaking Indians among the most powerful of peoples in vast areas of the western plains; but Siouan was also the language of some Indians in the Carolinas. The Algonkin, heard extensively to the far north of this continent and in some parts of the West, was spoken by some of the Southeasterners.

All these peoples prehistorically had been nomadic or had practiced seasonal migrations. Could some from above the natural boundary of the Ohio River have been lured to the Southeast with its rich Mississippian Culture and milder climate? Perhaps this was true. Perhaps, too, there were disagreements between strong leaders, as later Choctaw and Chickasaw myths indicate. There may have been divisions on religious issues or on how to live or even on which climate was the more invigorating. Historically, we find almost everywhere in Indian government the confederate idea with groups free to disassociate. Possibly this freedom, if it prevailed prehistorically—together with factors such as time, distance, and the system of communications—might account for Iroquoian, Siouan, and Algonkin speakers in the South, as well as in the North.

The southeastern Indian nations may be grouped generally into the inland peoples and the coastal peoples who lived along the Gulf of Mexico, Florida, and Atlantic coasts with some extension to the Piedmont. However, within these two groups there often were variations. For instance, the Mountain Cherokee had a modified inland culture. The Mountain Cherokee anciently lived on the Oconoluftee River in the southern Appalachian area of present-day western North Carolina.

The climate away from the coasts made possible the growth of corn, which doesn't grow well in coastal areas. The growing of corn, beans, and squash, with efficient techniques for storing and preserving, provided food for larger numbers of people and the time and freedom from want in which to develop a richer culture than the less

FRANK J. MILLER

Mountains reach into the Southeast. populous coastal tribes. These inland peoples were not tied to the whimsies of the sea for their food as were the Hatteras and the Pamlico of the Atlantic coast, the Ais of the Florida coast, and the Atakapa of the Louisiana and east Texas coast. The Cherokee of the mountains, numbering some sixty families in early historic times, raised corn but hardly to the extent of their kinsmen in less mountainous areas.

In general, there were striking similarities in the lifestyles of the large southeastern Indian groups and their neighbors on the margin of that fertile region, such as the Powhatans in their confederacy.

Some of the similar cultural practices were a religious system with a priesthood, rituals and ceremonies centered around corn, a sacred perpetual fire symbolizing the sun, and the use of temple mounds. There was village or town life and a military system in which skill in war could advance an individual in social rank. Government was usually by a chief or chiefs, and in some tribes the office

ROBERT B. FERGUSON

was so honored that the chief was carried everywhere on a litter. Women were influential in council, and in some places they cast the deciding vote for war or peace.

Pines and palmettos along the southern coast

From Virginia to Louisiana, from the Appalachian Mountains and valleys to the lower Mississippi, the larger Indian tribes associated together in confederacies. Within the confederacies there was division; and sometimes serious tension developed between the war towns, which took red as their color, and the peace towns, which took white. The inhabitants of war towns played major roles in the conduct of wars and fighting. But the presence of peace towns and their primary leadership in governmental affairs clearly shows the relative position of warfare in the lives of the people.

Centered in what is now Alabama and Georgia, the Creek Confederacy is an arresting example of Indian statecraft. There were fifty or more Creek towns with a total population that went up and down from approximately fifteen thousand to more than twenty thousand.

39

BILL WITSELL

Lush fields extend throughout the Southeast.

Although various Muskogean dialects were spoken in the extensive confederacy, one Creek might be unable readily to talk with another Creek. But the Creeks seem to have excelled in the arts of communication. There are reports of professional interpreters in larger towns, such as Big Tulsa, on the Tallapoosa River in present Tallapoosa County, Alabama, and Tukabahchee, in present Elmore Couty, Alabama. Black slaves sometimes interpreted Creek to Creek and Creek to white men and white men to Creek.

How did these peoples relate to each other? There was barter trading, intratribally and intertribally, in which sign language and a simple trade language developed by the linguistically adroit Choctaws were utilized. There was visiting back and forth. Within confederacies, "red" towns competed in ball games with "white" towns. Groups of towns competed for the "national" championship. The best team in the Creek Confederacy once took on the Choctaw champions in a ball game, the outcome of which was supposed to settle an argument over territory. The Creeks stand in history for yet another reason. From their confederacy came the later Seminoles of Florida.

The area comprising the present state of Mississippi was the homeland of three large southeastern Muskogean-speaking tribes: the Natchez in the south; Choctaws in the east central part; and the Chickasaws in northern Mississippi, western Tennessee, and Kentucky.

The Iroquoian-speaking Cherokees may once have quarreled with their northern Iroquois brothers, who then allied with the Algonkin Delawares to drive the Cherokees south into present-day North and South Carolina, east Tennessee, north Georgia, and northeastern Alabama. During their relocation they, as intruders, could well have incurred the anger of the Creeks which may explain the traditional enmity between Creeks and Cherokees in historic times. What the prehistoric quarrel was about is anybody's guess, but the first European visitors commented on a bristling pride of many of the Cherokees and their self-proclaimed taste for making war. In any family, qualities like these are apt to make for quarrels.

Though Cherokees and Chickasaws spoke different languages and were not always on the best of terms—displaying a touchiness that provided fine tinder for their acknowledged enjoyment of war—they cooperated in 1715 and again in 1745 to forcibly expel bands of Shawnees from the rich hunting lands on the site that is now Nashville, Tennessee. This type of combined military operation against other Indians regarded as enemies is not unusual in southeastern history.

The Tuscaroras who lived on the Roanoke, Tar, Pamlico, and Neuse rivers in present North Carolina were Iroquoian also. Known as the hemp gatherers, they were expert in military architecture as shown by their palisaded villages. It is not known why they had come from the north to which, eventually, they returned, but in 1600 the Tuscaroras numbered some five thousand.

After the Tuscarora War of 1711 to 1713, fought to

SMITHSONIAN INSTITUTION

Chickasaw warrior

By Bernard Romans in A Concise Natural History of East and West Florida, *1775*

41

escape pressure of white settlement and brutal raids of white militia with Indian allies, most of the surviving Tuscaroras migrated from North Carolina and were adopted on a basis of equality by the Oneidas of the Five Iroquois Nations. A few may have gone to Florida, but by about 1773 approximately one thousand Tuscarora men, women, and children had relocated in New York in a rather spectacular migration. University of Texas historian Caleb Perry Patterson, authority on North Carolina slavery, finds that the Tuscaroras in North Carolina would not be enslaved without the grimmest resistance to white-led raiders, and furthermore, they transferred their hatred of enslavement to blacks sometimes used in raiding parties. On the whole Atlantic Seaboard, Dr. Patterson concludes, the Tuscarora Indians were "the implacable enemies of Negroes."

To the south of the Tuscarora's North Carolina lands

A palisaded village in Florida

From an engraving by de Bry after a painting by Le Moyne, who visited Florida in 1564-65

SMITHSONIAN INSTITUTION

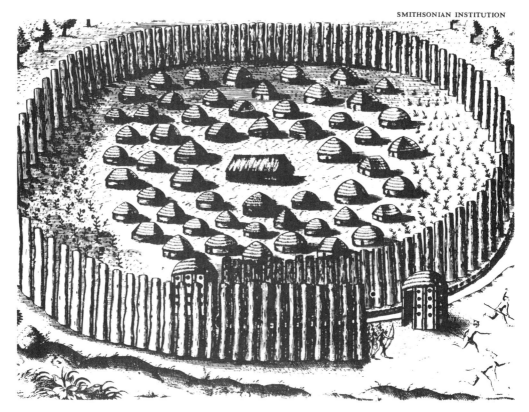

the Siouan-speaking Catawbas, numbering some five thousand in 1600, were by far the most numerous of the Siouan tribes in the Southeast. They lived mainly in what is now York and Lancaster counties in South Carolina. In the prehistoric migrations of the whole Siouan people undoubtedly there were numerous separations of smaller groups from the whole, and the Catawbas, finding a locale they liked, stayed. In historic times the Catawbas were punished by raiding parties of Delawares and Shawnees.

Two thousand Yamasees, a Muskogean-speaking people, lived at various times in northern Florida, south Georgia, and southern South Carolina. They were almost exterminated in the Yamasee War in 1715 by whites with Indian allies. The Yamasees, unwilling to be impressed into plantation slavery, rose in rebellion against the English in South Carolina and killed some two hundred settlers. At least 50 percent of the Yamasee population was killed; the survivors fled to Spanish Florida.

In 1635 the Spanish reported the presence of thirteen thousand Timucua Indians living in Florida between the Suwannee and the St. Johns rivers and in the area of present-day Tallahassee, seven thousand Apalachee Indians. South of what is now Tampa and ranging through the Florida Keys the three thousand, possibly Muskogean-speaking, Calusa Indians lived in an economy dominated by products of the sea. Contemporary historians believe that maize cultivation did not reach that part of Florida until the arrival of the Seminoles in the 1700s and 1800s. A unique factor in Calusa culture was gold, silver, and copper obtained from wrecked Spanish treasure ships and hammered by the Indians into arm bands, gorgets, and other ornaments.

Scholars are intrigued because the Siouan-speaking Biloxis, who numbered about four hundred and lived in the vicinity of present-day Biloxi, Mississippi, had as their constant companions the Muskogean-speaking Pascagoulas. Did their children learn both languages and also the well-known sign language?

When the Europeans arrived in the area now comprising Louisiana there were three major linguistic groups totalling approximately fifteen thousand Indians.

Ethnographer John R. Swanton identifies as Muskogeans the Acolapissa, Avoyel, Bayogoula, Okelousa, Quinnipissa, Taensa, and Tangipahoa who lived in what is now central Louisiana. After historic times the *Saktci Hooma,* Houma Indians who spoke their own brand of Muskogean, moved from the Mississippi side of the Mississippi-Louisiana line to below the head of Bayou La Fourche.

Louisiana's second linguistic stock, the Tunican, was represented by the three thousand Chitimachas in 1700 living on Grand River, Grand Lake, and Bayou Teche. Their culture was based on corn but was strongly influenced by harvesting the foods of the bayou. Koroas and Ofos, who were also Tunican, lived at different times on both sides of the Mississippi River near where the Yazoo River joined. Also in the Tunican linguistic group were some fifteen hundred Atakapas, who in 1700 were located along the coast of present Louisiana and Texas from Vermilion Bayou to and including Trinity Bay.

Indians in the Natchitoches Confederacy which centered on the Red River around present-day Shreveport and Natchitoches were members of the Caddoan linguistic family. Apparently renowned hunters even in prehistoric times, after about 1700 they adapted to the use of the horse in hunting, and agriculture diminished even more in importance in their life economy. They numbered some one thousand people in 1700.

West of the Mississippi River and north of present-day Louisiana, the most populous Indian nations on this margin of the southeastern region were the twenty-five hundred Siouan Quapaws at or near the mouth of the Arkansas River, and some 6,200 Siouan-speaking Osages north and west of them. An enmity rooted in antiquity existed between the Osages on the one hand, and the Choctaws and Chickasaws on the other. Bold hunters of the two southern tribes often went across the Mississippi River to hunt bison on Osage-claimed territory. That most famous Choctaw, the culture hero Pushmataha, earned fame as a youth on his first hunt by taking several scalps when his group was ambushed by an Osage party.

When we come to the historic dividing line of the Ohio, we find that north of it Algonkin-speaking tribes were the most numerous neighbors of the south-eastern Indians.

One Algonkin-speaking people in particular, the highly migratory Shawnees, who are associated generally with the Midwest, from time to time had bands living in the Southeast. In about 1740 a group was in what is now middle Tennessee, and some thirty years later was with the Creeks on the Chattahoochee and Tallapoosa rivers near present-day Montgomery, Alabama. Tecumseh, the famed Shawnee statesman and brave advocate of Indian unity, had blood ties with the Creeks. Tidewater Virginia, which John R. Swanton considers distinct from the Southeast, had in 1607 the nine thousand Algonkin-speaking people of the Powhatan Confederacy from which Pocahontas came.

Then there were the Iroquian peoples ranging from the valley of the St. Lawrence River to the area around Lake Erie and Lake Huron. From these people the Cherokees and Tuscaroras are said to have split for unknown reasons in ancient times.

Although Europeans had touched along the coasts of the Southeast, not until 1539 did they enter the heartland of the region. In that year Hernando de Soto led his well-equipped army to shore at Tampa Bay, the beginning of his search for gold and silver. From then until 1542 he and his army marched and fought from the Florida peninsula through what is now Georgia, into southeastern Tennessee, then to southern Alabama, across Mississippi, and into Louisiana territory where de Soto died.

De Soto's "chroniclers," the official writers with him,

45

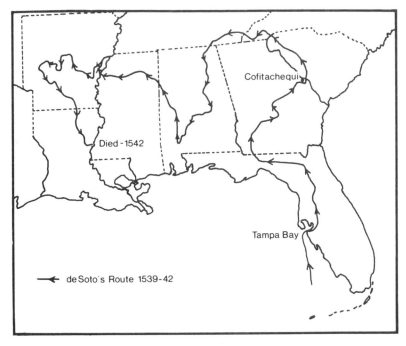

de Soto's Route 1539-42

introduced into written history the broad rivers and warm summers of the Southeast and its powerful peoples.

One of the strangest episodes was de Soto's encounter with the Lady of Cofitachequi, shortly after his soldiers had removed fresh-water pearls from burial places. The Lady was probably a high-ranking Creek, who traveled borne on a litter by male carriers. When they first met in the spring of 1540, she placed her own long string of pearls around de Soto's neck. (Enthnographer John R. Swanton, interpreting the Spanish account, locates Cofitachequi, or Cutofachiqui, in present-day South Carolina on the Savannah River near Augusta, Georgia; other interpretations place it across the river.)

An agreement was reached for the Lady to guide the de Soto expedition, and she was given a female slave to help guard the pearls.

For seven days the Lady guided the Spaniards to the northwest where present-day Georgia, Tennessee, and North Carolina meet. This had been Cherokee country since before recorded history began. Perhaps she guided

EARLY HISTORIC LOCATION

the European invaders intentionally into the country of the traditional enemies of the Creeks.

The chroniclers do not explain, for the Lady of Cofitachequi, her slave, and the store of pearls vanished on the seventh night and were never seen again.

The journey of de Soto marked the dawn of an age of change and ultimate misfortune for the Indian peoples of the Southeast. Today, except for scattered groups like the Mountain Cherokees, most of those earlier Southeasterners are gone.

How the Peoples Lived

Baltazar de Gallegos made a scouting foray for Gen. Hernando de Soto soon after the Spaniards landed in the vicinity of what is now Tampa Bay in 1539.

Probably visiting with the Apalachees, Baltazar reported that the Indians lived in villages and were busily engaged in cultivating maize, beans, pumpkins, melons, and several kinds of fruit.

He spoke of marching for two leagues through continuous fields of corn, which he mentioned to support his statement about the bountiful, well-organized life of the Indians. Baltazar wrote that the products he saw were "sufficient to sustain a large army without its knowing a want."

The good life of the Apalachees, like that of their counterparts throughout the Southeast, owed much to the beautiful corn plant, whose products made for a relatively stable and comfortable level of subsistence. Corn was revered by many southeastern Indians, who considered it a gift to the Indian from the Creator of life. Its versatility as a food knew no seasons of lack for it could be stored in granaries for later use, Baltazar reported. And this feature of corn made possible the social development in which the Southeasterners fitted themselves into village organization with their various relationships.

Villages—sometimes called towns by the first European

SMITHSONIAN INSTITUTION

visitors—generally were neighborhoods of single houses, often stretching along a stream or a creek, but sometimes extending into the woods for several miles, and connected by a network of trails. There was a center—sometimes a square—for social gatherings and major ceremonials which was also used informally for news-sharing and that gossiping, or light conversing, identified with villagers everywhere. The ceremonies were like festivals that provided good times. They were, however, augustly religious at their height. They renewed and strengthened ties that held village together with village and, ultimately, with the tribe.

Houses were designed to be as functional as possible and complement the climate. Noncoastal Southeasterners had one readily available building material, cane, that tall hollow member of the reed family. Strong and flexible, it could be put to many uses in a household. Often the characteristic raised shelf along the wall, used for sleeping

Timucuans in Florida tend and plant their fields.

From an engraving by de Bry after a Le Moyne painting made in 1564 or 1565

49

A town in what is now North Carolina. Cultivated crops include corn, tobacco, pumpkins, and sunflowers.

Watercolor made by John White, ca. 1585

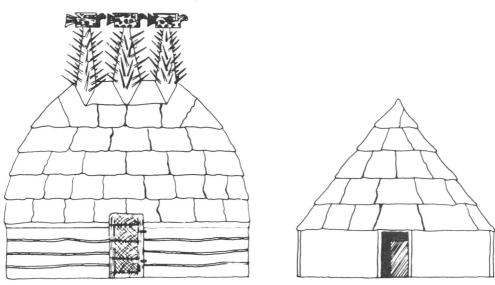

*Acolapissa temple
and house in Louisiana*

and sitting, was made of cane. Coastal people found the ever-available palmetto as useful as cane.

Types of houses varied but the whole idea of their construction was to achieve utility without clutter and elaboration. The Indian, in fact, saw no reason, or so he said to the first Europeans, for building a house that would outlive its original occupants and possibly become an object of contention among survivors.

However, as one of de Soto's chroniclers, a man known as Gentleman of Elvas, noted, Indian house construction was remarkably functional and intelligently adapted to the climate. Elvas observed that two houses, not one, was the style away from the coastal region of the Gulf of Mexico. The summer house, he said, had its kitchen and oven for baking bread and was detached from the sleeping and sitting quarters. There also was a winter house, plastered for strength inside and out with a compound of clay and locally available additives, such as crushed mussel shells, and warmed by a fire "so that it gets hot as an oven, and stays so all night long so that there is no need for clothing." However, he found widespread use of blankets, attractively woven from the inner bark of trees. Smoke holes were used by some of the housebuilders, who often did

51

their work under the supervision of an older man who knew what to do in making a good house.

The winter house was so designed that it provided a moist heat rather like that in a Scandinavian sauna. At times, the Choctaws would pour water on heated stones. Steam would rise. Many Indians made systematic use of steam and aromatic vapors in treating respiratory disorders.

Some Southeasterners were very skilled in choosing hickory, sassafras, and other fragrant woods for smoking as well as for barbecuing meat. Smoke holes were often made in houses of the Alabamas and Chitimachas to let the smoke out.

Père Marquette, who descended the Mississippi to the mouth of the Arkansas in the summer of 1673, noted of the Chickasaws,

> They raise a scaffolding, the floor of which is made of simple poles, and consequently a mere grate-work to give passage to the smoke of a fire which they build beneath. This drives off the little animals, as they can not bear it. The Indians sleep on the poles, having pieces of bark stretched above them to keep off the rain.[1]

The "little animals" could have been the mosquito, the gnat, the flea, or several varieties of the fly.

Palmetto often was used by the Chitimachas of Louisiana and the peoples of Florida. Winter hot houses were not used in these warmer areas. Seminoles developed the *chickee,* well-suited to a warm climate. These homes without walls were built on stilts for protection against dampness and snakes. Each member of a family had his or her own canopy for protection from sand flies, mosquitoes, and heavy dew. In the morning it was tightly rolled up and stored in the thatched-over palmetto rafters until needed. It was often a piece of unbleached muslin after the Europeans introduced that material to the Indians.

Among the Koasatis, a Muskogean-speaking group who lived where the Coosa and Tallapoosa rivers join to

Chickee

form the Alabama, there were well-defined differentiations between the speech of men and of women. In 1944, Dr. Mary R. Haas published her findings about speech differences in the Koasati (or Coushatta) in southwestern Louisiana, descendants of those once living at the junction of the Coosa and Tallapoosa. Dr. Haas was told, "Women talk easy, slow, and soft. It sounds pretty. Men's speech has too much *ssss.*" Women avoided using the *s* sound, men liked it.[2]

Many males of the Timucuas, whose more than forty villages and thirteen thousand people extended from the Suwannee River to the St. Johns River in Florida, favored long hair, as did Choctaws, Pensacolas, and others. Choctaws were known to Chickasaws as *Pansh Falaia,* meaning "long hairs"; and, apparently, many boys signified they no longer were children by letting their hair grow. Males in the Southeast usually shaved away most of the hair of the head. It was said that in Virginia there were women "barbers."

Girls learned early in life to groom their long hair with combs made of copper, cane, wood, or, perhaps, shell and bone. Copper was a native trade item before the coming of the Europeans. Body hair was removed by Acolapissa women with a depilatory of shells and hot water. Shells were used by both sexes as tweezers and razors. Use of flint razors was widespread.

Women and girls fashioned fine baskets from cane, a craft that approached real art among the Cherokees in their Appalachian coves and valleys and among the Chitimachas in Louisiana. They cooked and preserved foodstuffs. They spun and wove, and in many tribes they processed deer, bear, and buffalo skins and made them into clothing that delighted the eye and well-suited the human body. Pride in grooming definitely extended to clothing, and real pains were taken in making it.

Women taught girls to make pottery in sizes ranging from small objects to five-gallon containers. Among those noted for their pottery technology were the Catawbas and

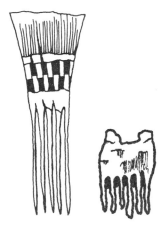

Combs made from bone or antler

Chitimacha baskets

the Cherokees, and on the fringe of the Southeast, the Chitimachas of present-day Louisiana. As in the Mississippian Culture, the early historic southeastern Indian artisans in many of the tribes stamped designs into the clay before firing it. Beautiful specimens of "negative painting" have been recovered by modern archaeologists. Negative painting is a method of making a design on pottery by covering parts of the vessel with wax, following the desired pattern, and then applying the color to the rest of the dish. When the wax melted as the pot was fired, the area the wax covered remained the original color of the vessel.

Negative painted pottery

Helped by their daughters, women pounded corn into meal, gathered nuts and acorns and extracted and stored their oils. Men and boys cleared the fields, the girls and women generally tended the crops. Men generally felled the trees. In some tribes women, occasionally helped by the older men, often cut and brought in firewood. They also brought in fresh water.

Men repaired and made tools and weapons. A man might be good at sewing, and, in fact, a task of many southeastern men was to repair or make new moccasins, which appear to have worn out rather quickly. Men prepared and staged the notable ceremonies. They were carpenters and builders, making the homes, corncribs, structures on the public square, and the great canoes. According to American botanist William Bartram, Timucua Indians of Florida's east coast had canoes that could make a round trip to Cuba for trading purposes.

SMITHSONIAN INSTITUTION

Making a canoe

Engraving by de Bry after a watercolor by John White, ca. 1585.
North Carolina coast.

Southeastern canoes generally were of dugout design and could be as much as forty feet long. Cherokee canoe-making skills are probably representative of many Southeasterners. A large tree would be cut down and the trunk hollowed out by a series of burnings and adzings.

Men also made drums, calumets, sticks for ballplay, bows, arrows, axes, and war clubs.

A calumet pipe

55

Father Jacques Gravier, a French Jesuit, observed the division of labor in the Tunica and Choctaw villages in present Mississippi: "The men do here what peasants do in France; they cultivate and dig the earth, plant and harvest the crops, cut the wood and bring it to the cabin, dress the deer and buffalo hides, when they have any . . . the women do only indoor work, make earthen pots and their clothes." [3]

The peoples varied in their activities. Some men farmed. Others fished, hunted, acted as traders, and took part in war. A few males at an early age were dedicated by their parents to the study of medicine; and a few of these eventually might discharge the role of physician-priest required in Indian medicine. Whatever the life-style of an Indian tribe, children contributed to the work which had to be done by their families.

Jean-Bernard Bossu said of marriage customs among the people he saw in the Mississippi Valley,

> Indian marriages, governed entirely by natural law, depend only upon the consent of both parties. Since they are not bound by civil contract, the couples merely separate when they are no longer happy together, claiming that marriage is a matter of love and mutual assistance. I have seen very happy marriages among these people; divorce and polygamy, authorized by [their] law, are not common. . . . Indian women generally work hard, since they are warned from childhood that if they are lazy or clumsy, they will have worthless husbands. [4]

Jean-Bernard Bossu noted that marriage had no form other than mutual agreement. A would-be groom made gifts of furs and food to his prospective bride's family. If the presents were accepted, there was a feast to which the entire village was invited and during which there was dancing and singing. The marriage ceremony the next day was the simple presentation made by the oldest man in the village of the girl to the suitor.

Infidelity was severely punished among most southeastern peoples. With the Alabamas, Outachepas, Tunican, Tallapoosas, and Pakanas, of French Louisiana, the wronged partner must witness with his own eyes his mate's misbehavior. The offended party then reported to the tribal leader who would pass judgment.

The guilty were forced to dance at a meeting attended by the whole tribe. At the height of their performance they were thrown to the ground and soundly switched on their backs and stomachs.

After her whipping and even before everyone reproached the woman for her conduct, her long braided hair was shaved off by her husband. Her lover's long hair, which was often worn parted in the middle, was shaved off, too.

The guilty parties were then exiled from the village by order of the tribal leader. Their life in society was ended.

Some of the Creeks punished misbehaving women by clipping the ears or nostrils. These women often became prostitutes.

When the Cherokees divorced, it was only after reconciliation efforts by the wife's mother and the husband's mother had failed. Cherokee women sometimes took the initiative in divorce and tossed their husband's things outside the house. The divorced man might be derided by his fellows. For, turned out of his home, he had to return to his mother.

The practice of polygamy was not uncommon in the Southeast. One of the best early English sources is James Adair who lived among the Chickasaws for nearly forty years prior to 1775. He reported that a man might take as many wives as he could support. Adair added that some Indians laughed at the white man for being disinterested in variety and having but one wife.

Whether a man had one wife or two wives or possibly more, the marriage relationship, like other relations of life, was influenced by the clan laws. For example, a member of the Panther clan of the Creeks could not marry another Panther, since this was considered incest, which ordinarily was punished by death. There are reports of executions, as death by flogging, of young violators of incest laws based on the clan.

Under the ancient law of matrilineal descent, one's father came from one clan and one's mother always from another, but a child automatically was a member of his mother's clan.

Clan membership entailed no little protocol and etiquette, according to ethnographer John R. Swanton. For example, one's father's family and its connections were to be spoken well of in every instance, even if that clan's claims for recognition were less than spectacular. There also were complaints in early historic times that many of the younger generation found it difficult to remember instantly that such-and-such a person from a remote village, who might drop in for a lengthy visit, was privileged because he was from one's father's clan's connections although not really kin in the blood sense.

Toward members of one's mother's clan, however, one need not be so self-consciously aware of the laws of politeness, which were so engrained into the young Indian that lapses from etiquette might bring forth that particularly devastating form of punishment, much self-reproach and embarrassment. An easy, relaxed relationship could be enjoyed with members of the mother's clan.

A much commented upon Indian trait—hospitality—was basic in clan law. Fellow clan members were entitled to it, particularly those who were infirm, widowed, or aged. It appears, for example, that older persons might go from village to village seeking out fellow clan members for aid. By the 1750s many younger Creeks, and apparently youth in other tribes as well, were unhappy with ancient hospitality laws. They did not object to caring for those who were older, but they pointed to the increasing number of the not-so-old, who, as semi-professional visitors, manipulated hospitality laws to their selfish benefit.

Annual clan councils occurred at the time of the annual busk ceremonies. At this meeting, which one was required to attend, the most distinguished member would review the history of the clan for the past year and then would give the names of members who deserved to be commended for some deed bringing honor to the clan. At the same time, those who had dishonored the clan were mentioned by name in the meeting. Apparently no one who participated in or observed these meetings ever wrote about it, but in 1911-12, interviewing aged Creeks in Oklahoma, John R. Swanton found some who still remembered the suspense and tension which preceded the calling of names of persons who had done well and those who had not done so well.

Thus, the clan expectations and practices were powerful agencies in socializing the maturing young Indian.

Aside from the various social requirements, some time was given by clan members to stories about the particular wild animal with which the clan had been identified from time too remote for the oldest clan member to remember. These animals were the emblems or symbols of the respective clans and may have indicated that legendary time when man and the wild animals could speak with each other and understand.

Animals commonly used as totems in southeastern clans included the bird (the type not always specified), deer, panther, fish, wolf, skunk, and alligator. Among the Creeks, Alligator clan members delighted in telling how the alligator obtained his crooked nose in a ball game with an unidentified variety of bird. The bird, which in one myth is described as monstrously large with great flapping wings, had possession of the ball and sought, most unfairly, to eliminate alligator from the game by dropping the ball from his beak on alligator's head. Alligator, however, avoided the main impact of the dropped ball by alertly dodging so that the ball descended on his nose. Though alligator suffered intense pain, for his nose was broken, he courageously seized and gripped the ball

Great horned owl totem from southern Florida

59

in his jaws, whose hold no bird could break. Details of the subsequent ball play aren't found in the myths, but perhaps the ideas of alertness, endurance of pain, and general resourcefulness were considered a great deal more vital as the alligator stories were told and told again through the generations; and the clan members thereby rejoiced that so great an animal was their special friend.

As Dr. John R. Swanton and Dr. Angie Debo, authorities on southeastern Indians in Oklahoma, have said, we can only speculate about the political importance of clans. For example, members of the Wind clan of the Creeks—a clan producing the preeminent Creek leader Alexander McGillivray—often had prominence in tribal councils. But was this inherited? Swanton points out that if a member of one of the more prominent clans (clans not being equal in prestige) first handled himself well in war, oratory, athletics, or council matters, his membership could be an advantage. Clans sometimes associated with two or three other clans, which could be helpful in building a following.

But Alexander McGillivray never left a record showing that being a Wind member ordained his advancement. Two of the front-ranking Indian leaders, Pushmataha of the Choctaws and John Ross of the Cherokees apparently made no mention of indebtedness to their clans. Pushmataha went so far as to boast to Gen. Andrew Jackson that he was one of a kind, born when a mighty oak tree was split by a bolt of lightning. John Ross married Quatie, a member of his own Bird clan.

These three examples, McGillivray, Ross, and the only full-blood, Pushmataha, come, of course, from historic times; but they are foremost individuals.

After an exhaustive study of Cherokee and Creek leaders, with some analysis of backgrounds of Chickasaw and Choctaw leaders, Dr. Swanton concludes that the individual character and abilities of the man and not his clan membership caused his star to rise. Yet, Dr. Swanton notes, some clans were prestigious, and some had privileges of an honorary nature, such as the best seats on the square to observe the ceremonials.

The preoccupation of Europeans with notions of inherited caste, which the first observers brought with them, hardly relates to American Indians. In the area that may be broadly thought of as southeastern, only Chitimacha society in Louisiana and Powhatan society in Virginia had hereditary ruling classes, and the evidence is skimpy. This lack of hereditary ruling classes among American Indians was admired by Benjamin Franklin and Thomas Jefferson when, in the 1770s, they were studying the ways in which men have organized their societies and governed themselves.

In summary, the southeastern Indian clan system was a social grouping in which family relations included persons in other villages and other towns. It was said that the Creeks with their far-flung territories in what is now Georgia and Alabama had clan brothers and clan sisters wherever they went, and these personal relations were the heart of the political ties of the Creek Confederacy.

After all the lessons of childhood and youth, what if one should bring dishonor not only to himself and his clan, but to his tribe? Marrying within one's clan was punishable by execution. Cowardice or desertion in battle, also high crimes, met with the scorn of the tribe. Men who had behaved as cowards in battle often would lose their wives or, if unmarried, would be doomed to a life of bachelorhood, because no girl wanted to marry a coward.

The final experience, death, was feared and sorrowed over in annual mourning periods that the first Europeans called cry-times. Cry-times seem to have been family matters in the usual sense of family. Some of the Choctaws still living in the state of Mississippi observe cry-time retreats during which they fast and cover their heads, mourning deceased family members.

Bodies of Biloxi and Pascagoula chiefs were embalmed or dried according to ancient ritual and placed with those

SMITHSONIAN INSTITUTION

Choctaw burials

By Bernard Romans in
A Concise Natural History
of East and West
Florida, *1775*

of their predecessors around the interiors of tribal temples. Choctaws, Chitimachas, Bayogoulas, and others placed the dead on scaffolds; professional men known as bone-pickers later removed the flesh from the bones. The tribal assignment of these specialists—who sometimes might include women—was to prepare the bones of the dead for honored placement in special baskets in the tribal bone-houses.

The veteran observer James Adair truly said of the Chickasaws that they knew much of death, since they were allied to the British and sandwiched between the Illinois and Louisiana segments of the pre-1763 French North American empire. They taught themselves to say, at hard moments, *"Netak intahah,"* which translates, "His days are completed."

If a noble warrior fell, there would be a public oration by the leading "long talker," or orator, of the entire tribe with high ceremonials. The main theme of the euology, according to Adair, was, they who died are only gone to sleep with their forefathers.

Religious Beliefs, Rituals, and Ceremonies

After spending some forty years with the southeastern "Children of the Sun," the English trader James Adair concluded that among Catawba, Cherokee, Creek, Choctaw, and Chickasaw, and other Indians, there once was no separation of the religious customs of their forefathers from the natural and supernatural considerations of life.[1]

To illustrate his point Adair gave the homely example of an Indian man and his little personal ceremony of an occasional pipe of tobacco, sending small puffs of smoke from the revered tobacco to the sky, as if they were offerings to the sun. This simple, unstudied ceremony suggested to Adair the importance of the Indian's religion in everyday life as well as in the grand solemnly thrilling annual ceremonials.

Stone pipe representing a bird

A rather gruff, even hard-boiled, practical man, Adair further remarked that possibly he could present much more imposing ceremonials to show the close connection between the Indian's religious customs and his life ways.

It appears from what the first white men were able to gather from the southeastern Indians that they, like their brothers elsewhere, worshiped the sun, but they also conceived of one whom the Creeks called *Sawgee Putchehassee,* which roughly translated means, "Giver and Taker of Breath." *Sawgee Putchehassee* gave breath to the Indian that he could live in the warmth of the sun and sustain himself with the corn that was itself sacred. That breath would cease was explained in this Creek song, the music of which ethnographer John R. Swanton could not recover:

> Great chiefs are dead
> Be ready to dig the grave
> Let the people bury them
> Let them be ready to cover them
> Let the water be ready for washing.[2]

Among the Mountain Cherokees at Qualla Boundary Reservation in western North Carolina in the 1890s, anthropologist James Mooney heard a religious myth that helps us better to appreciate southeastern Indian beliefs concerning man's relationship with the Creator. "At one time," Mooney was told, "all things living were in the sky, on the sky rock, and this was before the world was made." All the animals could understand man; and man could understand them. Then, most tragically, man dishonored the privilege and was "stricken deaf to the talk of animals and birds. The Great One who was over the sky rock punished man so that he could only understand the talk of his kind."

In relating to other creatures in this world—which many of the Southeasterners conceived of as a kind of island in the cosmos, according to Swanton—the Indians followed definite rituals, for these creatures also were given the power to breathe. Among the Creeks, albino animals were sacred, and they would not willingly kill a wolf or a rattlesnake. By many of the southeastern Indians the bear was regarded as a onetime man who had become disgruntled with his village and retreated to the woods. Did not bear show little fear of man? Did not he eat the foods man enjoyed, seeming to take delight in stealing from man? Was not his erect gait in time of battle like man's? And could not he be evil-tempered?

Before going on a hunt, the southeastern Indian fasted, prayed, and purified himself with the "black drink." The Hitchitis of the Creek Confederacy, like many other Indians, evoked the spirit of the deer in a beautiful ceremonial song. Sadly enough the music appears to have been lost long ago but the words of the Hitchiti song speak well for themselves.

> Somewhere the deer lies on the ground. I think; I
>   walk about.
>   Awake, arise stand up!
> It is raising up its head, I believe; I walk about.
>   Awake, arise, stand up!
> It attempts to rise, I believe; I walk about.
>   Awake, arise, stand up!
> Slowly it raises its body, I think; I walk about.
>   Awake, arise, stand up!
> It is now risen to its feet, I presume; I walk about.
>   Awake, arise, stand up.[3]

This song, or incantation, might be adapted to other animals hunted for food. For example, the initial words, "Somewhere the deer" could be "Somewhere the turkey," or "Somewhere the bison," or whatever the quarry.

When the deer, for example, was brought down by the hunter, a ritual of propitiation was required. The Choctaw hunter would say, "Deer, I am so sorry to hurt you, but the Indian is hungry." He would soothingly say to the spirit of the slain deer that, after all, it would be reincarnated. Would it not inhabit the body of a newly born fawn? Finally, the hunter would tell the deer's spirit that he, the hunter, was not of the deer clan, that he, the hunter, enjoyed an honorable relation with the deer clan, that the deer and man, therefore, were not alienated by this necessary deed.

The populous southeastern tribes by historic times were served by a priesthood with responsibility for teaching the hunting and other rituals that had been passed down to them by their teachers in a preparation that could last twenty summers or longer. Supported by the people they served, the priests might marry and have families. The highest degree in their formal instruction was that of medicine-maker. In this medical training there was great concern for the role of the spirit in a patient's health.

Magical songs or song formulas with appropriate words were used in administering the herb medicines. A Creek song for the treatment of dizziness, headache, and toothache is quite vivid in Swanton's translation:

> Gallop away,
> Gallop away
> Gallop away
> Red rat
> Red cloud
> My head
> Is hot
> Is roaring.[4]

These words were used as an incantation over the patient by an assistant medicine man who wasn't necessarily the one most highly trained in medical matters.

There were good spirits and malevolent spirits that the southeastern Indians, indeed many other American Indians, accepted as having real roles in causing sickness and bringing or preserving good health. Thus the careful Indian, at least, had his personal collection of amulets, the nature of which he kept secret. It is known, however, that among the Cherokees polished quartz sometimes had value as charms. Many other taboos were observed, such

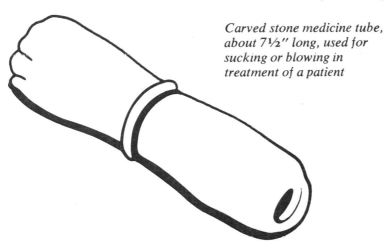

Carved stone medicine tube, about 7½" long, used for sucking or blowing in treatment of a patient

as not sleeping with the head to the west from whence came bad spirits, not looking at the weak-eyed mole lest the creature pass along to the observer his poor eyesight, and not eating the head of the turkey, for the poor fowl's head often was attacked by swarms of gnats and this affliction might be passed on to the careless eater. Throughout the Southeast, all flesh used for food was not to be eaten rare but well-cooked, since there were prohibitions about the sight of blood. Because its cry was thought to prophesy death, there were formulas for keeping the screech owl away.

In human relations also there were many taboos. The Cherokees, for example, did not address another person directly. To do so passed into the rudeness which so many Indians abhorred. This custom indicated reverence for another person's spirit, which was quite holy.

These considerations, as many ethnographers have said, were so "Indian" as to defy description in later times in another language. So far as we are now able to reconstruct, many of the Indians differentiated between body and spirit. For instance, the spirit might move at will during the night when the person was asleep. Dreams of wondrous experiences and sights, unknown places and unheard of events, were the experiences of the spirit. The Choctaws said that if the wandering spirit encountered a bear during its dream state there would be serious trouble in the future. Lesser ranking priests might be called on to explain the meaning of dreams.

Sorcerers by incantation could become the large horned owl of the forest, a heavy, strong bird free to travel at will through the darkness of the forest. If a large owl called many nights near one's dwelling, one could by special magic ask it to give its name, and perhaps hear a message that a medicine man could interpret as signifying either ill or good to the hearer.

Because the little people, beings no more than three feet tall, could cause sickness to strike a tribe, the medicine man used intricate special chants and secret charms to drive them away. Knowledge of these occult matters were handed down over generations and took long effort to master by hopeful young medicine men.

Widespread in the Southeast was the ceremony known to the Creeks as the *asi,* or the imbibing by the men of a purgative tea brewed sometimes by women of high status. Fashioned from the leaves of the shrub *Ilex vomitoria,* the tea, or black drink as it was sometimes called, produced nausea that was believed to purify both body and soul. It was imbibed before a war raid, hunt, ball play, in the yearly green corn ceremonies, and, in some tribes, in the morning. There is no evidence suggesting that males before puberty were eligible for taking the black drink. Among the Congarees, Waccamaws, Enos, Manahoacs, and others of the more than twenty-five small Siouan-speaking tribes on the Atlantic seaboard, a youth seems to have been partly initiated into young manhood by taking the black drink in a puberty ceremonial.

The Creeks believed that the Great Spirit or Master of Breath gave them the black drink, which suggests its importance in their life.

At stated times in the mornings the black drink would be brewed in Creek villages of any size, and the men would assemble on the square. Some villages banned small children from the square at these times.

Three young men of postpuberty age, perhaps priests in training, served as masters of ceremonies for the highly serious event, which they began by singing together the long black-drink note—*"Yohullah."* (This has never been translated.)

Then the three most distinguished men of the village would respond, holding the note, John R. Swanton says, for half a minute, *"Yohullah—"*

After this the youth sang, *"Choh!"* (also never translated). Each one of the three youths would serve the three distinguished men the black drink in a gourd, calabash, or conch shell. Then they would serve the remaining men in a rigidly formal ritual.

The Creeks observed the black-drink ceremony at other times, such as council meetings, when a youth had his war name conferred on him, and at the green corn ceremony.

Ceremony of the black drink. The women in the foreground prepare the drink.

Engraving by de Bry after Le Moyne painting made in Florida in 1564-65.

Conch shell drinking cup

69

Each summer the Creeks, and other Southeasterners, held their greatest annual ritual, the green corn ceremony or busk (*puskita* or *buskita*). It included a series of dances, and commemorated the arrival of new corn that, after fasting, the Indian could eat and enjoy as he

A dance by torchlight ends the green corn festival of the Natchez

Drawing by Le Page Du Pratz from Histoire de La Louisiane, *1758*

reaffirmed that corn was a life-sustaining gift. During the husk, which lasted eight days, old fires were extinguished and new ones made, broken pottery was discarded or replaced, the clans met and evaluated their past year, and the priests performed traditional rituals and uttered prayers at public ceremonials.

The *yatika,* the "long-talker" or orator, an official close to the purely political government but also working with the priesthood, having long been at work on his oration, would be given his opportunity to speak in the square. The chief himself never gave public addresses, relying on the *yatika* for that purpose although the long-talker enjoyed a certain independence of his own.

He would begin: *"Ta-a-a intukastci!"* which meant, "Now everybody's attention." He might continue:

New corn

> The young sporting among themselves.
> Laughing at each other as they ofttimes do.
> That must not be.
> That must not be, so he says.
> Therefore the people must be careful of themselves.
> As they two sit down,
> And if their friends shall come to them
> Victuals no matter how humble, you must break
>   with them. . . .
> As it is known to them.
> They must come up and stand by it, so he says! [5]

"So he says," refers to the chief, whose office was as religious as it was political.

For three hours in the heat of the day, the women —beautifully costumed and adorned with ornaments— danced ceremoniously in the square while the men watched. That evening and the next evening they had to dance again, but more informally. There were no guards with long "scratching" sticks on hand! There was a great deal of laughing in the evening when men danced, too, as the men and women tried to keep in step, weaving in and out of a complex pattern, not touching each other.

71

In the late afternoon on the third day, the warriors and young men began the "long dance" on the square, circling in and out of the area. Led by two singers whose voices rose higher and higher, the dancers' pace increased until the sun was behind the horizon. When darkness arrived, they stopped. There was nothing but silence. The dance was over.

The next five days were given to recreation, with social dancing every night and much singing.

Climaxing the ceremonial dancing and feasting was the forgiving of grudges, grievances, and many crimes. In this peace ceremony, the priests would reinstate former offenders to good standing, and newcomers were adopted into the tribe. These persons seem to have been on a kind of probation, a status never explained to European visitors. At the end of the green corn ceremony, the tribes were more firmly united. They had sung of friendship, law, and peace under the guidance of leaders of the white towns. The orators had spoken of the need to be virtuous, peaceful, and hospitable in the new year. The pipe of peace was used. Brotherhood was extended to new tribes wishing to join the confederacy. A new fire was made by the priest fire-maker's twirling a wooden drill between his hands, and as the first tiny clouds of white smoke came, many said, "It is good."

With their political talent the Creeks made use of the green corn ceremony to hold together their polyglot confederacy which covered a large territory. By eliminating causes of dissension among themselves, which the Cherokees never managed to do, they were that much stronger as a nation.

After many years of studying the life ways of the southeastern Indians, Dr. Swanton noted that the institution of war, which he found was liked by some of the Creeks, the Cherokees, the Catawbas, and the Chickasaws, hastened the destruction of many tribes. Originally Indian warfare was limited, sparing of manpower, devoid of supplies, and decided only in earnest council.

When the Europeans introduced the gun and ideas of supplying a military force for long-range operations, the war element in Indian societies took on strength, upsetting the social, political, and religious systems of those societies.

James Adair, looking in at war among the Indians, remarked that they, akin to other men, simply had enemies, and their enemies could inflict "crying blood," by slaying a relative, friend, or fellow clan member. As for the resulting warfare Adair declared, "Their hearts are fully satisfied, if they have revenged crying blood, ennobled themselves by war actions, given cheerfulness to their mourning country, and fired the breasts of youth with a spirit of emulation." [6]

Jean-Bernard Bossu was determined to find out why and how the Indians made war before European contact, and he reported of the lower Mississippi Valley Indians that they made war for such reasons as the kidnapping of women by another tribe, trespassing of hunting territory, or avenging wrongs.

Of the Alabamas, Arkansas, and Choctaws, Bossu said:

> They consider absolutely worthless a victory bought with the blood of their friends and their relatives. Therefore the chiefs are very careful to spare their warriors and to attack the enemy only when assured of victory either because of superior numbers or advantageous battle positions. Since the adversary uses the same strategy and knows just as well as anyone else how to avoid the traps set for him, the shrewder of the two contenders will win. Because of this, the Indians hide in the woods during the day and travel only at night. If they are not discovered, they attack at daybreak. Since they usually stay in covered terrain, the warrior in the lead sometimes holds a thick brush in front of him as camouflage. They walk in single file, and the last man covers their tracks by arranging the leaves and the earth on which they have stepped so that no telltale trace is left behind. The things which betray them most often to their enemies are

War party in Louisiana.
The warrior on the right
covers their tracks.

the smoke of their fires, which can be smelled a long way off, and their tracks. Indians can read these things with almost unbelievable skill. One day an Indian showed me, in a place where I had noticed nothing, the foot steps of Frenchmen, Indians, and Negroes, he even told me how long ago they had gone by.[7]

The Indian's total life, the real and the unseen, was shaped and influenced by spirituality. In many cases he departed from this life provided with a bowl of food and a bottle of water in his grave to nourish his spirit on the unknown journey. He had no conception of life as being only the experiences a person had on earth. His religious beliefs, rituals, and ceremonies accepted what the famous American philosopher William James in *The Varieties of Religious Experience* called the reality of the unseen. Attitudes, outlook, and practices of the Indian's day-to-day life were shaped and influenced by this great reality.

Menus of the Indians

In *A Concise Natural History of East and West Florida*, published in 1775, Bernard Romans said of the Muskogees, or Creeks, whose country he had visited,

> They make pancakes; they dry the tongues of their venison . . . they eat much roasted and broiled venison, a great deal of milks and eggs . . . also dried peaches and persimmons and other fruits and berries, as well as their particular boast, a prepared drink known as "hickory milk." . . . In a word, they have the greatest abundance available.[1]

A young Virginian, Lt. Henry Timberlake found Cherokee country in 1775 "yielding vast quantities of pease [peas], beans, potatoes, cabbages, Indian corn, pompion [pumpkin], melon, and tobacco, not to mention a number of other vegetables imported from Europe, but not so generally known to them. . . . There are likewise an incredible number of buffaloes, bears, deer, panthers, wolves, foxes, raccoons, and opossum."

James Adair and Timberlake both found only one complaint about Indian cookery, that foods were "overcooked" by European standards.

Le Page Du Pratz, an early historian, writing of the Indians of French Louisiana, pointed out,

> They never eat raw flesh, as so many persons have falsely imagined. . . . In Europe we have entire kingdoms which

A Natchez bison hunt

Drawing by Le Page Du Pratz
from Histoire de La
Louisiane, *1758*

do not give their meats as much time to cook as the natives of Louisiana allow to the most delicate morsels of bison, which is their principal enjoyment.[2]

Louisiana peoples such as the Atakapas, living in bayou, lake, or lagoon areas, were great eaters of fish products. Others, including the Bayogoulas, whose tribal emblem was the alligator, dined on alligator meat, which was a source of protein for peoples living on the Gulf, Florida, and Atlantic coasts.

The Jesuit priest, Father Du Ru, told in his 1700 journal of the Indian style of catching an alligator in Louisiana. The Acolapissas and the Washas, who lived just north of present New Orleans, would swim out to meet an alligator, carrying with them a sharpened piece of hardwood to lodge forcefully in the creature's gaping

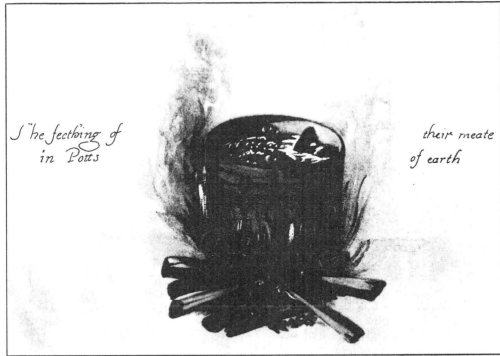

The feething of in Potts

their meate of earth

jaws to keep the sharp teeth from harming the men while they wrestled the alligator to the shore.

James Adair reported,

> It is surprising to see the great variety of dishes they make out of wild flesh, corn, beans, peas, potatoes, pompions, dried fruits, herbs and roots. They can diversify their courses, as much as the English, or perhaps the French cooks: and in either of the ways they dress their food, it is grateful to a wholesome stomach.[3]

Romans noted that corn was prepared by the Creeks in at least forty-two different ways. It was roasted, parched, boiled, stewed, ground up, and baked in several sizes and kinds of bread, combined with water to make an unfermented drink, and was eaten alone or in combination with other vegetables or meats or both! Adair liked the unfermented drink mentioned much better than water itself, though he explained that potable water was

Food cooks in an earthern pot.

Watercolor by John White, ca. 1585.

Timucuans in Florida storing their crops in the public granary

De Bry engraving after Le Moyne drawing made in 1564-65.

readily available. Finely ground particles from grains of corn, with the proper amount of water added, nourished countless hunters.

The Natchez cultivated mushrooms and sometimes made a succulent blend of them with corn, venison, fish, or other flesh. They, like others in the Southeast, enjoyed the combination of corn and several kinds of beans made delicious by a seasoning oil extracted from bear fat. Broths were popular.

Bear fat was cooked over a slow fire and the clear oil that rose to the top in the cooking pot was skimmed off. Then sassafras and wild cinnamon, or other spices, were added. Stored in large earthen jars, the oil would be sweet from one winter to the next.

Of the Enos, Sissipahaws, Congarees, and other Carolina Siouans he visited in the early 1700s, the English traveler and amateur botanist John Lawson wrote, "Sallads they never eat any; as for Pepper and Mustard, they reckon us little better than Madmen, to make use of it amongst our Victuals." Salt was mixed with "their Bread and Soupe," to give them a "Relish." [4] Salt substitutes were made from the ashes of herbs.

Salt—derived from either spring or sea water by boiling, or from mines, such as present Avery Island, Louisiana—was important in early trade. The Caddos, Tunicas, Koroas, Ouachitas, and Chitimachas developed a salt industry. Some of the Creeks made presents of salt to de Soto on his journey through the Southeast.

Away from the coastal areas corn everywhere was queen in the diet and her chief handmaidens were beans and squash. "Corn is their chief produce, and main dependence," James Adair wrote. "Of this they have three sorts . . . [One of these, a small variety, usually ripened in two months, from the time it is planted, though it was called by the English, the six-weeks corn.] The second sort is yellow and flinty, which they call 'hommony-corn.' The third is the largest, of a very white and soft grain, termed bread corn.' " [5] Popcorn, too, was known and relished by the peoples throughout the Southeast.

The chief big game animals were the deer and the bear. Meat was stewed, barbecued, dried, and smoked. A featured dish of hospitality was slivers of venison grilled over a fire on the end of grill sticks and served to guests by young girls who prepared the venison this way. Turkey, rabbit, and squirrel were favorite meats.

Deer

Probably some 60 percent of the food supply of southeastern Indians was plant foods. When game and fish weren't always available, peoples such as the Creeks and the Choctaws relied on their stores of corn and various dried vegetables, meats, and fruits.

Birds prevalent in southeastern menus were the wild turkey, passenger pigeon, and quail. Their eggs were sought after, also. Choctaws, reportedly, ate small game —rabbit, squirrel, beaver, otter, raccoon, opossum— more than most.

Almost everywhere, fishing was important, but especially along the Atlantic coast, the Florida peninsula, and the Gulf coast. The Chitimachas and others too, perhaps, sought the turtle and turtle eggs. In Florida, one of the first Spanish observers, Lopez de Velasco, reported that the Calusas and Tekestas hunted the sea cows, or manatee, for food, tusks, and raw material for leather.

Fish were caught with spears, arrows, hooks, nets, traps, dams, and by drugging when herbs or roots were spread over the water to stun them temporarily. The Chickasaws even practiced hand-to-hand combat. "They have," James Adair said of them,

> a surprising method of fishing under the edges of rocks that stand over deep places of a river. There, they pull off their red breeches, or their long slip of stroud cloth, and wrapping it round their arm, so as to reach to the lower part of the palm of their right hand, they dive under the rock to where the large cat-fish lie to shelter themselves from the scorching beams of the sun and watch for prey: as soon as those fierce aquatic animals see that tempting bait, they immediately seize it with the greatest violence, in order to swallow it. Then is the time for the diver to improve the favourable opportunity; he accordingly opens his hand, seizes the voracious fish by his tender parts, hath a sharp struggle with it against the crevices of the rock, and at last brings it safe ashore.[6]

In addition to raising sunflowers for their seeds, Chitimachas gathered seeds of the pond lily and the palmetto. Wild grapes were enjoyed throughout the Southeast. The great American artist, George Catlin, made a painting of Caddos gathering wild grapes.

Along the Gulf coast, wild rice and wild sweet potatoes were available.

In Virginia and the Carolinas and as far south as northern Georgia, maple sugar trees were tapped. Both maple sugar and maple syrup were important industries with the Cherokees, who used these delicious products in barter. Also gathered were scuppernong grapes, strawberries, huckleberries, crab apples, peanuts, and persimmons.

THE THOMAS GILCREASE INSTITUTE, TULSA, OKLAHOMA

Among leading users of the persimmon were the Tunicans, located on the south side of the Yazoo River. Their diet is said to have been centered around this fruit one entire month each year. They also made persimmon bread as did the Natchez. Baked loaves of this bread one and a half feet long, a foot wide, about as thick as a finger won a good market in New Orleans.

As early as 1775, the Choctaws were taking hogs and poultry (European introductions) to Mobile, some 120 miles from the nearest Choctaw town.

With ease the southeastern peoples adapted to the horse, poultry, cattle, and swine from the European. The watermelon, introduced by the Spaniards, was widely popular when the first English and French arrived.

A common practice of the peoples of the Southeast as well as throughout North America was sharing of food

"Caddo Indians Gathering Wild Grapes" by George Catlin

81

with those who needed it. If a man's home were to burn and with it stores of food, neighbors would come and, as John Lawson relates of the Atlantic seaboard peoples he visited, "every man, according to his Quality, throws him down upon the Ground some Present," most often, food.

> It often happens, that a Woman is destitute of her Husband, and has a great many Children to maintain; such a Person they always help, and make the young men plant, reap, and do every thing that she is not capable of doing herself.[7]

Similar care was given the infirm, and the aged. Lawson calls these helping scenes "feasts of charity," which clearly implies joy in sharing.

Vessels of pottery often were used for storing foods. Pottery bowls, pitchers, and bread molds were found widely in the Southeast. James Adair told of seeing five-gallon containers widely used in the region.

Some of the men of the Pamlicos, Tuscaroras, Pedees, and Woccons were "sorry hunters," according to John Lawson. In winters, in "Spare-hours, the Women make Baskets and Mats to lie upon, and those men that are not extraordinary Hunters, make Bowls, Dishes, and Spoons, of Gum-Wood, and the Tulip-Tree." [8] Lawson reported that others made white clay tobacco pipes. These items were traded to other Indians for raw skins, which were dressed in the summer.

Muskogean Indian Recipes in Use Today

Shuckbread or *Bunaha.*

2 cups cornmeal	about 1½ cups water
1 teaspoon soda	corn shucks

Mix dry ingredients, add water until mixture is stiff enough to handle easily. Form into balls about the size of a tennis ball. Wrap each ball in a corn shuck that has been boiled for ten minutes in water. Drop the shuck-covered ball into a deep utensil of boiling water. Cook one hour. Serve as a bread.

Abuskie.

Parch dry yellow corn in skillet over an open fire or in a hot oven. Pound into fine pieces or powder; put in large utensil; cover with water; stir it well. Serve to drink with water sweetened to taste. Abuskie may be kept several days and used for meals. Today it is often served at special Indian meetings or social gatherings.

Canutchie.

Gather hickory nuts, hull, dry over slow fire. Store to use as needed. Crack nuts. Put nutmeats in wooden bowl (Indians used tree stump, hollowed out). Pound fine with wooden wedge. Roll substance into balls about the size of baseball. These balls keep for quite a long time.

Melt ball with boiling water, add more water and strain all through a sieve. Use it in corn dishes or sweeten with honey and use as a drink.

Games of the Southeast

Athletics among the southeastern peoples were often highly charged with drama. He who excelled came into prestige in his tribe or nation, so the stakes of the meets were high.

René Laudonnière, who commanded a 1564 French expedition to Florida, published *L'Histoire notable de la Floride* in Paris in 1586. He wrote:

> They exercise their young men to run well, and they make a game, among themselves, which he winneth that hath the longest breath. They also exercise themselves much in shooting. They play at the ball in this manner: They set up a tree in the midst of a place, which is eight or nine fathoms high, in the top whereof there is set a square mat, made of reeds, or bullrushes, which whosoever hittith in playing thereat winneth the game.[1]

One of the oldest field games in North America is Indian stickball. Early French explorers in the northeast called the form of the game they saw "La Crosse," because they thought the single ball stick wielded by each player resembled a bishop's crozier.

In the Southeast each player was (and still is) equipped with two rackets. They differed in form and length from tribe to tribe, but usually they were fashioned of dressed wood handles, with a fully curved end. Leather thongs

SMITHSONIAN INSTITUTION

*Games and exercises
of young Timucuans*

*Engraving by de Bry after
a painting by Le Moyne
in 1564-65*

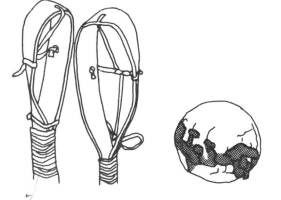

*Ends of stickball
rackets and leather ball*

criss-crossed the curved end to form a pocket in which
the ball could be picked up or caught in flight.

Generally, the ball, about the size of a golf ball, was
made of woven or laced deerskin.

Although goal posts were usually 500 feet apart,

85

They were sometimes much more. Some tribes used slender poles for goals; others, such as the Choctaws, preferred goal posts like those used in football.

The Catawbas, living in the area of present-day South Carolina, played this game with two sticks hollowed out like large wooden spoons. One of their rules of play, which was shared in common by most southeastern tribes, was that no one must touch the ball with his hands. Players could retrieve it, toss it, or catch it only with their rackets.

According to Smithsonian Institution anthropologist James Mooney the object of the game among Eastern Cherokees usually was to carry the ball between the goal posts twelve times. However, the winning score where large numbers of players were involved could be one hundred points as will be indicated below. If twelve was the winning number the first team to have twelve counting pegs put in the ground by an official medicine-man scorer won. This system was also used in scoring larger totals.

Sometimes a game might last until dark, if the two teams were well matched. There was no time limit on how long a game could last; once it was started it was not over until one team had won.

Preparing for a ball game was a serious matter. It involved "purification" of the players and a lengthy invocation of powerful spirits to assure a win. Just before a ball game, Mooney reported of the Cherokees, there was a special preparation of the athletes. The medicine man inflicted on their bodies, arms, and legs the ritualistic scratching and prayed for the spiritual aid of the panther and other animals which were swift and strong and to be admired.

The long night of dancing and preparation according to Cherokee sacred history was the climax of a period of seven sunsets. During this time, players did not eat rabbit flesh, hog-sucker fish, frogs, or the flesh of any other weak or sluggish animals. Infants were not touched since they are weak and helpless. The husband of a pregnant woman was ineligible to play because much of his strength was being lent the coming child.

A special diet of the flesh of animals known for their speed and courage was eaten. Though the raccoon was small, it was cunning and ferocious. It was eaten to lend its heroic qualities to the players.

In 1834, artist and writer George Catlin watched a ball game played by the Choctaws in Indian Territory. He made both a painting and a word picture of the great *Tulli Okchi Ishko* ("He who drinks the juice of the stone"), the champion ball player of the tribe. The painting shows a powerful man, with heavy thighs and legs, and the long hair style typical of the Choctaws. Of the game Catlin said:

> In every ball-play of these people, it is a rule of the play, that no man shall wear moccasins on his feet, or any other dress than his breech-cloth around his waist, with a beautiful bead belt, and a "tail" made of horsehair or quills, and a *"mane"* on the neck of horsehair dyed of various colours.
>
> The game had been arranged and "made up," three or four months before the parties met to play it, and in the following manner:—The two champions who led the two parties, and had the alternate choosing of the players through the whole tribe, sent runners, with the ball-sticks most fantastically ornamented with ribbons and red paint, to be touched by each one of the chosen players; who thereby agreed to be on the spot at the appointed time and ready for the play. The ground having been all prepared and preliminaries of the game all settled, and goods all "staked" (wagered), night came on without the appearance of any players on the ground.[2]

Soon after dark, a procession of lighted torches came from the two encampments. Then the players assembled. To the beat of drums and the chants of the women, the two groups of players began the ball-play dance, which Catlin also painted. Each group danced for a quarter of

Tulli Okchi Ishko,
champion stickball player

Paintings by George Catlin

"Ball Play of the Choctaws—Ball Up"

an hour, "in their ball-play dress; rattling their ball-sticks together in the most violent manner, and all singing as loud as they could raise their voices." [3]

The women of each party—(who had placed the bets, which even included personal clothing)—then formed into two rows on the line between the teams of players to dance and chant. In addition to calling the spirit powers to their assistance, they sang out to their teams to play the game with vigor. Indeed there was much at stake— horses, weapons, household goods!

Meantime, four old medicine men, who would start the game and be the judges, smoked ceremonial pipes at the very center of the playing field. The puffs of smoke were prayers to the Great Spirit to make them impartial in judging.

"This dance," Catlin said, "was one of the most picturesque scenes imaginable, and was repeated at intervals of every half hour during the night, and exactly in the

Stickball played by Mississippi Choctaws today

JIMMY MOORE

Young Choctaws begin a stickball game.

"Ball Play Dance. Choctaw"—Painted by George Catlin in Indian Territory in the 1830s

same manner; so that the players were certainly awake all the night." [4]

Play began, finally, at nine in the morning as judges threw up the ball. An instant struggle began between *the six or seven hundred players*. One can imagine the shouting of the crowd.

The players tried to catch the ball in their sticks and throw it home between their goals for a score of one point. There was running, leaping, darting between other players' legs, tripping, throwing, foiling one another, leaping over one another's heads, shouting, and, even, shrill yelping and barking sounds! Catlin saw fist fights between players, while others swirled past ignoring them. Fighting was permissible, but the ball sticks were not to be used in such brawls.

The ball often disappeared from sight when it fell to the ground, and a confused mass of players fought to pick it up with their sticks.

Finally an hour before sunset, the successful team scored one hundred points and the game was over. To the victors went the wagers made by the opposing side.

Catlin commented, "This wonderful game, which is the favorite one amongst all the tribes, and with these Southern tribes played exactly the same, can never be appreciated by those who are not happy enough to see it." [5]

Ball play was often time to let off steam, tension, and friction, a game could settle built-up bad feelings. Some of the southeastern peoples told the first Europeans that ball play was "little brother to war."

The game was a major undertaking for the medicine men, who moved among the players on the field. Since all life and power came from the sun, they carried small looking glasses to reflect the rays of the sun onto the bodies of their players. They would try to will the ball to go to their given goal posts. If a medicine man's team lost, he was apt to be blamed. His following might decline and certainly his powers would be questioned.

Jean-Bernard Bossu earlier wrote of the Choctaws,

> When the men's game is finished, the women get to-
> gether to play to avenge their husbands losses. Their rackets
> are different from those that the men use in that they are
> bent. The women, who are very good at this game, run
> swiftly and push each other around just as the men do.
> They are dressed exactly like the men, but with a little
> more modesty. They put red paint on their cheeks only
> and apply vermilion instead of powder to their hair. . . .
>
> After having played hard all day long, everyone goes
> home in glory or shame. There is no bitterness as each one
> promises to play another day when the best man will win.[6]

Another popular sport which was played in slightly
different ways throughout the Southeast was chunkey.
Usually a specially smoothed and rounded stone was
rolled along the ground, and two players each threw a
long slender pole after it. The thrower whose pole hit the
stone or was nearest the stone when it rolled to a stop
made a point. Poles varied in length among tribes from
A form of chunkey eight to fifteen feet, some with crossbars, some in the
played in Mississippi today shape of an F, some notched for counting, but most

JIMMY MOORE

straight. The Bayogoulas and Mugulashas are said to have played this game for days at a time.

The Creeks constructed special large enclosed courts with sloping sides which could seat many spectators. However, a common use of the public square in many southeastern towns was for sporting events and gaming.

Colonial Virginia explorer John Lederer in 1672 reported of the Enos of North Carolina: "Their town is built round a field, where in their sports they exercise with so much labor and violence, and in so great numbers, that I have seen the ground wet with the sweat that dropped from their bodies; their chief recreation is slinging of stones [playing chunkey]." [7]

Dice games were played by women in the North Carolina area who used the seeds or stones of persimmons for dice. Natchez women played games of chance with split canes; Choctaws used grains of corn, charred on one side;

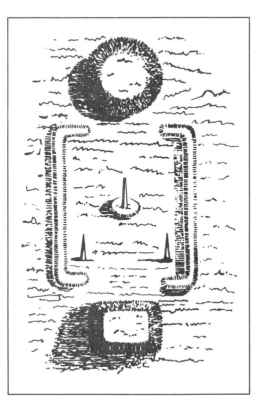

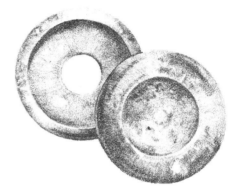

Plan of an early Creek chunkey yard and carved and polished chunkey stones

and women of the Cherokee, dried lima beans. The tireless English traveler John Lawson related of a group of Congarees,

> The Women were very busily engaged in Gaming: The Names or Grounds of It I could not learn, 'tho I looked on above two Hours. Their Arithmetick was kept with a Heap of Indian Grain.
>
> Their chiefest game is a sort of Arithmetick, played with a parcel of small, split reeds, fifty in number, and each about seven inches in length. Some of the reeds were tossed to the opponent; and the Art is, to discover upon sight, how many you have, and what you throw to him that plays with you.[8]

He found that a good set of the reeds had "the value of a dress'd doe skin."

Pioneer Louisiana historian Le Page Du Pratz found that among the Natchez "The young people, especially the girls, have hardly any kind of diversion but that of the ball: this consists in tossing a ball from one to the other with the palm of the hand, which they perform with a tolerable address."[9]

Childhood games of the southeastern Indians were like those of most children—imitations of their parents. They drew the bow, ground the corn, performed the various dances.

Cherokee boys had a game of gliding a stick or cane pole in the snow; the boy who made the longest toss-glide won. Girls and women in Choctaw and Congaree lands played games not unlike jackstones and modern dice.

Dr. Mary R. Haas wrote about Creek intertown relations in Oklahoma, based on memories of older Creeks, stories told them by their parents and friends, as well as other research.

Dr. Haas found that ball play often was a match game between war and peace towns, or red and white towns as they were called. These towns weren't always on the best of terms, but the ever-popular ball play relieved hostility and distrust. Match games were held in the summer, shortly after the green corn ceremony. Since preparations for the game took much time, one game a year for a town was enough.

If a town was defeated by the same town three or four times in a row, it was required that the loser become a dependency of the winner. For example, a white town could become a red town.

Indian stickball is still played today both in Oklahoma (where many southeasterner tribes now live) and in the Southeast.

Dance and Music

John Lawson who visited many of the Carolina tribes in the early 1700s commented,

> For every sort of Dance, they have a Tune, which is alloted for that Dance; as, if it be a War-Dance, they have a warlike Song, wherein they express, with all the Passion and Vehemence imaginable, what they intend to do with their Enemies; how they will kill, roast, sculp, beat, and make Captive, such and such numbers of them; and how many they have destroy'd before. All these Songs are made new for every Feast; nor is one and the same Song sung at two several Festivals. Some one of the Nation (which has the best Gift of expressing their Designs) is appointed by their King, and War-Captains, to make these Songs.[1]

In the early 1790s American botanist William Bartram told a tale of song theft. "Some of their most favourite songs and dances," he said of the Creeks, "they have from their enemies, the Chactaws [Choctaws]; for it seems these people are very eminent for poetry and music; every town amongst them strives to excel each other in composing new songs for dances; and by a custom amongst them, they must have at least one song, for exhibition, at every annual busk." [2]

A young Creek who was also part Choctaw traveled into the Choctaw country from Mobile in order to learn the secrets of their music and poetry. He was soon found out and denounced as a spying Creek and a song thief and was hotly pursued by the Choctaws.

Then the spy became an employee of a trader at the Creek town of Mucclassee where he was something of a hero because of his Choctaw song piracy. "Having learned all their most celebrated new songs and poetry," Bartram declared, he was pressed by the youth of Mucclassee to give out some of these new songs, which he did.

In due time, the young people of the town staged a great dance and festival, in which a young Choctaw slave girl was forced to lead the dances. During the singing of one of the songs, she began weeping.

Bartram, much moved, learned that when she was taken captive, her father and brothers were slain. The

A religious dance performed about 1585

From an original watercolor by John White made in what is now North Carolina

SMITHSONIAN INSTITUTION

chorus of the song, stolen from her people, reminded her of her family. This is the chorus as given by Bartram:

> All men must surely die,
> Tho' no one knows how soon
> Yet when the time shall come
> The event may be joyful.[3]

There were martial, romantic, festive, social, and religious dances, some of them combining so many elements that they were major ceremonials. Each dance had its own song. Instrumental music was provided among many tribes by the drum, the rattle, and a kind of flute made of a joint of reed (or cane) or the large bone of a deer's leg. Among the Creeks, the flute apparently was played only by individuals, often by young men, and never used in ceremonials. The Creeks evidently used the flute for personal enjoyment. The Creek women prior to the dance fastened rattlers prepared from tortoise shells to the calves of their legs.

John Swanton, John Lawson, and William Bartram agree that there were several styles of singing with sweet

Eastern Cherokee gourd dance rattle, Choctaw drum made from the trunk of a black gum tree, and Choctaw cane flute

and low tones prevalent. Bartram maintained that "moral songs" were the most popular among the Indians he knew, the Seminoles, Creeks, Choctaws, and Cherokees.

Below is a Choctaw song for success in the ball game. Although written music can't capture the full flavor and rhythm of Indian music, it does give some idea of the melody.[4]

Lawson reported that there were wallflowers, or plain girls who were not selected by the dance leaders for the company of those who entertained visitors.

Bossu tells of a war dance among the Arkansas, or Quapaw,

All the young men are painted red. The one who does the discovery or surprise dance remains in a crouching position as he spies on the enemy. He jumps up suddenly, club in hand, and utters piercing screams as he attacks his foe in simulated battle. The dance partner falls as though struck by lightning and stiffens his arms and legs like an epileptic. After this, the victor does a scalping dance. He pretends to make an incision in the forehead and around the neck of the enemy. The then goes through the motion of digging his long fingernails into the cut and places his knees on

Ceremony of the calumet performed by Chitimachas in 1718

Drawings by Le Page Du Pratz from Histoire de La Louisiane, *1758*

the victim's shoulders. He then pushes forward quickly with his knees as he yanks back with his hands, removing the dead man's scalp, hair and all.[5]

The warriors fasted, prayed, swallowed the black drink, danced, and sang.

About three miles from the present town of Charenton, Louisiana, on a little bay of Grand Lake, the Chitimachas had a tribal dance temple, which French explorers called Maison de Valeur, a 12-foot square building with a pointed roof. In it were kept the special costumes of dancers and red, black, and white body paint.

On the day before the new moon, presumably in the summer (the accounts leave no clues as to precisely when), families arrived at the temple in dugout canoes for the six-day festival of initiating young males into manhood.

Women and girls weren't permitted within the temple as young men underwent a program of dancing and fasting under the watchful eyes of priests. It is said that part of a young male's initiation was dancing until exhaustion came. Drinking of water was prohibited. These requirements probably were intended to teach endurance and resistance to fatigue.

Far to the east in the Carolinas John Lawson observed puberty initiations among a number of Siouan-speaking tribes such as the Cheraws, Keyauwees, Sissipahaws, Waterees, Woccons, Congarees, and others. He reported confinement of youths without food and water, partaking of the black drink afterwards, followed by the individual performances of singing and dancing if the youths could stand on their feet. Lawson also said that the youths had to take potions, the ingredients of which he could not ascertain but which induced temporary delirium after which they were pronounced men by venerable elders of the tribe. These potions were not the ubiquitous black drink.

A Chitimacha ceremony, found in varying forms in the Southeast, honored the bones of the dead. Special officials were in charge of the bone house in which a perpetual fire was kept. Annually these men in a solemn ritual would open the graves of the recently buried, take out what remained of the bodies, and remove the remaining flesh from the bones. Then the bones would be wrapped in a new burial mat that often had a checkered design.

When the people assembled they walked six times around a blazing fire after which the bones were placed in a mound. If the dead were a chief, his widows and male orphans had to take prominent roles in the ceremonial dance which followed.

Of a social dance in the grand village (Natchez) of the Natchez, a French visitor observed an apparent separation of generations in dances, men dancing with women and boys with girls in groups of twenty or thirty, evenly divided in sex. A married man could not dance with the girls or married women with the boys. After midnight the young unmarrieds were left to themselves to continue dancing until daylight.

A Natchez self-renewal ceremonial saw the women, girls, and old men seated in a circle on the square ground with a lead singer in the middle. He would lead them as they sang, *"Honothea, honothea"* (evidently a religious word, which has not been translated), in cadence, striking their abdomens with their palms to make a kind of echo.

Then the women and girls would rise and circle around the fire, gracefully waving feathers with their left hands, and shaking gourd rattles with their right hands. This had to have been practiced at length to achieve coordination. One may wonder about what persons born with poor coordination did but alas! the accounts are silent.

The dance ended dramatically when the men and boys, each in a dead run, struck a symbolic post with his tomahawk to express fidelity and bravery.

According to John R. Swanton, the purely social dances of the Creeks began at sunset when the moon was full.

Noted anthropologist James G. Swan classifies the dance forms of the Creeks in three ways: social dances, busk dances, and animal dances. In all these dances the most common step was a slow, shuffling one, alternating first the right foot foremost, and next the left. Good form in dancing was prized so highly that hours might be spent in practicing.

A popular social dance among the Creeks was the friendship dance. Around a night camp fire young, unmarried men would form a ring about an inner ring of young, unmarried women. The men would then move in a circle simulating the course of the sun, the females moved in the opposite direction. As they did the slow, shuffling step the men would strike their arms with their open hands. The girls would follow, clapping their hands, and, in Bartram's phrase, "raise their shrill sweet voices, answering an elevated shout of the men at stated times." Often there was an interlude during the dance when the girls performed as a separate chorus.

Another variation of the friendship dance began when a man sitting on a bench at night by the camp fire would sing, and drum on an instrument often made of a hollow cypress stump. He sometimes was assisted by a second male singer. Two men would come into the light of the fire, step around it, and then go out and bring in two women, after which the four individuals would move around the fire. Next, the two women stepped out to bring in two other men; then these two men would bring in two more women; and this was kept up until all were brought in.

A colorful animal dance was the fox dance performed exclusively by Creek women. It began with the dancers moving very slowly round and round the fire, increasing in pace to a rapid finish. Older women nicked the dancers' legs slightly with gar teeth or crawfish claws to make sure they were lively.

Small children were taught to dance as part of their education. Among the Seminoles they had dances of their own, and in 1933 the great authority on Indian music Frances Densmore recorded the music for some Seminole children's dances. Below are two of the songs:[6]

The corn dance of the Seminoles was a religious activity featuring a song leader, who also led the line of dancers in which men and women alternated, usually holding hands. A long line was formed that moved counter-clockwise around the fire. The leader sang one phrase, then all joined in the singing. There was no drum, but the sound of small turtle shell rattles worn by women below the knee of each leg marked the time. Each shell contained sun-hardened, handmade pellets of mud. The

corn dance, obviously, praised most solemnly the marvel-
ous plant that made a comfortable life possible for the
Southeasterners.

With some variation, the corn dance of the Seminoles
found a counterpart in the dances of the busk, or green
corn ceremony, that important religious and new year
ceremony of the Creek peoples.

One of the corn dance songs goes like this:[7]

Traditional dances may be seen at annual fairs of
southeastern Cherokees and Choctaws and the annual
powowows of the Florida Seminoles. Annual cele-
brations, to which guests are welcome, bring colorfully
dressed Indian families together in Oklahoma from mid-
June to early September.

Indian Childhood

Among some southeastern peoples, the first few days of life were critical. James H. Malone, historian of the Chickasaws, reported that during the first days of an infant's life, the mother evaluated the baby's fitness for living. Chickasaw mothers felt an obligation to the tribe and also to the physically imperfect infant to spare it the ordeal of living longer.

The Yuchi thought a newly born child, during its first four days, was closely associated with the spirit world from which it came. If the infant survived entrance into the world, it was given the spirit name of an ancestor. As a token of having been so named, a string of small white beads was placed around the baby's neck.

Numerous tiny skeletons that lacked these beads were excavated by University of Tennessee archaeologists Thomas M. N. Lewis and Madeline Kneberg in east Tennessee. Because so many infants had not survived, they surmised that the child, spirit-human, wasn't nursed or clothed those first four days.

John R. Swanton reports that Creek mothers, perhaps to comfort themselves, sometimes buried infants who died under the floors of their houses.

Cherokees, and a good many others in the Southeast, bathed daily in streams or lakes near their homes. In fact, proximity to running water largely determined where a given village was to be situated. Babies also were bathed each day and their bodies anointed with oils derived either from bear fat or the passenger pigeon.

In what is now North Carolina, the father-husband made from wood a flat cradle board some two feet long and one foot wide. The mother carried the baby in it on her back.

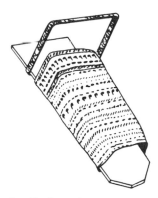

In the Carolinas, "diapers" were moss placed in the bottom of the cradle board which was changed by pushing a lever.

Cradle board

Foreheads of male Waxhaws, Catawbas, and other Siouan-speaking tribes, of Choctaws and Chickasaws, and Caddos generally were flattened at birth. One method was to hinge a board so that it gently pressed the skull of the infant in his cradle board. Children might nurse up to six years of age. Boys, the first to wear clothes, began wearing the breechclout when they were about four or five years old. At three or four, boys and girls were separated. Boys began the serious business of learning to be a man. No longer could girls ramble unattended about the village.

Usually boys were instructed by the oldest uncle on their mother's side. Sometimes a bachelor uncle had more to do in their upbringing than their fathers, who were busy with farming chores, hunting, fishing, and the defense of the village and tribe.

Swanton theorized that the oldest aunt on the mother's side instructed the girls in Creek society. Among some present-day Seminoles and Miccosukees in Florida the maternal grandmother's wisdom is sought and cherished.

Boys, among the Chickasaws who valued valor, slept on panther skins to acquire that animal's strength and courage. Sleeping on doe skins made Chickasaw girls more graceful. Parents and children slept on comfortable cane "mattresses." They went to sleep with their heads to the east, the direction from which the sun came. It was not good to sleep headed west, for trouble and bad spirits came from that direction.

Many southeastern peoples looked closely for signs of special promise among children. Twins were especially watched, for the younger, if a boy, might have the gift of prophesy. If not detected and developed, it would vanish before he had seen ten summers.

There does seem to have been a great amount of planned activity for children. Le Page Du Pratz, a Frenchman in early Louisiana, noted that among the Chitimachas, Alabamas, Choctaws, and Natchez, ten-year-old girls had to walk two or three miles, one way, to help in the village corn fields. Boys of the same age carried home fish and venison caught by their fathers.

By the time a boy was eight, he was expected with the clever use of the blowgun to bring in quail and rabbit to add to the family larder. His life was competitive. There were contests of archery, running, wrestling, weight-lifting, chunkey, and ball play, with his "uncle" insisting on both strength and courage. He probably also practiced with the rabbit or throwing stick, which Choctaws called *iti isht nipa*.

JIMMY MOORE

A young Choctaw aims the blowgun.

Efforts to get around the morning bath in the stream were punished by the uncle, with scratching of arms, backs, or legs with a snake's tooth, or the teeth of a gar fish.

The English trader, James Adair, noted that the chief manly virtues were honor, and love of country, or the tribe, which were " prized above life." Feminine qualities were "a mild, amiable, soft disposition: exceedingly modest . . . and very seldom noisy, either in the single, or marired state." This character molding in the young was accomplished mainly by sweet words. For instance, a boy who disgraced himself by cowardice would be praised by uncle for his exemplary courage. Adair says, "I have known them to strike their delinquents with those sweetened darts [words], so good naturedly and skilfully, that they would sooner die by torture, than renew their shame by repeating the actions." [1]

Jean-Bernard Bossu, who in 1753 visited many Indians living in the colony of Louisiana, also reported on the Indian's skill with words. Children grew up understanding about character by example and *word*.

JIMMY MOORE

*A toss of the rabbit stick
at a moving target
in present-day Mississippi*

The infant at first was deemed a kind of representative from the unseen world to which the native was attuned. Missionary Augustus Ward Loomis was told by a white trader, "They see ghosts and witches, and such, a lot sharper than you."

Some of the children in Creek villages were given much counsel about the ten-foot giants, whose eyelids opened vertically, not horizontally. According to this bit of folklore their heads were small, their arms very long. They often kidnapped the prettiest of the young girls. If they caught a lazy boy they would flay him alive. Boys had to know how to run swiftly!

Boys needed to be fleet runners to elude the little people as well. Choctaw children were told these beings, who were no more than three feet tall, liked to steal small boys.

Childhood training was to help boys and girls to behave themselves, to respect their elders and learn from them, to know clan and tribal histories, and especially to attend spiritual matters—the most important agencies of all.

In puberty ceremonials for males among Creeks and Choctaws, boys were tattooed to signify early manhood. By puberty some Choctaw males had pierced the gristle of their nostrils and were wearing bear claws there. Ear lobes sometimes were pierced and made large by stuffing them with buffalo wool. Young men learned the art of applying red, white, and black body paint for ceremonial occasions.

Ear spools

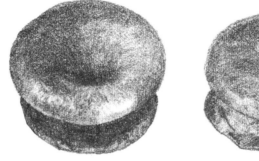

Mistippee,
a Creek youth of the early 1800s,
wears facial decoration.

From The Indian Tribes of North America
by Thomas L. McKenney and James Hall

Catawba young women were learning the famed Catawba art of properly styling and wearing feathers. When a Caddo girl in what is now northwestern Louisiana became a teen-ager, great flowers were tattooed on her body by artists. Soot from pine might be used for this tattooing. Using pine soot and herbs, women of the Natchez and Bayogoulas periodically blackened their teeth.

And so childhood and adolescence passed, and the young person was ready for his mature role in society.

Traders and Imperial Rivalry

After de Soto's journey through the Southeast, the Europeans began moving in from all directions.

Spanish explorers and missionaries advanced up the Florida peninsula, across the Gulf of Mexico and up the Georgia coast. English settlers pressed from colonies on the Atlantic Ocean in the present-day Carolinas and Virginia. With hunters moving down the Mississippi from Canada and out from New Orleans and Mobile, France approached from the north and west and south.

Struggling with one another for power, each national group sent traders traveling through Indian lands and often to live in their villages. In return for deer, bear, and beaver skins, the traders supplied goods such as metal knives, iron kettles, guns, and woven cloth.

To woo tribes to their side or to keep them neutral, representatives of the three European governments also presented the Indian nations with gifts of these items.

Choctaws, their Mississippi River lands near the French settlements in New Orleans and Mobile, became friends of the French. Often in conflict with the Choctaws, the Chickasaws allied with the British. Though close to the British colonies, the Cherokee often traded with both the French and the British.

The peoples of the Creek Confederacy were in the most delicate position of all, for they were in direct contact with all three European groups. Agents from French Mobile, Spanish Pensacola, and British Charleston plied the Creeks with gifts, each urging them to ally with his particular nation and to turn against the others. Master diplomats, the Creeks skillfully played one nation against the other.

In his journal of 1729 a Frenchman, Lt. Régis Du Roullet, reveals the European rivalry for the Indian favor. When Lieutenant Du Roullet made his journey, the British were doing well among the southeastern peoples. English traders swarmed out of Charleston. The British Isles were pouring forth manufactured goods priced cheaper than those turned out by the less-booming French industry.

Lieutenant Du Roullet recorded his orders for August 21, 1729, from Gov. Etienne oucher de La Perier in New Orleans,

> Sieur Regis will be freiendly with all the chiefs . . . ask them whether they prefer . . . a warehouse for goods established among the Choctaws . . . they must promise me to guard [it] . . . it will be placed under their protection and since there will be only one officer and few soldiers there, for whose safety they will likewise keep watch.[1]

The lieutenant was also to determine the reason for the Choctaws' displeasure with the French.

Presents of about eight hundred pounds in weight were to be taken with him to be given to the "Great Chief of the Choctaws."

Lieutenant Du Roullet went from New Orleans to Mobile, where he made the friendship of Patlaco, the youthful chief of the Chickasawhays (a small tribe allied with the Choctaws), who guided him to the Great Chief's headquarters in east-central Mississippi. Seventeen strong men were needed to bear the gifts on their backs.

> When I arrived there I had the soldiers and the Indians who were following me fire a volley. This had a very good effect.

After this I sat down on one of these mats [which he had found spread on the ground in the shade of four big trees]. . . . From there I perceived two or three hundred men with the Great Chief accompanied by the other chiefs under his authority coming to me singing the calumet song. At a certain distance from the Great Chief I rose. He came to me, gave me his hand and embraced me in the French manner. The principal chiefs of his escort did the same thing. After this I sat down.[2]

More ceremonies followed, which included smoking the pipe of peace and enjoying a feast prepared for this ambassador from the "Great Chief" of the French at New Orleans.

I remained for some time according to their custom without saying anything and after this interval I began my speech. [Through his interpreter he said:] "The Great Chief who sends me is in a position to supply you more abundantly than the English with the limburg cloth [standard woolen fabric used in trade by both the English and the French, usually dyed scarlet or blue, and named for Limburg province in the Netherlands], the white blankets, the guns, the powder, the bullets, the kettles, the vermilion, the beads, the mattocks, the hatchets, the gunflints, the pistols, the swords, the coats, the hats, the shoes, the stockings, the ribbons of all colors, the belts, and in general all the goods that you and your nation will need.

"Listen well. The Great Chief tells you furthermore that the English are seeking to detach you from the French only to destroy you more easily by means of the Cherokees and other nations who listen to the word of the English."

[Then he had the heavy gift packages untied.] I began first by giving the Great Chief a gun, a pair of leggings, a shirt and the equipment. . . . I addressed myself to the Great Chief and told him that as this present concerned him he only had to make the distribution of it. This he did at once and everybody was satisfied.[3]

Each village chief received a coat, a gun, a pair of leggings, a breechclout, a blanket, two shirts, a hat, two axes, a tomahawk, round beads of white and colored porcelain glass, a pair of scissors, two pickaxes, a comb, some nails, two awls, some vermilion, some brass wire, twelve small bells, and various other items.

November 11, 1729, Lieutenant Du Roullet arrived back in New Orleans and reported that over 160 Choctaw village chiefs, sub-chiefs, principal men, or politicians had been given the present. The Choctaws wanted the warehouse.

Referring mainly to the Chickasaws but generally to all the peoples of the interior Southeast, British trader James Adair observed in his book published in 1775, "The Indians, by reason of our supplying them so cheap with every sort of goods, have forgotten the chief part of their ancient mechanical skill, so as not to be as well able now, at least for some years, to have independence of us.[4]

Earlier, in 1728 William Byrd, an American colonial writer, planter, and Virginia official, had written of the Nottaways in Virginia to whom guns were being made readily available, "Bows and Arrows are grown into disuse except only amongst their Boys. Nor is it ill Policy but on the contrary very prudent, thus to furnish the Indians with Fire-Arms, because it makes them depend entirely upon the English, not only for their Trade, but even for their subsistence."[5]

Flint lock musket

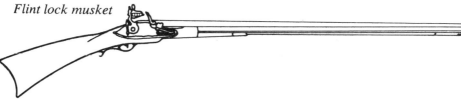

Guns are more effective for hunting and war than arrows and spears. Metal implements are sturdier, more lasting than flint and wood. Manufactured cloth requires less work than tanning hides or weaving bark.

The items the Europeans had were desirable. But what differences their introduction brought! Basketry, pottery-making, and other crafts began to disappear. Adequate defense against those using guns was the use of guns.

To obtain the European products, the peoples of the Southeast hunted the fur-bearing animals of their forest and fields—the deer and beaver and bear, even the bison.

Trading was heavy. For example, from 1739 to 1759, a million and a quarter deer skins were shipped to England from Charleston, South Carolina, alone. In the rivalry between Great Britain and France for dominant influence in the Indian nations, the French bought so many unneeded beaver skins that great quantities were burned in Quebec.

The herds of bison that roamed the Southeast vanished before the hunter's gun. Nor did the hunter any longer thank the spirit of the animal he killed in order to provide food and clothing for his needs. Use of the products of Europe brought changes. The people of the Southeast were indeed becoming dependent on the Europeans and their trade goods.

"Like Little Birds Before the Eagle"

In 1733 there was a meeting between Gen. James Oglethorpe, founder of the colony of Georgia, and a number of Creek Indian leaders one of whom was an aged Coweta who told Oglethorpe through his interpreter that his heart was heavy.

He explained to the general that his and other Creek tribes had been "scattered like little birds before the eagle."

One of the many other "little birds" which had been scattered by 1733 were the Sewees, a Siouan-speaking people whose home had been on the Santee River in central South Carolina and around the Charleston Harbor, which they had shared with the Cusabos before they were displaced by the Spanish. In 1600 there were said to have been eight hundred Sewees. When the English colonists arrived in the vicinity of Charleston in 1670, the Sewees hospitably shared their corn, meat, and other foods with them.

Within forty-five years, however, only fifty-seven Sewees were left. Seeing them about 1700, John Lawson later wrote that their fortunes were a "classic study" showing that "all other Nations of *Indians* are oberv'd to partake of the same fate, when the *Europeans* come.

"The Small-Pox has destroyed many thousands of these

Natives," he related. This disease, and others, such as measles, mumps, and cholera, that came with the European contact, fanned out like waves "within 200 miles of our settlements." [1]

Many Sewees ill with smallpox jumped into rivers in an effort to treat the new disease. The shock to the body that resulted often caused death.

Historian Robert H. White, who made special studies on historical effects of smallpox, found that the Cherokees also resorted to rivers and streams when attacked by smallpox. For to them, as to the Sewees, cleanliness and daily bathing were important. He added that the scars of smallpox, even if a victim survived, were too frightful to tolerate. Some took their own lives, because of their badly scarred faces.

John Lawson estimated that the Indian population of North Carolina and South Carolina was reduced through disease by five-sixths in fifty years.

Another new health hazard for the Sewees, as others, was drunkenness. John Lawson reported of them that they liked to drink rum, drink it fast, and take it "straight," usually during "night frolics" that started out as fun but became orgies. Drinkers fell into fires, and deeply burned arms and legs or to death. Others fell from cliffs. Brawls, murder, and stealing were common. Adultery went unpunished. Women became prostitutes to obtain liquor; men sold their wives and daughters.

Leaders of the Sewees met with authorities from North Carolina, where the rum was coming from, and asked that they cease trading the liquor with the Sewees.

The authorities promised to take the matter under advisement. But after the conference, the young Sewee braves threatened their leaders with death if the liquor traffic were stopped.

The liquor trade was profitable, John Lawson reported. Tuscaroras were employed by traders to carry the Caribbean rum from seacoast ports where it had been exchanged for corn, deerskins, and other Carolina products.

Some Indians refrained from drinking because of its ill effects on self-control. This was a hard thing since getting intoxicated had become almost a way of life among many of the Sewees. As with many people today, drinking was an outlet for frustration. The Sewees, their old way of life vanishing, were not part of the new culture, although caught up in it.

Apparently the first Europeans to have visited the Muskogean Cusabos in their lands between Charleston Harbor and the Savannah River were Lucas Vazquez de Ayllon and two Spanish caravels from Santo Domingo in 1521. Pietro Martire d'Anghiera, also known as Peter Martyr, author of *De Orbe Novo,* one of the first accounts of Spanish New World explorations, wrote in 1530,

> When the Spaniards landed, he [a Cusabo] received them respectfully and cordially, and when they exhibited a wish to visit the neighborhood, he provided them with guide and an escort. Whenever they showed themselves, the natives, full of admiration, advanced to meet them with presents, as though they were divinities to be worshipped. What impressed them [the Indians] most was the sight of the beards and the woolen and silk clothing.
>
> But what then! The Spaniards ended by violating this hospitality. For when they had finished their explorations, they enticed numerous natives by lies and tricks to visit their ships, and when the vessels were quickly crowded with men and women they raised anchor, set sail, and carried these despairing unfortunates into slavery. By such means they sowed hatred and warfare throughout that pleasant and peaceful region, separating children from their parents and wives from husbands.[2]

This slave-hunting expedition probably landed slightly north of Charleston Harbor.

The Catawbas of Siouan stock lived in what is now the western Carolinas and eastern Tennessee. Once there were almost five thousand Catawbas, who, in the estimation of contemporary observer James Adair were renowned in many of the arts, but under European influence came to glory in military prowess.

Catawba fortunes began ebbing in 1715, when to avoid being made slaves they joined the Yamasees in war against the English colonists. The war was short but frightful, with reports of some one thousand of the Catawbas and Yamasees killed, certainly a national calamity for them. Peace was made between the English colonists and the Catawbas in the same year, the surviving Yamasees taking refuge in Florida on the St. Johns River from which some joined the Creeks in what is now Alabama.

For the Catawbas after 1715 it was epidemics, spreading alcoholism, population decline, and sporadic fighting with Iroquois and Shawnees. These northern tribes had once apparently been intimidated by Catawba fighting qualities and numbers, but after 1715 they seem to have raided them almost at will. By 1775 only some four hundred Catawbas remained.

Another scattered people, the Apalachees, lived in what is now northwest Florida. In a frontier war between England and Spain, Col. James Moore of South Carolina, with fifty colonist volunteers and some one thousand Creek warriors fell upon the Apalachee nation at present-day Tallahassee. In his official report to the colonial government at Charleston of May 1, 1704, Colonel Moore observed that his force had totally destroyed all the people of four towns. Some thirteen hundred Apalachees were taken to Charleston to be sold as slaves. Some four hundred escaped to Mobile.

Official French sources in Mobile said that the raiders "have killed and made prisoner six or seven thousand Apalachees, . . . and have killed more than six thousand head of cattle and other domestic animals such as horses and sheep." [3]

The Timucua had some forty villages with an estimated population of thirteen thousand in 1650 in their territory which extended from the Suwannee River to the St. Johns in Florida. They are considered by many to be a Muskogean people. When they first met the Spanish the Timucua occupied not merely central and northern areas of the Florida peninsula but Cumberland Island, Georgia, and a part of the adjacent mainland. Spanish conquest of the Timucua and other Florida peoples began after they destroyed a French fortification on the St. Johns River in 1565, the end of French efforts to colonize in Florida and the Carolinas. Doña Maria, a Timucuan chieftainess of a town near St. Augustine, was married to a Spaniard, and she greatly helped the Spanish infantry and the Franciscan friars as they moved slowly out from St. Augustine. In an effort to woo them away from the French to the Spanish Doña Maria received and entertained many Indians.

The friars proceeded so vigorously in converting the inhabitants of the land that by 1606 the Bishop of Cuba made an official visit and is reported to have confirmed 2,075 Indians in the Catholic faith.

In a dramatic event in 1609, the chief of the Timucuas and leading men of the tribe were baptized in St. Augustine. A friar, Francisco de Pareja made Timucua catechisms, manuals, and a grammar.

By the end of the seventeenth century, Creek and Yuchi Indians and English settlers from the north were making frequent raids into Florida. The Apalachee functioned as a quasi-buffer between the English and their Indian allies and the Spanish-influenced Timucua. After the Apalachee were routed from their lands west of the Timucua more than thirty-two Timucuan settlements and almost as many Spanish missions were destroyed. Many Timucuas were killed or carried into slavery.

From the province of San Augustin de la Florida, Gov. Dionisio de la Vega, reported August 27, 1728, to the king of Spain,

Provinces having been destroyed by virtue of many invasions, and all the towns deserted and many of the Indians, converted as well as infidels, killed or made prisoners, while the majority of them revolted and joined the English.[4]

After the destruction of these provinces and towns, wars continued to rage between the converted and infidel Indians, the latter assisted and fomented by the English.

As shock troops, he reported, the English brought in "a large number of Caribe Indians," who could have come from the British colony of St. Kitts, Leeward Islands, West Indies. It is possible that the Timucua ultimately became part of the Seminole.

The Calusa, whose lands stretched below the Timucua, lived along the west coast of Florida south of Tampa Bay and in the Florida Keys. It is estimated that in 1650 they had more than fifty villages with some three thousand inhabitants. The main Calusa village was protected by a Spanish garrison and served by a Jesuit missionary. Though a fort was built in 1566, it did not last more than three years. When the chief and fourteen of his principal men were killed by the Spanish for plotting against them, the Calusas burned their village and retreated into the forests leaving the Spanish without supplies.

Groups of Calusa lived on the west coast of Florida until the end of the second Seminole war in 1842. They are believed to have been absorbed by the Seminole or to have emigrated to Cuba.

In 1729 and 1730, the Natchez nation fell before the French and their Choctaw allies. Some four hundred captured Natchez were sent to the West Indies as slaves. Others who escaped to western Louisiana were defeated by the French and the Natchitoches.

Houma Indians along the Mississippi, who befriended escaping Natchez, were then attacked by the French,

Choctaws, and Chakchiumas; Bossu reports that about one thousand of them were captured and taken to New Orleans to be sold as slaves on the island of Santo Domingo.

Many Natchez took refuge among the Chickasaw, traditional enemies of the French, and later settled among the Cherokee, the Upper Creeks, and in South Carolina. Although a few Natchez still retain their identity in Oklahoma, the intervening years have seen that once mighty people absorbed into the culture and blood of its host nations.

Of the Houmas, who suffered with them, only some three hundred were reported ten years after the Natchez war.

And so thousands had been "scattered like little birds before the eagle." The days when the Indian lived in harmony with the earth, his fellows, and himself, finding the will of the Maker of Breath in all the life of which he was part now were faded memories. All things had been scattered and blown about.

The Changing Scene

Rivalry between France and Great Britain finally culminated in war in 1754. In addition to competition for trading rights among southeastern Indian tribes, there had been disputes between Frenchmen and Englishmen in Nova Scotia and along the New England borders and on the Great Lakes. War began, however, when France built a line of forts along the Allegheny River in western Pennsylvania to keep the English out of the Ohio Valley.

The treaty of peace in 1763 which ended French and British hostilities affected many Indian tribes in the Southeast. As a result of losing the war, France ceded Canada and her southeastern territories and claims east of the Mississippi River to Great Britain. The year before, French Louisiana lands west of the Mississippi had been secretly ceded to Spain. To regain Havana, captured by the English during the war, Spain turned Florida over to Great Britain.

Thus, France was gone, Spain was in Louisiana but out of Florida, and Great Britain, unchallenged by another colonial power, claimed control from the Atlantic Ocean to the Mississippi River.

Indebted to Cherokees and Chickasaws, among others, for military support in the contest with France, the British government in the Proclamation of 1763 announced that the area from the Appalachians to the Mississippi River

SMITHSONIAN INSTITUTION

Cherokee chiefs, including Attakullakulla (far right), visit London in 1730.

Engraving in the British Museum by Isaac Basire, after a painting by Markham

was closed to white settlement. But, enticed by Daniel Boone's glowing reports in 1760 of what was called the Tennessee country, settlers were already there. Choice hunting lands in what is now middle Tennessee were luring the "long hunters," whites who spent three months or more hunting bison, deer, and bear.

For the Cherokees the British Proclamation of 1763 announcing no white settlement west of the Appalachians must have been an ironic, empty decree, especially since the British made no effort to enforce it. Cherokee lands were the first to know the white frontiersmen restlessly rushing west from the English seaboard colonies, and border incidents in which blood was shed became common.

That the Creeks had fine lands was known in the Carolinas and colonial Virginia and Georgia. Georgia colonists like those in Virginia and the Carolinas were not

126

Tchow-ee-put-o-kaw,
*a Creek,
painted by George Catlin*

SMITHSONIAN INSTITUTION

to be confined by the Proclamation of 1763. At first moving westward in a trickle, the English colonials and blacks—both bondsmen and freemen—began western movement that eventually was to take the new Americans to the Pacific Ocean. It happened that the southeastern Indians were among the first to confront the trickle of white settlers that by the 1780s were a small torrent on the way to becoming a spreading flood of intruders on Indian homelands.

After 1763 the Creeks were a people favored lavishly by the British with guns, lead, powder, and farming equipment. Great Britain could always use Indian allies against the likelihood of the Spanish moving northward and eastward from their New Orleans base.

Pressed by Britain from the north, Spain from the south, and France from the west, the Creeks had long played an important role in colonial history of the Southeast. Throughout this time, the diplomatically astute Creeks had been guided by the 1716 doctrine of Chief

Old Brim, who said they should use a balance-of-power diplomacy, playing one colonizing nation against another, and gain as a consequence not only trade goods but, ultimately, a more durable independence.

Creek groups from towns on the lower Chattahoochee River had begun to push southward into north Florida after the Apalachees were destroyed. This movement increased greatly after Florida was ceded to Great Britain in 1763. By 1800 the Seminoles were to develop from these Creek migrants, runaway black slaves from Georgia, and remnants of other Florida tribes, such as the Calusa. Although there was some ethnic intermarriage, there is no evidence suggesting that Seminoles are not an Indian people.

OKLAHOMA HISTORICAL SOCIETY

Tishomingo,
*last war chief
of the Chickasaws*

The Choctaws, most agricultural of the southeastern peoples, and long friendly with the French, experienced some internal dissension after the departure of their European allies. There were those mourning the passing of the French presence who counseled isolation. Among these Choctaws there was no particular affection for the Spanish and none for the British, although Choctaw warriors did not participate to any great extent in the French-British War.

The Choctaws had had dealings with British colonials out of Charleston that led to friendship. But the Choctaws in what is now southeastern Mississippi were not obliged to maneuver diplomatically in the style of the Creeks or to confront white settlers directly—at least for a few years —as had the Cherokees.

Their neighbors to the north, the Chickasaws, a people of renowned military skill, had long allied with the British and were favored by them in lower prices for trade goods. The Chickasaws were regarded by some of the Choctaws as plutocrats spoiled by the British.

A number of tribes moved after the French and British War in an effort to stay near the European power considered most friendly. The Koasati, or Coushatta, of the

NEW ORLEANS MUSEUM OF ART, GIFT OF MR. W. G. GROVES

"Louisiana Indians Walking Along a Bayou"—painted by Alfred Boisseau in 1847. The boy carries a cane blowgun and two darts.

southern groups of the Creeks, who lived where the Coosa and Tallapoosa rivers joined, crossed the Mississippi and settled on Red River in Louisiana with a few bands going on to present-day Polk County in east Texas. Some of their friends from the Alabama tribe joined them in St. Landry Parish and in what is now Allen Parish, Louisiana, but most went on to Polk County.

The Louisiana area also received bands of Biloxi, Pascagoula, and Tunica, who settled near Marksville, small bands of Choctaw settling near Jena and Lacomb, and some Houma who made their home in Ascension Parish near New Orleans.

The migrants intermarried with the native Atakapas, Avoyels, Ofos, and Chitimachas. The latter had numbered some three thousand souls in 1650 but in 1784 had an estimated population of one hundred. The once numerous Natchitoches in northern Louisiana numbered only two hundred in 1831, one-fifth of what they had been before European intervention began in 1700.

In thirteen short years, when the colonies along the

Atlantic seaboard went to war with England, the scene for the Southeasterner was to change again.

In the quarrel between the English colonies and their mother country, the Cherokee were at a loss to understand what issues like taxation without representation meant. Too, the Cherokee had a long friendship with the British.

However, a war faction principally of young Cherokee appeared under the leadership of Dragging Canoe, Old Abram, and The Raven. Dragging Canoe argued that now was the time to destroy white settlements in upper Tennessee, and seven hundred young fighting men made ready to attack.

At this point Nancy Ward, the Beloved Woman at Chote, told her trader-friend, Isaac Thomas, the plans, and he alerted frontier military leader, John Sevier.

After the defeat of the Cherokee war party by the Tennessee frontier militia, the Cherokee met with Sevier and others July 20, 1777, at Long Island, now Kingsport, and surrendered claims to land in upper Tennessee. The treaty established a boundary line which the whites promised was "to remain through all generations and to be kept by our Children's Children . . . like a wall, high and strong, that none can pass over or break down."

Although many Cherokee now were arguing that the only way to survive was peace and adjustment to the white man's civilization, other Cherokee, including those who hated and feared white civilization, wanted to drive the white intruders away. By 1780 it appeared obvious the Americans were gaining the upper hand over the British and would probably win the war.

In the American Revolution, the Choctaw policy was one of friendly neutrality toward the colonials, but the Chickasaw fought in important American campaigns in the Old Northwest to keep that area from the Great Lakes to the Ohio River from the British. Had the British won, their hunting lands between the Tennessee, Mississippi, and Ohio rivers in what is now western Tennessee and Kentucky would have been opened to northwestern Indians friendly to Britain.

Preserving the integrity of their hunting lands was a fixed principle of Chickasaw policy during and after the American Revolution and in the renewal of American-British discord in the War of 1812.

Following the Revolutionary War, the Chickasaws and Choctaws negotiated treaties with the infant United States which defined the traditional boundaries of their lands.

During the Revolution the Creeks in their confederacy —approximately 84,000 square miles including Georgia's highlands, and from near the present Tennessee-Alabama line to Montgomery—remained friendly with the British, who controlled Florida.

By 1783 the European powers surrounding the Southeasterners had shifted again. The new, young United States was in control along the Atlantic; Spain, still in Louisiana, returned to Florida; Great Britain, active though distant, was in Canada and the Bahamas.

Chief Etch-ee-fix-e-co, *or Deer without a Heart, and his daughter,* Chee-a-ex-e-co, *Yuchis. Their tribe was part of the Creek Confederacy.*

Paintings by George Catlin

SMITHSONIAN INSTITUTION

SMITHSONIAN INSTITUTION

Although small groups were scattered throughout the area, four major nations, who had not been surrounded and all but absorbed by the encroaching Europeans, remained in control of their ancient lands: the Cherokee, Choctaw, Chickasaw, and Creek.

Each had absorbed remnants of other tribes. Through the years their villages had hospitably taken in Europeans and blacks, some of them free. Thus each of the four groups had a number of mixed-blooded members. The people in each of these nations were often better housed, clothed, and fed than many of the first white settlers.

Black slaves were found in all four nations, but generally their children were born free. Sometimes the blacks served as interpreters. Runaway slaves often added to the Indian's knowledge of agricultural techniques.

Agriculture had become even more important for the Southeasterner, who adapted to raising poultry, cattle, hogs, melons, and various fruits, while continuing to cultivate corn.

The Cherokee domain in east Tennessee, west North Carolina, and north Georgia had been close to the war scene and afterwards was a kind of portal to western lands that white settlers wanted.

Guerrilla-style frontier war between the whites and the Cherokee was waged off and on until about 1794, centering around Chickamauga in the vicinity of present-day Chattanooga. This was two years before the state of Tennessee entered the Union.

By 1809, the twenty thousand Cherokees were an enclave in a fast-increasing, aggressive white population, for in Tennessee there were almost three hundred thousand whites. Treaty by treaty, Cherokee lands were reduced to less than half what they had been in 1777.

The Cherokees made every effort to communicate with the U. S. government. In 1809 a deputation of Cherokees went to Washington to seek Pres. Thomas Jefferson's counsel and to inquire about his idea of an Indian Territory west of the Mississippi.

Teh-ke-neh-kee, *or Black Coat,*
a Cherokee chief who settled
in Arkansas

Painted by George Catlin

SMITHSONIAN INSTITUTION

President Jefferson said, or the Cherokees thought he said, that the Indian could best preserve his identity by going west. Perhaps thinking that there would be time to find the money, the President added that federal assistance would probably be made available to those who would go at once to the Indian Territory.

Later that year the Cherokee traditionalist Tahlonteskee and several hundred Cherokees left east Tennessee and migrated to the Arkansas River in what is now western Arkansas. Federal assistance proved unavailable, but unsurveyed lands were set aside for the West Cherokee nation.

The lands of the Choctaws and Chickasaws away from the westward moving United States were relatively safe from white settlement until 1803. In that year France, which had regained the Louisiana Territory, sold it to the United States.

Like water down a mountain, streams of traders and settlers moved toward the Mississippi and down to New Orleans. Goods to be sold would be put on rafts and

133

floated to the Mississippi and down to Natchez and New Orleans. The homeward journey was through Chickasaw country on an Indian trail—the Natchez Trace. The pressure for their lands had begun.

Following the Revolutionary War, with the vigorous new state of Georgia alive to the issue of states' rights and with Georgians moving west, the Creeks sought diplomatic recognition from the British in Canada and particularly from the Spanish in Louisiana and Florida. To be thus recognized would mean that the Creek Confederacy would be treated as a nation by the two European powers that their statesman Alexander McGillivray considered to be far better established than the new American republic. Being recognized as a nation meant not only identity as a people but, more important, as holders of an area of land.

McGillivray's clever letters, his state visits to Pensacola and to the American capital of New York City as Pres. George Washington's guest, and his continual boasts of his "army" of ten thousand warriors, backed by the strategic location of the Creek Confederacy, bore fruit. The Americans, British, and Spanish competed to supply the Creeks and shower McGillivray with favors.

The Northwest Ordinance of 1787, authored by Thomas Jefferson, said in part that no land or property should ever be taken by the U. S. government from the Indians without their consent. This was reaffirmed in 1789 when the U. S. Constitution was ratified.

McGillivray thereupon in 1790 negotiated a treaty of recognition for the Creek Confederacy with the United States, which he soon repudiated to accept an offer of recognition from Spain.

After Alexander McGillivray's death in 1793 there was no man with his diplomatic and political skills to succeed him, and the Creek Confederacy broke into factions.

These included the anti-American Red Sticks, who

Tecumseh

took their name from the color and insignia of war; the pro-Americans, many of whom were sons of white men who had married Creek women; and an increasing number of those who wished no part of the troubled lands of their forefathers. These last Creeks migrated from Alabama to Spanish Florida and became part of the loosely gathered Seminole, as the latter were being called.

In 1811 the United States yielded to demands from Georgia and cut out a road for horses and wagons from a point on the Chattahoochee River to Mims Ferry on the Alabama River in Alabama Territory. Alabama and Mississippi at this time were parts of the Alabama Territory which was attached to Georgia. Creek country was violated by this road.

In the fall of the same year, Tecumseh, the famous Shawnee statesman, undertook a mission from the northwest to the Chickasaws, Choctaws, and Creeks, urging a tribal confederacy of Indians against the whites.

He failed to arouse the Choctaws and Chickasaws. The Choctaw leader, Pushmataha, pointed to the rising

135

Pushmataha

From Indian Tribes of North America
by Thomas L. McKenney and James Hall

strength of the United States. A war would be suicidal, he argued. Piomingo and the influential Colbert brothers of the Chickasaws concurred.

Tecumseh's Creek visit fired dissension already underway between the Red Sticks, who wanted no part of the white civilization, and the pro-American faction, who argued that farming and schools and other white systems were the path to survival of their people.

Accepting British arms brought in from the Spanish port of Pensacola, the Red Sticks attempted to win over the pro-Americans by force, and a Creek civil war ensued. A group of Creeks were attacked by Alabama whites on Burnt Corn Creek in Spanish Florida, and in reprisal Fort Mims, a temporary stockade near the junction of the Alabama and Tombigbee rivers, was overrun by the Red Sticks on August 30, 1813, resulting in the death of from 350 to 500 soldiers and settlers.

One of their leaders, William Weatherford, half-Creek son of a Scottish trader, appears to have sent a warning to the commander that Fort Mims was to be attacked. Lax

136

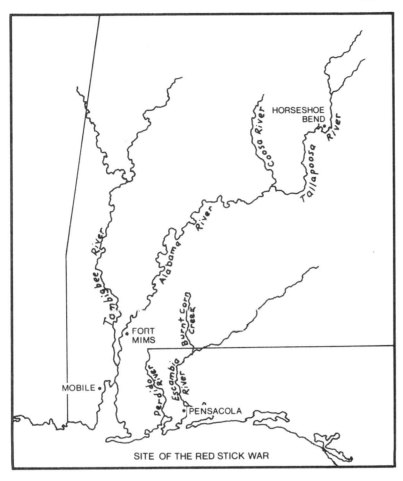

SITE OF THE RED STICK WAR

to begin with, the commander reportedly was drunk and the gates were not even closed.

After Fort Mims, Georgia and Tennessee militia, armed settlers, Chickasaws, Choctaws, Cherokees, and other Creeks fought against the Red Sticks. Finally, Gen. Andrew Jackson and his composite American-Indian forces attacked the Red Sticks in their last stand at Horseshoe Bend on the Tallapoosa River, March 27, 1814. At the close of the terrible battle over six hundred Red Stick warriors had been killed.

One of the few Red Sticks who survived was Menewa. Hit seven times by rifle bullets and left on the littered battlefield for dead, Menewa recovered consciousness to

137

see a militiaman looting a fallen comrade. He weakly seized a discarded rifle and shot the soldier, who, in turn, put another bullet in him. Although Menewa miraculously lived, his thousand cattle, hogs, and horses, his general store, and his comfortable home were taken.

William Weatherford was another survivor. After the battle, he appeared before General Jackson offering his life for that of the Creek people, an offer that was declined. He lived ten years longer as a farmer, in present Monroe County, Alabama, dying in peace.

In August, 1814 General Jackson by the Treaty of Fort Jackson forced the Creeks to surrender to the United States about one-half the present state of Alabama, or, as he put it, "20 million of acres of the cream of the Creek Country, opening a communication from Georgia to Mobile." Much of this territory had been the homeland of tribes who fought beside the Americans in the Battle of Horseshoe Bend. Stripped of a great portion of its land, its people scattered, the Creek Confederacy was weakened beyond repair.

After the Red Stick War, migration of Creeks to Spanish Florida quickened. Legend says that during the hail of rifle bullets at Horseshoe Bend a Creek mother, pretending to be dead, placed her body over that of her infant son. Later she took her baby to Florida, where he grew up to be the renowned Seminole patriot Osceola.

Living in central and northern Florida, the Seminoles raised corn, or maize, a fact that greatly interested Georgia white men in Florida's possibilities. The Seminoles also provided sanctuary to fugitives, including black slaves fleeing Georgia and Alabama plantations, which added antagonism to covetousness in the hearts of many neighboring whites.

In 1817 the Seminole began the long defense of his freedom, his wish to be left alone. In an expedition unauthorized by his superiors in Washington, General Jackson invaded Seminole country in Spanish Florida because

Seminole woman

Painted by George Catlin

of alleged border incidents involving Seminoles and Georgians. War between the Army and the Seminoles was to last off and on for the next forty-one years.

Florida was purchased by the United States from Spain in 1819, and thus the villages of the Seminole and the still smaller Miccosukee became the target of land-hungry whites in Georgia and Alabama.

With Spain out of Florida, the last European was gone from the Southeast. France had left in 1803 when she sold the Louisiana Territory to the United States. Great Britain, without territory after she retroceded Florida to Spain in 1783, had still used freely the Spanish port of Pensacola. Now, they were entirely gone, and the Seminoles and other Indian nations in the Southeast were engulfed in the ever more powerful United States.

A Small Gallery
of Notable People

We come now to a small gallery of men and women who lived lives often filled with conflict and storm.

Hagler

Hagler (or Arataswa or Oroloswa or Haigler), last of the great Catawba chiefs, is almost lengendary. Nothing is known of how he came by his name, though some traditions mention the possibility of his having English blood, or of his having been reared by English colonists in South Carolina. However, "there is no evidence that he was not all Indian," writes Douglas S. Brown in her excellent history.[1]

There is evidence that Hagler was an orator of high ability, addressing himself to the issue of alcoholism among his people.

Hagler may be thought of as an example of Indian leadership in crisis. When Hagler assumed Catawba leadership about 1753, boundary lines between the English colonies of Virginia, North Carolina, and South Carolina were not firm. Catawbas for a long time had been friendly to the point of ruin to all the colonial governments. Catawba blood had been spilled freely enough for all three colonies.

He was appointed to be Catawba "king" by the royal

140

governor of South Carolina, a common practice of colonial administrators. This position was not necessarily given to the elected chief.

Hagler deserves recognition because he tried to make the white officials help him save the Catawbas still intact as a tribe, others having gone to the Cherokees in western Carolina.

Meeting in 1754 with North Carolina commissioners to talk about matters of common interest, a listener, Matthew Toole, reports Hagler's remarks:

> Brothers, here is One Thing You Yourselves are to Blame very much in, That is you Rot Your Grain in Tubs. You sell it to our young men and give it [to] them, many times; they get very Drunk with it [and] this is the Very Cause that they oftentimes Commit those Crimes that is offencive (sic) to you and us and all thro' the Effect of that Drink . . . many of our people has (sic) Lately Died by the Effects of that strong Drink, and I heartily wish You would do something to prevent Your People from Dareing (sic) to Sell or give them any of that Strong Drink, upon any Consideration whatever for that will be a great means of our being free from accused of those Crimes that is Committed by our young men and will prevent many of the abuses that is done by them thro' the Effect of that Strong Drink.[2]

The crimes mentioned were usually not murder but the stealing of horscs, pigs, and cattle, which weren't always fenced-in.

Hagler finished his speech with a call for reconciliation addressed to the hearts and minds of both the Indians and the Europeans present. Arranged to show the poetic form of Indian oratory and in the spelling of the old North Carolina colonial records, Hagler continued,

As to our Liveing on those Lands
we Expect to live on those Lands wc now possess
During our Time here
for when the Great Man above made us
he also made this Island

he also made our forefathers and of this Colour and Hue
(showing his hands and breast)
he also fixed our forefathers and us here
to Inherit this Land and Ever since
we Lived our manner and fashion
we in those Days, had no Instruments
To support our Living
but Bows which we compleated with stones,
knives we had none.
And as it was our Custom in those days to Cut our hair . . .
we Did by burning it of [off] our heads and Bodies
with Coals of Fire,
our Axes we made of stone
we bled ourselves with fish Teeth
our Cloathing were Skins and Furr
instead of which we [now] Enjoy those Cloaths
which we got from the white people
and Ever since they first Came among us
we have Enjoyed all those things
that we were then destitute of
for which we thank the white people,
and to this Day
we have lived in a Brotherly love and peace with them
and more especially with Three Governments
South Carolina, North Carolina, and Virginia
and it is our Earnest Desire
that Love and Friendship
which has so long remain'd
Should ever continue.[3]

Understandably European scissors and razors were popular in trading with the Indians. Cuplike devices for bleeding, an Indian as well as European practice, were useful. There were hundreds and hundreds of "all those things" for the Indian to acquire and learn to use.

At the meeting in North Carolina, Hagler may have had on the beautifully made round headdress with tail feathers from wild turkeys worn by Catawba leaders. He probably had his own standard, or flag, perhaps of swan feathers, and with a man chosen to bear it. His standard would have fluttered in the wind over his home when he was there.

To the last Hagler sought to live by the laws of the whites, although he complained that when an Indian horse thief was delivered to South Carolina justice, the punishment was more severe than that given a white thief taken in by the Indians.

The Rev. William Richardson, a Presbyterian minister, often spoke with Hagler about salvation as he understood it. Hagler listened patiently, but that was all. He never accepted the white man's religion. That these two men could be friends highlights Indian tolerance of the convictions of another if he were a good man. This accounts for Indian acceptance of the earliest Roman Catholic missionaries in Florida, French Jesuits in the lower Mississippi Valley, and Protestant workers among the Cherokees, Chickasaws, and Choctaws after the turn of the eighteenth century.

In 1762 Hagler persuaded the 150 to 200 people remaining in his tribe to go to a reservation 15 miles square on the Catawba River near what is now Rock Hill. This is said to have been the first Indian reservation in the Southeast. He was killed the next year by a raiding party of Algonkin Shawnees, people whose warriors long had tormented the Siouan Catawbas.

Nancy Ward

Nancy Ward was the last Beloved Woman of the Cherokees. The national office that she held is described by Ben Harris McClary, modern authority on Nancy Ward,

It was believed that the Great Spirit often used the voice of the Beloved Woman to speak to the Cherokees and consequently her words were always heard, if not always heeded. In the matter of what to do with prisoners she did have absolute authority, which she did not hesitate to use. But perhaps most important, the Beloved Woman was the head of the influential Woman's Council, made up of a

143

representative from each clan, and she sat as a voting member of the Council of Chiefs.[4]

Nancy Ward was born in 1738 in the old Cherokee capital, Chota (or Chote), on the Little Tennessee River in eastern Tennessee. Her mother, Tame Doe, was the sister of Attakullakulla, an important civil and political leader of the Cherokees. "Nancy" is a corruption of her name *Nanye'hi,* which derives from the Cherokee word for "spirit people."

Sometime in the 1750s a marriage for Nancy was arranged by Tame Doe and other members of the Wolf clan. It was a brilliant match. Kingfisher, of the Deer clan, showed vigor, purpose, and judgment. But in battle against the Creeks at Taliwa, near what is now Canton, Georgia, in 1755 Kingfisher was killed. Nancy was with him at the time, and strangely moved, she rallied the Cherokees and led them to a great victory in which she personally captured one of the Creek slaves.

Back at Chote, Nancy found herself revered. Even before she was twenty, she was chosen by the seven clans to fill the vacant office of *Agi-ga-u-e,* or Beloved Woman. Her second marriage was to a white trader named Bryant Ward, but she remained the Beloved Woman until her death in 1822 when she was eighty-four.

Alexander McGillivray

Before the birth of Alexander McGillivray, it is said that his mother Sehoy Marchand dreamed of the paper and ink and quills used so cunningly by the Europeans.

Alexander later showed that the ancient Indian belief in dreams might have had some basis for he wrote hundreds of letters in his successful effort to win recognition from the new United States and Spain for the Creeks as a nation.

Scottish on his father's side, one-fourth French and one-fourth Creek on his mother's, McGillivray was born in the important Creek town of Little Tallassie on the Coosa River in Alabama, probably in 1759.

His father, Lachlan McGillivray later returned to his native Scotland when Great Britain lost the Revolutionary War. Although said to have lost one hundred thousand dollars in support of the British, Lachlan McGillivray remained wealthy. Alexander's mother was a member of the important Wind clan. She named her son *Hoboi-hili-miko,* or the "Good Child King."

When Alexander was about fourteen, his father sent him to his cousin Farquahar McGillivray, a Presbyterian minister in Charleston, to be tutored in Greek, Latin, English history, and literature.

He was then placed in the Savannah counting house of Samuel Elbert, later governor of the state of Georgia. The work was dull, so he returned to Charleston for additional study. He found that city a stimulating enough place although smelly and dirty with no system for its wastes. But the lure of his Creek village Otciapofa was strong. He returned and, as a member of the Wind clan, took up an inherited good status.

Victory of the colonists in the American Revolution distressed Alexander McGillivray because of his royalist attitudes but mostly because of the aggressiveness of the new state of Georgia in asserting its ownership of land from the Atlantic Coast to the Mississippi River.

"For the good of my country, I have sacrificed my all & it is a duty incumbent on me in this Critical Situation to exert myself for their Interest," [5] he said of himself and his people.

A sharp observer of the Europeans and the new Americans, McGillivray wrote in 1784 that the United States was torn by violent dissension. "The whole continent is in confusion," he wrote. "Before long I expected to hear that the three kings [English, French, and Spanish] must settle the matter by dividing America among them." [6]

Again, he said, "The protection of a Great Monarch is to be preferred to that of a distracted Republic." [7]

145

He made a useful and penetrating observation about Indian politics and white efforts to operate within them, "No Wisdom or foresight can form any plan in the closet that can always suit to manage Indians, as nothing but a long experience & knowledge of them can direct them properly." [8]

In 1793, he boasted that he could not be bribed by "Washington himself had he the thirteen United States in his belly." [9]

Subject to painful rheumatism, sometimes drinking heavily, and playing a dangerous game of bargaining with the Americans and the Spanish, Alexander McGillivray poured out letters by the dozens. These letters often were mocking, ironic, and sarcastic about those in his midst like Tame King and Fat King, subordinate chiefs the Georgians wooed to McGillivray's worry that they might stir up trouble against him. His letters never sparkled with contentment or happiness. Many of them he wrote at his plantation "Apple Orchard," a two-story structure at Little Tallassie. Constant attendants were David, who had white blood, and Paro, a black, both of whom may have worked as interpreters, for McGillivray is said to have spoken mostly French and English. Other aides were a French brother-in-law Leclerc Milfort, and the Creek war leader, Taskiniahatkic.

While on a diplomatic mission to Pensacola in Spanish Florida, Hoboi-hili-miko died at age thirty-four from gout, rheumatism, and other complications. Left were two wives with separate houses, three hundred head of cattle, many horses, and much land. He was given Masonic Order burial in the garden of his friend and adviser, the trader William Panton who had said of him, "His efforts will always be directed toward the ends that he conceives to favor the Indians, his tribesmen." [10]

In writing of the king of England's contest with the American Congress, Alexander McGillivray gave his own epitaph, "I would rather remain governor of my savages than change places with him." [11]

Sophia Durant

Sophia Durant, one of McGillivray's sisters, was the wife of a French Huguenot, Benjamin Durant. She gave heroic service to her brother when he was negotiating with President Washington in New York City.

In McGillivray's absence, rival politicians in the Creek Confederacy conspired against him. They were joined by dissident war leaders and by others who hated the white man's civilization. Why not eliminate the puny white settlements in Tennessee? Why not push back the encroaching Georgians?

Learning of this, Sophia McGillivray Durant with a Negro companion-servant made a four-day horseback ride to reach the hidden meeting place of the conspirators. She then made a surprise appearance at a night meeting and berated them. Did they not realize they were fools in their scheming? That big talks were going on with the newest of the foreign powers? That these would be collapsed if war was made at this time. Were they willing to lose their strength by dividing the people? Her words turned aside whatever schemes were being made for war. Two weeks after that meeting Sophia gave birth to twin daughters.

The Colbert Brothers

In the 1700s a Scottish trader in English service, James Logan Colbert, began a forty-year residence in the Chickasaw country, settling in what is now Bissell, Mississippi. Colbert married three Chickasaw women. His sons, William, George, Levi, Samuel, Joseph, and Pittman (or Pitman, sometimes called James) provided important Chickasaw leadership that lasted for over a century, constituting a kind of board of directors of the relatively small Chickasaw nation much of the time.[12]

William Colbert, the eldest son, once visited President Washington, who gave him a sprig of willow. Planted on

147

Colbert's large farm, the sprig is said to have originated the weeping willows of the state of Mississippi. Influential in guiding the Chickasaws to friendship with the United States in its rise to power, William Colbert served in General Jackson's campaigns against the Creek Red Sticks in Alabama in 1813-14. Although he died in the 1830s, the exact dates of his birth and death have not been established.

The second son, George Colbert, was born in 1764 near the Tennessee River in what is now north Mississippi and died November 7, 1839 at Fort Towson in Oklahoma Indian Territory. In the War of 1812 he served with the Americans in campaigns in the Old Northwest. George Colbert possessed the Colbert flair for business and had a farm of some five hundred acres near present-day Tupelo, some one hundred fifty black slaves, and a lucrative Tennessee River ferry. Some idea of his wealth is suggested by the feeding from his own resources of approximately three hundred Chickasaw western migrants in addition to his own family and servants.

Levi Colbert, James Logan Colbert's third son, became the unofficial chairman of the board in Chickasaw council matters before his death in 1834 on the eve of the removal to Indian Territory. His Indian name, Itawamba, was earned when a boy in a brave solo confrontation with a party of Creek raiders. Itawamba County in Mississippi is named for him. In the early 1820s to help his people face the encroaching American nation, Levi Colbert welcomed Presbyterian missionaries to Chickasaw country and aided in the building of Charity Hall mission school near Cotton Gin Port. Hospitality to visitors in his home near Tupelo made him popular almost to the point of legend.

Samuel Colbert and Joseph Colbert, the fourth and fifth sons, although sharing the Colbert affluence, were overshadowed in leadership roles by Pittman Colbert, the sixth son. He was educated in the East, specializing in bookkeeping and surveying, subjects of great practical value to the Chickasaw nation and the Colberts. Pittman Colbert helped pay the expenses of fifty Chickasaw families unrelated to him when the nation removed to Indian Territory. There his properties included a five-hundred-acre cotton plantation worked by over one hundred slaves. Pittman Colbert was one of those who in the 1840s led the successful effort to separate Chickasaw and Choctaw lands and governments.

Third generation Colbert men in what is now Oklahoma included Holmes, who helped write the Chickasaw constitution in the 1850s; Benjamin Franklin, who ran

Above:
*Betsy Love Colbert,
wife of Holmes Colbert*

Left:
Holmes Colbert

BOTH PHOTOGRAPHS COURTESY
OKLAHOMA HISTORICAL SOCIETY

149

Winchester Colbert

OKLAHOMA HISTORICAL SOCIETY

a strategically located ferry on the Red River near Sherman, Texas, often used by travelers going to Texas and California; and Winchester, Civil War governor of the Chickasaws.

An index to their standing in Indian Territory was provided in 1854 when Methodist missionaries named a new school for Chickasaw youth, Colbert Institute. Located at present Perryville, Colbert Institute admitted both male and female students for study of the Bible, the traditional curriculum, and vocational subjects. It was an educational trailblazer until the Civil War brought havoc to the new homes of the former Southeasterners.

Wild Cat

Coacoochee, or Wild Cat, was born in the Seminole village of Yulaka on the St. Johns River in present-day east Florida about 1816. His twin sister did not live long, but because he was a twin, Coacoochee was felt by some of the villagers to have great gifts that in time would be developed. Had he been the surviving one of male twins, he probably would have undergone intensive training for the priesthood. Coacoochee's father, the elderly Ee-mat-la, called King Phillip by the whites, was chief of the Yulaka band of Seminoles, brother-in-law of Micanopy, one of the most influential of Seminole chiefs, friend of

Ee-mat-la, *or King Phillip*

Painted by George Catlin

Osceola, and so important that the American artist George Catlin made a life portrait of him.

Probably from boyhood Coacoochee had black friends, for runaway plantation slaves had been coming to Florida since well before 1800. Descendants were free; those who were Seminole slaves had no fear of being sold.

Assuredly Coacoochee grew up in a wartime atmosphere that began in 1817 when Gen. Andrew Jackson burned the village of Old Mikasuki in present-day Jefferson County, Florida. That First Seminole War, which lasted through 1818, was partly touched off by white bordermen's anger at Seminole reception of valuable fugitive slaves. In 1822 Florida became an organized territory, and white-Indian incidents, many of them centered around fugitive slaves, increased. Border trouble was often generated because Georgians claimed that Seminoles enticed and then hid away black slaves. Although the Seminoles in some cases seem to have sent word to plantation black slaves that they would be welcome, there is no evidence that Seminole-black parties liberated black slaves.

After a long series of incidents on the Georgia border the so-called Second Seminole War began in 1835, eventually involving virtually all of the U.S. Army.

In 1837, the Army captured Coacoochee's aged and infirm father Ee-mat-la and held him in the grim former Spanish fortress Castillo de San Marcos, renamed Fort Marion, in St. Augustine. Meantime, Coacoochee, now known by his war name Wild Cat, though not a chief, had attracted a following of Negroes and Indians. To him Gen. T. S. Jesup sent the news of Ee-mat-la's imprisonment. If Wild Cat would come in and agree to removal to Indian Territory or what is now Oklahoma, the general would promise the Seminoles that "their allies shall be secure in their lives." By "allies" the general meant the estimated two hundred black slaves and one thousand free blacks among the population of about thirty-five hundred Seminoles. Black slaves weren't

Coacoochee,
or Wild Cat

Engraving by N. Orr Co. from The Exiles
of Florida, *1858, by Joshua R. Giddings*

absolutely prohibited from marrying Seminoles and might
obtain freedom thereby; as with other southeastern
Indians, offspring of black slaves were free.

On a spirited horse, wearing a colorful turban with
white plumes to show peace, Wild Cat and a Negro com-
panion appeared at St. Augustine in September, 1837
to talk with General Jesup.

By this time, Wild Cat was a most important war
leader and had strong ties with Arpeika of the Miccosukees, who were much smaller than the Seminoles but
even more opposed to removal. Wild Cat's interpreter,
who could have been the man known only as Louis, said
that Wild Cat considered the Negroes as his people, and
they would follow him.

General Jesup gave no assurances that the Seminoles
and their Negro allies would be together if they agreed
to remove to Indian Territory. At the time blacks among

the Seminoles were alarmed about slave hunters from Georgia who were active in Florida.

Through his interpreter Wild Cat informed General Jesup that he would faithfully report to his Seminole Indian and Negro people that his interview was inconclusive. He would ask their feelings about removal and report back to General Jesup.

In October, 1837 Wild Cat and Louis reappeared at St. Augustine and presented General Jesup a peace pipe and a white plume of peace belonging to the fiery Seminole patriot, Osceola, a friend of Ee-mat-la. Osceola, Wild Cat said, would confer with the Army about peace, under a flag of truce. When the Seminoles and Army leaders met later that month, both Osceola and Wild Cat were captured and imprisoned despite the flag of truce.

Wild Cat and his party of eighteen, some of whom were black, escaped from the twenty-foot room in which they were held at Fort Marion. They improvised ropes which they threw around the bars of the single window eighteen feet above them. Wild Cat later said that he and his companions had fasted for six days to reduce their bodies so they could work their way between the bars which were about eight inches apart.

After this, Wild Cat became the great leader of the Seminole resistance. On Christmas Day, 1837, Wild Cat and Arpeika, leader of the Miccosukees, defeated forces commanded by Col. Zachary Taylor, later president of the United States.

In 1839, Ee-mat-la died en route to Indian Territory. The Army now was promising that the Seminoles and their Negro allies would be taken to the west together and on arrival there, the Negroes could not be seized by the slave-owning element of the Creeks. But Wild Cat and his associate, the free black, known as Gopher John, refused to present themselves and their followers to the Army. In 1841, Wild Cat officially became the Army's "most wanted" Seminole.

Finally with his people suffering hunger and in rags,

Wild Cat agree to meet with Army personnel. Near Fort Pierce on Indian River Lt. William Tecumseh Sherman met the party of about a dozen young Indian men and asked if they knew where Coacoochee was, whereupon, Sherman later wrote, "a handsome young fellow" slapped himself on the chest and said, "Me Coacoochee."

Wild Cat and a following of about two hundred Indians and Negroes arrived at Fort Gibson in Indian Territory in November, 1841, where he said, "I was in hopes I should be killed in battle, but a bullet never reached me." In 1842 the Army ended the guerrilla war that began in 1835 and formally announced that the war was over.

In Florida Wild Cat, who apparently was full-blooded Indian, was a prime military leader of the Seminoles, a diplomat for them with the fiercely independent Miccosukees, and a steadfast champion of the right of Negroes to remain in Seminole society and be transported west with them. The position of the Negro was one of the cardinal principles for which the Seminoles fought. Without Wild Cat some of the blacks might have been taken into slavery by Georgians or in the west by Creek slave owners.

When he died in 1857 at the age of forty-one, Wild Cat was developing a colony of Seminoles and free blacks in Mexican territory with that country's blessing.

Henry Berry Lowry

Although they were not banished from their lands during the Removal of the 1830s, those Indians living in and around Robeson County, North Carolina, and the few hundred more across the border in South Carolina were subject to abuse and misuse.

Known today as the Lumbees, they were not then allowed to vote or even to attend school. During the Civil War, Lumbees were refused service in the Confederate army, though some were willing. Instead, male Lumbees were forced to work on fortifications at the sea port of

155

Wilmington, North Carolina. Poorly fed and brutally treated, many died. Others escaped to the swamps along the Lumber and nearby rivers. Along with enforced slavery, Lumbees were hounded by the Home Guard in its efforts to keep non-whites in their "places."

Against this background there emerged in Robeson County a guerrilla band led after 1864 by Henry Berry Lowry (sometimes spelled Lowrie or Lowery). One of ten sons, he was still in his teens when his leadership began.

In his band of perhaps a dozen men were blacks, browns, and at least one white, drawn together by friendship or kinship and by harsh experiences with the Home Guard and with forced labor for the Confederacy.

In times of almost unimaginable social upheaval in the South, when violence was everywhere, the Lowry

band raided big plantation houses and then distributed corn and meat to the poor of Robeson County's three races.

A hardened guerrilla who asked no special treatment and gave none, Henry Berry Lowry acquired the reputation of being bulletproof. He is known to have escaped from three different jails in 1866, 1868, and 1869, perhaps aided in one of those escapes by his young wife Rhoda. Her brother Boss Strong, who was only fourteen in 1864 when his participation in the Lowry band began, is thought to have been Lowry's chief lieutenant.

The Lowry band, slipping in and out of the Lumber River swamplands, confronted the Home Guard, then U.S. troops, and then the Ku Klux Klan. They did much to thwart the KKK's post-Civil War terrorizing of non-whites.

On July 10, 1871, a unit of eighteen militiamen sought to surprise Lowry at Wire Grass Landing on the Lumber River, but, when they opened fire, he ducked over the side of his canoe into the river, leaving his rifle on the floor of the boat. Then, keeping afloat with one hand and his feet, he took up the rifle, sighted over the edge of his craft, and returned the fire of the militia. Instead of disappearing into the lowlands, Lowry swam toward his attackers, shielding his body with the canoe and firing his rifle. At least two of the eighteen militiamen were wounded, and the rest fled in panic.

Not only an outstanding rifleman, Lowry is said to have been an excellent player of the fiddle and the banjo, although he was not given to oratory or even to much speech. Lowry was described by his wife Rhoda in 1908 as "the handsomest man I ever saw."

After 1872, according to historian W. McKee Evans, Henry Berry Lowry disappeared as if swallowed up in the mists of the Carolina swamps. The then-huge bounty of twelve thousand dollars, offered by the state of North Carolina for him dead or alive, was never claimed. His death was never established, and in the 1930s some

Lumbees insisted that he yet lived which was possible since he was in his teens in 1864.

According to Evans, Lowry was a folk or culture hero who helped give the Lumbees the sense of being a people at a critical and violent time in national history when their identity might well have been lost. Moreover, Henry Berry (as he is sometimes called) led men of different ethnic groups yet was dedicated to his Indian people. In 1885 the North Carolina General Assembly enacted legislation giving his people full legal status as Indians, an action Lowry would have applauded.

Words attributed to him well express Henry Berry Lowry's life and courage:

> My band is big enough . . .
>   They are all true men . . .
> We mean to live as long as we can
>   —and at last, if we must die,
>   to die game.[13]

Race to Survive

Twenty-eight-year-old John Ross was president of the Cherokee national committee and a former officer in General Jackson's campaigns in the Red Stick War. On July 3, 1819, he wrote a white friend [The original letter is in the Tennessee State Library and Archives at Nashville.] that he and other Cherokees had been giving the most searching thought to ways to survive as Indians outside the voluntary exile from their remaining ancient lands. The only way was to accept white civilization as a fact and make use of it. And to begin immediately. Ross explained.:

> I am convinced of the favorable disposition of the Government toward the object of ameliorating the conditions of the American aborigines—and also of the more liberal sentiments which are beginning to prevail among the people, generally, toward them. I hope the time is now at hand when the dark cloud of prejudice (which has so long hung over the Heads of Indians) will vanish—and the tongues of calumny which have been pointed at their intellectual powers silences into shame. . . . I trust the period is not very far distant when the Cherokees will evince to the world, that American Indians, are capable of civilization and improvement in the highest degree.

Almost frantically Ross appealed to humanitarians everywhere, telling about the churches, schools, and out-

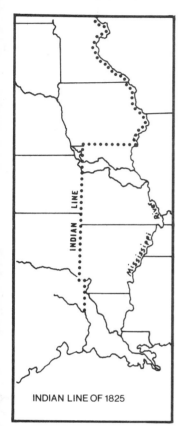

INDIAN LINE OF 1825

standing farms found in the Cherokee nation, and he succeeded in winning the support of many powerful men, including Henry Clay of Kentucky and Sen. Daniel Webster of Massachusetts.

At the time that enlightened interest in the Indian seemed to be on the increase, Thomas Jefferson's idea of an Indian Territory—that unorganized area generally corresponding with present-day Oklahoma—was revived.

Accepting the proposal of Secretary of War John C. Calhoun, Pres. James Monroe on January 27, 1825, urged the Congress to enact legislation that would remove all Indians in the eastern half of the United States to Indian Territory. The President further recommended that an imaginary "Indian Line" should be drawn, with all Indians to stay west of that line. The line would follow the boundary of western Michigan Territory, northwest Illinois, northern and western Missouri, and western Arkansas Territory. White settlement would be forever prohibited west of the Indian Line.

John Ross was a handsome, privately educated man, whom Gen. Andrew Jackson had called "that scamp." Ross led in the effort to preserve the Cherokee through taking on the new civilization.

By the 1820s the results included good roads, schools, churches, government modeled on that of the United States, widespread literacy as the result of the development of a syllabary by Sequoyah, a newspaper with the symbolic title of *Cherokee Phoenix* printed in both the Cherokee language and in English, advanced animal husbandry, dairying, meat processing, and general agricultural accomplishment.

As the decade was waning the Christian Book Society was operated from Brainerd Mission, established by the American Board of Commissioners for Foreign Missions on Chickamauga Creek near present Chattanooga. Any Cherokee might be a member for one year of this "book club" by payment of "any sum," for no amount was

stipulated. Members receive half of their subscription's value in books or tracts printed in Cherokee, and could purchase religious books or tracts recommended by the Society.

In 1829, the Cherokee Christian Book Society distributed among the Eastern Cherokees (so called to differentiate them from those on the Arkansas) five hundred copies of the Gospel of Matthew, one thousand copies of the Gospel of Mark, and reported circulating numerous tracts and books of hymns, all in Cherokee.

The Cherokees also did well in business. John Ross was one of a number of capable Cherokee business entrepreneurs, and his interests included a general store, ferry, wharves, and real estate at Ross Landing, later to become Chattanooga.

In the 1820s the Chickasaws were also welcoming missions and schools, exporting cotton and corn from their farms mainly in Pontotoc and Union counties in Mississippi.

161

Levi Colbert, one of the six brothers who were important Chickasaw leaders, made missionaries welcome and was instrumental in founding Charity Hall, a kind of free vocational high school for young Chickasaws, near Cotton Gin Port, Mississippi. He gave consistent backing to the Cumberland Presbyterian Monroe Station after helping organize it in 1821. The Chickasaw by 1829 had a written code of laws which, among other things, banned whiskey from the nation. A mounted police force of one hundred men, twenty-five for each district, enforced the law.

A federal census made of the Chickasaw nation in 1827 disclosed there were approximately four thousand Indians and some one thousand black slaves in the nation. Government agents reported the metamorphosis of Chickasaw life, partly attributed to the work of missionaries, from an economy in which hunting provided meat but agricultural products were obtained by trade from the Choctaws, to one basically agricultural.

From their black slaves the Chickasaws had learned about cotton so that they exported a thousand bales of cotton in 1830 from their then severely reduced domain in northeastern Mississippi.

The Rev. Cyrus Kingsbury in 1827 was transferred by the American Board of Foreign Missions from Brainerd Mission in Cherokee country to Yellow Busha, Choctaw Nation.

There missionary Kingsbury soon was teaching the Choctaws the skills of the blacksmith, explaining that every village should have its own smithy to make agricultural tools. He taught an English school enrolling sixty Choctaw young people, ages six to twenty. With the backing of the mixed-blood Folsom and Pitchlynn families, Kingsbury established five other English schools, and his Board sent a dozen or more missionary teachers to instruct youth in the three Rs, practical arts such as sewing and cobbling, and in Christianity.

In the year 1820 the three districts of the Choctaw nation comprising some twenty thousand people contributed six thousand dollars for mission schools and new blacksmith shops where iron plows, blades of hoes, rakes, and other implements could be made to improve Choctaw farming. This sum, large for the time, came from annuities paid Choctaws for lands ceded to the U. S. government.

During this period another process also was underway in the lives of the Cherokee, Chickasaw, and Choctaw Indians. Pressed and pressured from all sides by whites who desired their lands, treaties were being made in which the nations gave up portions of their territory.

Ancient cultural ways which had bound the tribes together were beginning to relax if not disappear. Clan organization was one. People might not even know their clans, or, if they did, it might have no significance. For example, John Ross, who took pride in identifying himself as Indian, married Quatie in 1812, though she was a member of his own Bird clan. Twenty years earlier, perhaps, this would have been ruled incest and punished by execution. The Choctaw word for clan, *iksa,* came to mean "church denomination," as Baptist Iksa, Methodist Iksa. Some members of tribes in the 1820s still traced descent from their mothers rather than their fathers. Ceremonials continued to some extent; tribal lore was available from the elderly but was not systematically taught growing children, as before. Wild game was not as available; the bison were gone, and the beaver and wild pigeon were quickly vanishing. The fur trade, itself, was all but forgotten.

So much was being wrought so frantically, in less than a score of years compared to the thousands of years in which the ancient ways had evolved, as Cherokee, Chickasaw, and Choctaw coped with life in a nation that in itself was an example of remarkable change and growth.

John Ross, easily one of the ablest southeastern Indian

statemen, saw the ultimate task facing the Indian. He wrote of those who, like him, were trying to relate to the new world around them, "I hope their foundation to build upon will be rightly laid in the first place, and that their workmen may understand and judiciously conduct the job they undertake."

The Removal

But the race to survive in their ancestral homelands was not to be won by the five great southeastern nations.

By the time Andrew Jackson reached the presidency in 1828, the southeastern Indian nations were just so much unfinished business. Nowhere did the map of the United States show so many self-contained Indian *nations* as in the Southeast.

One southeastern state, Mississippi, with only a small portion of the state opened for white settlement, had a rapidly increasing white and black population that had passed seventy-five thousand by 1820. With an estimated Indian population of 23,400 in 1827, Mississippi had almost as many Indians as all the northern states combined.

For the dominant whites in the Southeast, it was time to tidy up the map. For the Indian nations that remained there, time was running out.

The machinery for bringing the Indian lands in the Southeast as well as the midwestern border states under state control was the Indian Removal Bill passed by the U. S. Congress on May 28, 1830. At once the new Jackson administration launched a tremendous treaty-making operation with Indian tribes. No less than ninety-four separate Indian treaties were ratified by the U.S. Senate in Jackson's first term alone.

Choctaw

The Choctaw were first to depart, perhaps as a kind of experiment by leaders in Washington. Here was a large nation, friendly toward the United States, nonmilitaristic, democratic almost to a fault in their government, and, as Secretary of War Calhoun earlier had noted, not so prone to lodging protests and appealing on humanitarian, moral, and legal grounds as the Cherokee. If the Choctaw, one of the largest Indian nations east of the Mississippi River, could be removed beyond the Indian Line to Indian Territory, or what is now Oklahoma, an important precedent would be quickly set.

In the year 1830, Choctaw national life, which now had some forty Methodist, Baptist, and Presbyterian missionaries, eleven English schools, and a code of laws, was drastically altered. That year the state of Mississippi, following Georgia's example in regard to the Creeks and the Cherokees and Tennessee's policy toward the Cherokees, declared that Mississippi laws were henceforth in effect everywhere within the state. Up until then the Choctaws had retained full authority on their own lands and dealt with the federal government as an autonomous unit. Now the office of chief was declared out of existence by the Mississippi legislature. Any Indian who presumed to exercise authority as a chief was liable to a fine of one thousand dollars or twelve months in jail, or both. In short, government of Choctaws by Choctaws was now a criminal offense in the eyes of the state of Mississippi.

Concurrently the Jackson administration arranged for a treaty-making conference with the Choctaws at Dancing Rabbit Creek in Noxubee County in central Mississippi near the Alabama line. The conference was zealously promoted by government agents sent to the Choctaws, who told of the free food and entertainment that would be available for up to six thousand. Some six thousand Choctaws came.

Along with the Choctaws, the worst elements of white

166

society also came, gamblers, saloonkeepers who made portable bars out of wagons, prostitutes, and the inevitable frontier rowdies. Had Thomas Jefferson, who fathered the general idea of Indian removal from contaminating influences, been alive and aware of the carnival atmosphere at Dancing Rabbit Creek, he would surely have grieved.

Secretary of War John Eaton ordered all missionaries away from the treaty grounds but ignored the swarm of corrupting whites. Why? Missionaries had warned the Choctaws not to allow themselves to be cheated.

On September 27, 1830, the Treaty of Dancing Rabbit Creek was signed. It conveyed to the United States for sale to settlers a total of 10,423,130 acres in Mississippi, in exchange for lands in the southeast portion of Indian Territory. The U.S. government was to pay for the removing. Three years were allowed for removal. However, those Choctaws who wished to remain in Mississippi might do so under provisions of Article 14 of the treaty, which stated that heads of families were eligible for an allotment of 640 acres. The article futher declared that single persons over ten were eligible for 320 acres; those under ten, 160 acres. Land eligibility, however, must be formally documented. For instance, a person had to prove he was a Choctaw, prove his or her age, prove that he was head of a family in ways that white courts would accept.

After the revelry and the treaty-signing, depression settled over many of the Choctaws. Chief David Folsom of the Folsom family, so instrumental in the coming of the missionaries, their schools and smithies, to the Choctaw, wrote in a letter to Presbyterian ministers in the nation, "We are exceedingly tired. We have just heard of the ratification of the Choctaw Treaty. Our doom is sealed. There is no other course for us but to turn our faces to our new homes toward the setting sun." [1]

Choctaw Peter Pitchlynn, who had attended the University of Nashville, sadly wrote a federal official:

David Folsom

I beg, sir, that for a whole nation to give up their whole country, and remove to a distant, wild, and uncultivated land . . . is a consideration which, I hope, the Government will always cherish with the liveliest sensibility. The privations of a whole nation before setting out, their turmoil and losses on the road and settling their homes in a wild world, are all calculated to embitter the human heart.[2]

After the removal began, in one month, September of 1833, the Choctaw Agency in southeastern Indian Territory reported the death of one hundred Choctaw migrants. It reported that of the three thousand migrating up to that time, some six hundred, or one-fifth, died either on the 500-mile journey west, or soon after arrival. Cholera, dysentery, influenza were common causes of death, but official reports indicate that numbers simply expired as if they no longer wanted to live.

The high incidence of fatalities is primarily the result of conditions of travel and the country through which the Choctaws had to pass. If a removing party, for instance,

Ha-tchoo-tuc-knee,
or Peter Pitchlynn

George Catlin

SMITHSONIAN INSTITUTION

chose to go overland it faced the seemingly endless swamps of eastern Arkansas. Cholera ran rampant on barges and boats proceeding up the Arkansas River, their primitive sanitary facilities overtaxed by overcrowding. Whether on land or on the Arkansas, the Choctaws were not used to the wintry storms blowing down from Canada. Sometimes, migrating parties of Choctaw relatives and friends were poorly supplied because of bad planning by private contractors or by outrageous graft on the part of supply agents with lucrative government contracts. Seeking to curb waste, the War Department ordered that cost of removal be held to a bare minimum. Unfortunately there were contractors and supply agents who abused both government and the Choctaws by leasing barges unfit for humans, buying wormy pork, and the like.

Though the Choctaw were selected to begin the government's process of removal, the expectation of swift completion proved illusory. Removal went through a cycle of on again, off again until 1846 and even then the Mississippi map still showed clusters of Choctaw.

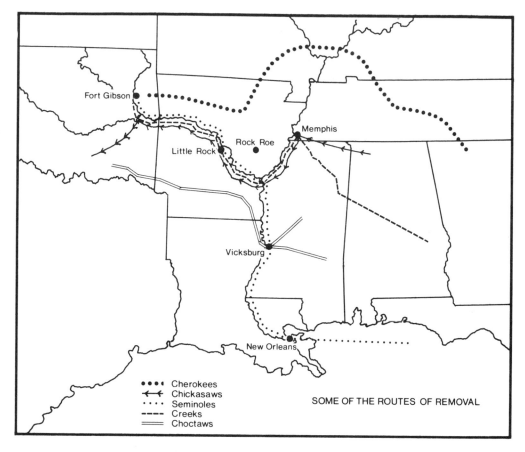

Fort Gibson

Memphis

Rock Roe

Little Rock

Vicksburg

New Orleans

●●●● Cherokees
←─← Chickasaws
· · · · Seminoles
---- Creeks
═══ Choctaws

SOME OF THE ROUTES OF REMOVAL

Chickasaw

In three treaties before 1830 the Chickasaws had had to relinquish claim to most of their lands.

Gen. James Robertson, founder of Nashville, Tennessee, began the whittling away of Chickasaw lands in a treaty made with them in 1805. In exchange for title to lands north of the Tennessee River the Chickasaws received twenty thousand dollars. In 1816, Gen. Andrew Jackson negotiated a treaty by which the Chickasaws yielded title to all land from the south side of the Tennessee River to the west bank of the Tombigbee River in exchange for twelve thousand dollars a year for ten years.

In a three-week meeting that began October 1, 1818, at Chickasaw Old Town near current day Tuscumbia, Alabama, General Jackson, agent for the United States and the state of Tennessee, aided by Isaac Shelby, former governor of Kentucky, threatened, coaxed, and argued elements of the Chickasaw nation into selling some seven million acres of their lands in western Tennessee and western Kentucky for twenty thousand dollars a year for fifteen years. These lands, among the best in the two states, were between the Mississippi and Tennessee rivers. Memphis, Tennessee, soon was founded at Chickasaw Bluffs as a real estate promotion by General Jackson, his law partner John Overton, and Gen. James Winchester.

After the Indian Removal Bill, the U.S. government on October 20, 1832, concluded a treaty for all the lands remaining to the Chickasaws at the Chickasaw Council House on Pontotoc Creek, Mississippi. With principal Chickasaw spokesmen Levi Colbert ill and unable to attend the conference, their 6,422,400 acres were ceded for a promised three million dollars that still had not been paid at the time of the Civil War. Chickasaw support of the Confederacy in the Civil War forfeited their claim for payment.

The preamble of the Pontotoc Treaty stated:

The Chickasaw Nation find themselves oppressed in their situation; by being made subject to the laws of the States in which they reside. Being ignorant of the language of the laws of the white man, they cannot understand or obey them. Rather than submit to this great evil, they prefer to seek a home in the west, where they may live and be governed by their own laws.

In January, 1837, Chickasaw leaders concluded an agreement with Choctaw spokesmen permitting the Chickasaw nation to move to the western portion of the Choctaw part of Indian Territory. The Chickasaw paid their kinsmen $530,000 for these new lands between the

Canadian and Washita rivers and the north and south forks of the Red River.

Compared to the experiences of other southeastern Indians, the actual migration of the Chickasaws was accomplished without great loss of life. The Chickasaw were not so numerous, for one reason. Said to have been the most affluent of southeastern Indians at the time, they were accustomed to sharp trading practices. With business expertise their leaders insisted that supplies and food be good. Even so, Chickasaw inspectors were cheated at every turn and given short weights in grain and beef sent overland across Arkansas from Memphis.

Left, Sho-ni-on, *Chickasaw man, prior to 1877*

Three thousand and one Chickasaws went by boat from Memphis landing to the mouth of the Arkansas and then up the Arkansas to their new homes.

Right, A young Chickasaw brave before 1868

One detail may suggest what the trauma of exile from the land of their ancestors was like. According to government regulations for those who went by boat, and some

three-fourths of the Chickasaws did, thirty pounds of baggage per person was allowed. A Congressional committee moved to challenge the thirty pounds as extravagant.

Who can measure the range and depth of anguish? In some cases there were Chickasaws who wept not only because they were leaving their Mississippi homes, but because they were parting from white friends. Chickasaw Billy and another youth, Kapia, both fine athletes who lived near Ripley in Tippah County, had many friendships among white youths. They asked T. J. Young, a friend with whom they ran footraces and wrestled, to go with them when they left, and even offered him money if he would, but Young did not go.

For some years after their removal, Chickasaws and Choctaws were identified as a composite nation.

Among the complaints of the Chickasaws in their new homes was the service required of them against the angry Osage, Cheyenne, and other plains tribes who claimed that they rightly owned the lands to which the Southeasterners moved.

Creek

General Jackson by the Treaty of Fort Jackson in 1814 had taken only part of the Creek lands. They still held much of the western part of Georgia, the largest state east of the Mississippi.

Many acres of their lands gone, hundreds of their men killed at Horseshoe Bend, and others of their people emigrated to Florida, the almost eighteen thousand Creeks yet in Alabama and Georgia were to know further ordeal.

Before the Indian Removal Bill in 1830, ownership of the remaining Creek lands was already disputed. William McIntosh, Scot-Creek cousin of Gov. George M. Troup of Georgia, and twelve other Creek chiefs in the Treaty of Indian Springs, February 12, 1825, reaffirmed a cession of fifteen million acres they had made two years earlier and ceded ten million more acres—the remainder of the Creek lands—to the state of Georgia. Already on

William McIntosh

the Georgia payroll, McIntosh was given one hundred thousand dollars more for division among the signers of the treaty.

Although the Creek Confederacy no longer existed as it had once been, Creek law still stipulated the penalty of death for any Creek selling land without the consent of all Creek leadership. The thirteen signers of the treaty, representing only about one-tenth of the Creek people, were condemned by the thirty-six other Creek chiefs for high treason.

Chief Opothleyoholo (aso known as Hopothleycholo) and many town chiefs and subchiefs approached the home and inn owned by McIntosh in what is now Carroll County, Georgia. The leader of the outraged Creeks stood on a large rock in the yard and cried:

> Brothers, the Great Spirit has met here with his children of the woods and their pale face brethren. I see his golden locks in the sunshine: he fans the warrior's brows with his wings and whispers sweet music in the winds; the beetle joins his hymn and the mocking bird his song. You are charmed! Brothers, you have been deceived! A snake has been coiled in shade and you are running into his open mouth, deceived by the double tongue of the pale face chief, and drunk with the fire water of the pale face. Brothers, our grounds are gone, and the plow of the pale face will soon turn over the bones of our fathers. Brothers, are you tame? Will you submit? Hopethleycholo says NO! [3]

Then turning with a finely controlled gesture of contempt to McIntosh, who was standing with Georgia officials at a window a few feet distant, he continued, "As for you, double tongue snake, before many moons have waned, your own blood shall wash out the memory of this hated treaty. Brothers, I have spoken." [4]

On May 1, 1825, McIntosh and his son-in-law were shot to death by a party of Creek soldiers. Their appointed leader was the great Creek patriot Menewa, who had been a leader of the Red Sticks.

Menewa

From Indian Tribes of North America *by Thomas L. McKenney and James Hall*

Because the Treaty of Indian Springs was illegal, Menewa went to Washington in 1826 and negotiated a treaty with the administration of Pres. John Quincy Adams, who had publicly declared his intention to treat the Indians honorably. This Treaty with the Creeks— sometimes more simply called Menewa's Treaty or the Treaty of 1826—affirmed Creek possession of their remaining lands and acknowledged Menewa's loyalty to the U. S. government.

But Governor Troup of Georgia, personally incensed because of McIntosh's execution, ran up the flag of state's rights and proceeded as if the Treaty of Indian Springs

175

Both paintings by George Catlin

Stee-tcha-ko-me-co,
or Ben Perryman

SMITHSONIAN INSTITUTION

were valid. He actively encouraged and protected with the Georgia militia, land speculators, gamblers, bootleggers, "land lawyers" specializing in shyster land deals with Indians, and white squatters in their intrusion upon and obtaining of Creek lands.

In December, 1831, Chief Eneah Micco made formal protest to President Jackson of the incursions onto Creek lands in violation of the Treaty of Washington five years before. In reply President Jackson stated that he and his administration did not feel bound by the treaty of former President Adams with the Creeks. The Creeks soon were persuaded to remove to Indian Territory within five years, and, in exchange, the federal government promised to keep white intruders from Creek lands.

However, this new Treaty of 1832 included a provision which gave each tribal member the right to sell his land—or remain on it if he chose—if the President approved each action. Unlike the provision for removal, President Jackson and the Secretary of War ignored this

Hol-te-mal-te-tez-te-meek-ee,
or Sam Perryman, his brother,
Creek chiefs during removal

provision for individual tribal members. On the local level federal agents either could not, or in many cases would not, interfere with the traffic in Indian land that mushroomed. With good land to be obtained from Creeks for whiskey, five or ten dollars, fancy promises, and the most flagrant confiscation—often with the Georgia militia casually standing by—white intruders overran the Creek country.

Within a year, their homes and crops taken, the Creeks were driven into the forests and swamps. Some continued to join the Seminoles in Florida. A U.S. marshal looking at the rush of white speculators on the Creek lands across the Chattahoochee River from Columbus, Georgia, wrote of "the most lawless and uncouth men I have ever seen."

The Treaty of 1832 had promised the Creek five years of grace from avaricious white men. Why did it fail? Responsibility for its failure can be attributed to President Jackson's perhaps deliberate neglect of the provision concerning individual Creeks who might sell their land, the inability of federal agents to stop such unauthorized sales, and the support given white intruders by the Georgia militia.

By 1836, when extensive Creek removal was underway, Eneah Emathala emerged as leader of the Lower Creeks south of what is now Phenix City, Alabama. Advocating noncompromise, the eighty-four-year-old Eneah Emathala's following included elements of the Muskogees, Hitchitis, and Koshitas. Their desire was only to be left alone in their homeland, to live without harming any people.

But the wish to be left alone fanned into active resistance when Eneah Emathala's group secured arms in ways never explained. On grounds of preventing Indian warfare, the War Department ordered the Army to remove all the Creeks from Alabama.

Gen. Winfield Scott was ordered to capture Eneah Emathala and in June, 1836, with the aid of Jim Boy, a Creek, General Scott succeeded in bringing Eneah Emathala in irons to Fort Mitchell, Alabama. Captured with Emathala were some one thousand other persons, ranging in age from one year to one hundred. Their colors were black, red, and white.

The aged Eneah Emathala and his warriors, all in chains, were marched by the Army some ninety miles west to Montgomery, capital of the state of Alabama. There, the Indians had to climb aboard wagons to be paraded through the streets. One young man who had secreted a knife on his person killed himself rather than be so humiliated.

In July, 1836, in intensely hot weather, some twenty-five hundred Creeks were jammed aboard two small river steamboats, each towing two barges. Thus began a long, hopeless journey down the Alabama River to Mobile, across the Gulf of Mexico to New Orleans, and then up the Mississippi to Rock Roe in Arkansas Territory. Their hardships were not lessened by the next lap of the trip—overland to Little Rock and Fort Gibson in Indian

Territory, where they arrived in September, two long months and some one thousand miles from their beloved streams and woodlands in Georgia and Alabama.

In one incident involving this group, green fruit, muddy Mississippi water, and army salt rations caused dysentery and diarrhea that claimed eighty-one lives.

The following year, a similar incident caused the death of 311 Creeks when the small steamboat *Monmouth* sank in the Mississippi River. During the Removal, more than one thousand Creeks lost their lives mainly from cholera and dysentery.

Some fifteen thousands Creeks were removed to lands between the Canadian and Arkansas rivers in Indian Territory where ancient enemies, the Cherokees, were destined to be their neighbors to the northeast.

Some Creeks had hoped to stay in the Southeast by finding sanctuary with the Chickasaws, but in 1837 they were removed to Indian Territory with their hosts. There the fugitive Creeks were forced by the government to rejoin the Western Creeks; for administrative purposes it was decided to keep the tribes distinct. The government on December 28, 1837, reported completion of Creek removal to the west.

However a number of Creeks—no one kept any records on how many—stayed on their ancestral lands and endured separation from their brothers who had gone west. Of this remnant, some were impressed into slavery. Others isolated themselves in Mobile, Dale, and Escambia counties, in the impenetrable country near the west Florida Panhandle, and their descendants are found in this part of Alabama today.

Cherokee

We have seen that in 1809 some of the Cherokees left the Cherokee nation to migrate west. In the 1820s Chief John Jolly vigorously administered the affairs of some 3,700 Cherokees in what is now Pope County, Arkansas.

Chief Jolly, or Jol-lee

Etching from a George Catlin painting

He was the chief who adopted Sam Houston before he re-signed the governorship of Tennessee and found refuge with the Western Cherokee. Houston later married a niece of Chief Jolly.

Some ten million acres of land claimed by the Cherokee nation in the east were exchanged in the Treaty of 1819 for approximately thirteen million acres in Arkansas where the Western Cherokees were. The Treaty of 1819 ended the Cherokee nation's claim to territory in North Carolina: Now their eastern lands were principally in north Georgia and southeastern Tennessee.

The Treaty of 1828 then exchanged the Cherokee lands in the newly organized Arkansas Territory for seven million acres in northeastern Indian Territory and for the so-called Cherokee Strip, some 50 miles wide and 25 miles deep to the west. Thereupon, the Western Cherokees moved to the new territory. Under Cherokee national law the new land was held in common with all the other

Cherokee citizens, in other words, with the more numerous Cherokees in the eastern part.

On June 26, 1829, Yonagusta, Long Blanket, Willnota, and fifty-six other Mountain Cherokees made their legal separation from the Cherokee nation to become citizens of what was then Haywood County in western North Carolina near the Great Smoky Mountains. This gave formal status to the reality of the situation.

At this time, the Mountain Cherokees of North Carolina agreed to give power of attorney for their group of some sixty families to a suitable lawyer. They were not a tribe but a settlement of Indians on the Oconaluftee River and, as with most communities, needed an attorney. No longer a part of the Cherokee nation, they were not to be directly involved in the Removal.

Soon after the Indian Removal Bill of 1830 several thousand Eastern Cherokees removed under government supervision to their brothers in the west, but the greater part of the Cherokees declined to exile themselves voluntarily from their ancient homeland.

Led by John Ross, the Cherokee, remaining on their much-reduced territory in the east, fought removal through the courts. Chief Justice John Marshall of the Supreme Court in a renowned opinion in 1831, ruled that the Cherokee nation, having been formally recognized as an entity by the government of the United States, the state of Georgia could not impose its laws on the self-governing Cherokees. Pres. Andrew Jackson is supposed to have roared, "John Marshall has made his decision, now let him enforce it."

Discovery of gold in present Lumpkin County in north Georgia added a new element to the complex situation the Cherokees faced.

On December 23, 1835, the Rev. John Schermerhorn as government agent called for a national meeting of all the Eastern Cherokees at the national capital of New

Echota in what is now northwest Georgia to make a treaty ceding the remaining Cherokee lands in the east, some ten million acres, to the United States in exchange for thirteen million acres of land in northeastern Indian Territory.

The Treaty of New Echota which resulted specified that some four and one-half million dollars were to be paid the Cherokees. There was no provision for those who might wish to stay behind.

John Ross boycotted the New Echota scene, thinking he could negotiate a better treaty. In fact, only about three hundred of the Cherokees actually were at New Echota when the removal treaty was made, and of these only seventy-nine were voters.

Although John Ross later presented a petition to Congress signed by 15,665 Cherokee indicating the illegality of the Treaty of New Echota, the Jackson administration rushed the treaty through the Senate. After one of the most bitter debates in its history up to that time, the treaty was ratified by the Senate in 1836 and the Cherokees ordered to leave their old homes.

An example of the aggressions against the Cherokees was the seizure by the commander of the Georgia militia, in 1834, of the home of "Rich Joe" Vann, a Cherokee businessman. The militia commander contended with a white boarder of the Vanns to take over the two-story house facing the federal road (now U.S. 76), at a point betwen Dalton and Chatsworth, Georgia. After forcing out Joseph Vann and his family, the commander set fire to the stairway to smoke out the traitorous white boarder. The Vanns fled to a farm they owned in Tennessee. Visitors to the Vann House can see the charred floor to this day. Dating from 1804, the solid brick house is said to be the oldest example of cantilevered construction in Georgia.

Joseph Vann lived through the forced Cherokee migration, to settle at Webbers Falls on the Washita River in what is now Oklahoma and to amass another fortune in

David Vann

The Vann House near Dalton, Georgia

Cherokee removal,
"Trail of Tears"
by Robert Lindneux

From the original at
Woolaroc Museum,
Bartlesville, Oklahoma

the operation of his farm and business. The duplicate of his former Georgia house built at Webbers Falls was destroyed during the Civil War.

Other Cherokees, however, did not live to see their new western homes.

Determined to end the Cherokee presence in east Tennessee and north Georgia, the government in 1838 sent some seven thousand troops under Gen. Winfield Scott to drive the Cherokees out of their homes, herd them into concentration camps, and then transport them west.

As with the Creeks earlier, a few thousand Cherokees were transported on steamboats as prisoners. But more than twelve thousand Cherokee traveled overland in thirteen parties through Tennessee, Kentucky, Illinois, Missouri, and Arkansas, journeys that took from three to five months.

Although the government never released a report of the number of fatalities, the leading authority on the Cherokee, the Smithsonian's James Mooney, estimated that over four thousand died as a result of removal.

Quatie Ross, wife of John Ross, was buried at Little Rock, Arkansas on February 1, 1839, one of the many victims of utter exhaustion and pneumonia. Several nights before during a winter storm she had given her blanket to a sick infant, perhaps saving the child's life. When daylight came, Quatie was quite ill. Former Pvt. John G. Burnett, U.S. Army, recalled years later:

> I was on guard duty the night Mrs. Ross died. When relieved at midnight I did not retire, but remained around the wagon out of sympathy for Chief Ross and at daylight . . . was detailed . . . to assist in the burial . . . her uncoffined body was buried in a shallow grave by the roadside far from her mountain home, and the sorrowing calvacade moved on.[5]

The government reported that the last of the thirteen parties reached Indian Territory on March 26, 1839. The end of the "Trail of Tears."

Seminole

Before the Red Stick War or, as it is also called, the Creek-American War of 1813-14, the Seminoles probably numbered about two thousand. Creek migrants after the Battle of Horseshoe Bend increased the total to about four thousand, which may have been the peak. One band of Seminoles, the Miccosukee, are believed by the noted ethnologist John R. Swanton to have had a population of about fourteen hundred when General Jackson raided the Seminoles in 1817-18, the so-called First Seminole War.

At Payne's Landing, Florida, on May 9, 1832, the government agreed to provide a blanket, shirt, and food to each Seminole who would migrate to Indian Territory where the Seminoles would unite with the Creeks. At the time, the Seminoles were surviving on roots and on the

A Seminole woman in Florida

Etching from a George Catlin painting

cabbage of the palmetto tree, their crops having been destroyed in a severe drought the year before.

An exploring delegation led by Jumper, often called the Sensekeeper, and including Abraham, the black interpreter, made a river and land trip to Fort Gibson, where they learned from the Creeks that the Kiowas, Comanches, and other Plains tribes, unhappy with the presence of the former Southeasterners, were stealing their horses. Jumper indignantly told the government that it was trying to put the Seminoles with bad Indians, and the delegation returned to Florida with that report.

This seeming bad faith on the part of the government only fanned the fears of the influential black element, both free and slave, some of whom once had been Creek-owned slaves and had no wish to rejoin their former owners. The Seminoles also included Creek "separatists," as averse as the blacks to rejoining the Creeks.

Meantime, Georgians were loudly crying that the Seminole were inciting black slaves to run away to Florida.

In November, 1835, Che-cho-ter, the young wife of Osceola, was seized by a white force and carried off into slavery, according to Osceola, who bitterly resisted the removal the government was advocating so forcefully. (It has often been said that Che-cho-ter's mother was a fugitive Negro slave.)

On December 28, 1835, near the Great Wahoo swamp six or seven miles north of Withlacoochee River a large party of Indians and Negroes ambushed a company of army troops that was attempting to round up the Seminoles for enforced removal. All but three of the company of 110 were killed. The Second Seminole War was underway.

In January, 1836, Osceola sent a letter to the Army in Florida in which he declared: "You have guns, and so have we—you have powder and lead, and so have we—you have men and so have we—your men will fight, and so will ours, till the last drop of the Seminole's blood has moistened the dust of his hunting ground." [6]

Osceola

Etching from a
George Catlin painting

Taken by ruse during a supposed peace parley, Osceola died in a damp cell at Fort Moultrie in Charleston Harbor on January 30, 1838. He had roused his people to resist and humiliate an invading army of more than ten times their number. Later, Civil War general William Tecumseh Sherman, a young Army officer in Florida in the 1840s, wrote his wife Ellen that it was a dirty, ungallant business to burn small villages and banana trees, and to have to search for an enormously outnumbered enemy.

The Seminoles showed astonishing genius in guerrilla fighting as they retreated farther and farther into the Everglades. Finally, the Army ended this Second Seminole War—literally—by saying it was over.

Except for a few hundred who escaped the soldiers, the Army completed the removal of most of the Seminoles immediately after the war ended in 1842. Merger of the Seminoles with the Creeks in Indian Territory was still required. After years of distress for Seminoles in the old lands and the new ones, the Treaty of 1856 was negotiated in Washington between the Creeks, Seminoles, and the United States conveying from the Creeks to the Seminoles a long narrow strip of some 2,169,000 acres between the Canadian River and the North Fork of the river, northwestward to the one-hundredth parallel, or the present western boundary of Oklahoma.

A few years before and after the Treaty of 1856, what has been designated the Third Seminole War took place in Florida, which had become a state. Acknowledging that it was yielding to the demands of white settlers to clear Florida once and for all of Indians, the Army endeavored to capture the Seminole remnant.

May 4, 1858, the Army declared that the operations in Florida were over. On that date a small party of 165 Seminoles, of whom 121 were women and children, left Fort Myers on the steamboat *Quapaw*. Proceeding by way of New Orleans up the Mississippi and Arkansas rivers to Fort Smith, they traveled by wagon to their new homes arriving June 16. No tally was kept on the numbers of the last Seminole migrants known to have died on the journey.

While many Indian tribes were moved into Indian Territory, the largest contingent—some sixty thousand people—was the former Southeasterners, who by the 1850s were being called the Five Civilized Tribes because of their high degree of cultural development.

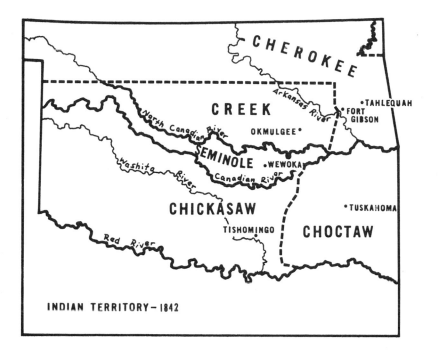

INDIAN TERRITORY—1842

Cherokees were in the northeastern part of what was to become Oklahoma, Creeks in the center, and Choctaws in the south. In 1856, the Seminoles, as we have seen, were given separate identity and separate territory. In that year, too, the Chickasaws were accorded separate existence from the Choctaws, with their land district west of the Choctaw lands.

Soon after arrival each of the Five Civilized Tribes was recognized as a separate nation under the protection of the United States. The Cherokee national legislature met at Tahlequah, the Chickasaw at Tishomingo, the Choctaw at Tuskahoma, the Creek at Okmulgee, and the Seminole at Wewoka. Churches, schools, farms, stores, mills, and other businesses were going concerns by the time of Civil War.

In the new country many adjustments were required, especially in human relations: Creek had to reunite with Creek and with the Seminoles, placed in their midst by the government because many of the Seminoles had a Creek background.

191

Slaveholding Creeks kept alive the charge that the Seminoles had lured away their slaves before removal and in Indian Territory were still encouraging blacks to run away. Chickasaws tried to be content with being officially fitted into Choctaw territory. The Cherokees needed years to straighten out their differences about removal. The Cherokees who had gone west earlier flaunted their status as "old settlers" before all. But all five nations wrote constitutions modeled on that of the United States and built strong societies in the new land that had become their home.

Tuko-see-mathla,
a Seminole Warrior

From Indian Tribes of North America
by Thomas L. McKenney and James Hall

*"Trail of Tears"—painted by
Jerome Tiger, Creek-Seminole*

John Ross,
principal chief of the Cherokee

From Indian Tribes of North America
by Thomas L. McKenney and James Hall

Opothleyoholo,
Creek Chief

From Indian Tribes of North America
by Thomas L. McKenney and James Hall

Chittee Yoholo,
*a Seminole chief
who had been Creek*

Both paintings from Indian Tribes of North America
by Thomas L. McKenney and James Hall

Tooantuh, *or Spring Frog,
Cherokee warrior
and champion ball player*

*Choctaws of today wearing
tribal costumes that are
decorated with handmade braid
and lace beadwork*

ROBERT B. FERGUSON

JIMMY MOORE

Mrs. Eva Wolfe, Cherokee, weaves a basket from river cane.

ROBERT B. FERGUSON

Charlie Billie Boy, Seminole medicine man, sings at the annual
Florida powwow.

*Choctaw dance. The women wear long cascades
of ribbons in their hair.*

*A fast stickball game
played by Choctaw boys in
Mississippi and a player
at rest against the goal post
during the time out*

BOTH PHOTOGRAPHS BY JIMMY MOORE

"Cornstalk Shoot"—painted by Franklin Gritts, Cherokee

Penny Otter,
Cherokee girl,
in tribal costume

Cherokee surveyors
in North Carolina

"Seminoles in Everglades"—*painted by Fred Beaver, Seminole*

Florida Seminoles wearing traditional patchwork costumes

ROBERT B. FERGUSON

The Remnant

In a message to Congress on December 3, 1838, Pres. Martin Van Buren announced that the removal of the eastern Indians to the west was completed. Concerning one of the largest Indian groups north of Mexico, he added, "The measures authorized by Congress at its last session have had the happiest effects. . . . The Cherokees have migrated without any apparent reluctance."

No doubt, the bland presidential statement was based on what Van Buren had been told. If so, he was misinformed. There was reluctance, abject misery, and there were tears—many, bitter tears. That some of the Osage, Comanche, Arapaho, and other Plains people were far from happy about the relocation of Southeasterners on their home or hunting lands was something else again.

Choctaw

By treaty rights, some of the Choctaw stayed on their ancestral lands in Mississippi. Others went to Louisiana and some, perhaps, to the Seminoles.

From 1845 to 1847, the Office of Indian Affairs (OIA) made a determined effort to remove at long last the Indian presence from Mississippi. Some four thousand Choctaws, or the largest number since 1833, were removed. Still, a remnant doggedly clung to the land and resisted efforts of the OIA as well as appeals from their western brothers to come. Why?

In 1843, a Mississippi Choctaw known only as Cobb sought to explain to an OIA agent:

> Brother: When you were young, we were strong; we fought by your side; but our arms are now broken. You have grown large. My people have become small.
>
> Brother: My voice is weak; you can hardly hear me; it is not the shout of a warrior but the wail of an infant. I have lost it in mourning over the misfortunes of my people. These are their graves; and in those aged pines you hear the ghosts of the departed. Their ashes are here, and we have been left to protect them. Our warriors are nearly all gone to the far country west; but here are our dead. Shall we go, too, and give their bones to the wolves?
>
> Brother: Our hearts are full. Twelve winters ago our chiefs sold our country. Every warrior that you see here was opposed to that treaty. If the dead could have counted, it could never have been made. But alas! though they stood around, they could not be seen or heard. Their tears came in the raindrops and their voices in the wailing wind, but the pale faces knew it not, and our land was taken away. . . .
>
> Brother: When you took our country, you promised us land. There is your promise in the book. Twelve times have the trees dropped their leaves, and yet we have received no land. Our houses have been taken from us. The white man's plow turns up the bones of our fathers. We dare not kindle our fires; and yet you said we might remain and you give us land.[1]

Cobb was right. The Treaty of Dancing Rabbit Creek had promised land to those who chose to remain in Mississippi. The total amount expressly reserved for distribution to the Choctaws measured approximately 150 square miles. It was all there in the book as Cobb said.

But there was a catch. Application had to be made to receive a land allotment; and there were certain tests for applications. For example, proof that a man was head of a family had to be given. Proof of age, even, was required.

These were uncertain, difficult matters to prove in a time when written records were sparse.

April 25, 1846, sixteen years after the Treaty of Dancing Rabbit Creek, or time enough for a young man and woman to marry and begin a family, the OIA signed and sealed the land claims of the Mississippi Choctaws. During that time over one thousand families formally presented claims. Of these, only 143 were acceptable to the government. What had happened?

It was not unlike the scene at Dancing Rabbit Creek, though more prolonged and widespread. The understandable tendency of many Indians to become disheartened grew pronounced. Many gave up. Many made no effort even to survive. Within their midst, hundreds traded land for whiskey. No longer permitted, by edict of the Mississippi legislature, to govern themselves through their traditional chief system, the Choctaws lived in a kind of limbo. White land speculators bought land claims from Indians with free treats of ball games, food, and whiskey. Land sharks operated openly. The Choctaw was encouraged to flirt casually with debt—a condition which he once had regarded with horror.

Moreover, the Choctaw was subjected to race prejudice, with a kind of three-way segregation—white, black, and red—developing. Many an otherwise respectable white said in gracious Mississippi accents that the only way to deal with the lying Indian was to cheat him first. Legal aid, if it could be found in such an environment, was incompetent, poorly done, and expensive.

As the Mississippi Historical Society once reported, an estimated four million acres of land was swindled from the Mississippi Choctaws.

Yet, remnants remained. They became sharecroppers on land that once was their own. Stern segregation, plus a desire on the part of the Choctaws to retain racial purity, froze much of Choctaw culture at the 1830 level. Their language often seemed old-fashioned to Western Choctaws.

SMITHSONIAN INSTITUTION

"Choctaw Settlement" —painted by Frances Bernard in 1869. The women before the fire appear to be brewing dye to color the nearby strips of cane in preparation for making baskets.

For almost a century in the midst of juggernaut-strong white culture, they existed with very little change from the customs prevailing during the days of the Dancing Rabbit Creek Treaty. The *alikchi,* or medicine men, continued to practice. The great stickball game was played on occasion. And the *bohpoli,* or little people of the forest, continued to play pranks and pop stones against hollow trees. Except for the songs of the people, the voice of the Choctaw was stilled. Their governmental system was gone. Their pioneering school system had been removed with the bulk of the tribe. The people who stayed behind struggled for bare survival.

Cherokee

Unlike some of the agreements with Indians in other areas, the Treaty of New Echota made no provision for qualified applicants to receive parcels of land and remain in their beloved homeland. But were *all* the Cherokees really uprooted from the Southeast?

We need only remember the sixty families of Mountain Cherokees in North Carolina who in 1819 formally separated from the Cherokee nation, people small in number, true, and often ignored by history, but in their own way as remarkable as any element in the whole Cherokee people. They did not go; and in a certain persistence, staunchness, and in separation by preference, these isolated few were very "Cherokee."

And there are others. A story is told of Tsali, or "Charley," a Cherokee man well along in years. He wasn't a member of the Cherokee aristocracy, but he lived a good life far back in the reaches of the Great Smoky Mountains. He farmed a little. His family consisted of his aging wife, his three sons and their families, and his brother-in-law, Lowney.

One day in May, 1838, Lowney brought some disturbing news: A lot of soldiers were down in the great valley, come to deport all the remaining Cherokees to the west.

Two soldiers with bayonets on their rifles came to Tsali's cabin. They ordered Tsali and his family to come with them to the concentration camp for Cherokees at Bushnell, North Carolina. This was one of a number of stockades built by the Army to hold the Cherokees until all could be moved away.

The old Cherokee offered no resistance to the soldiers, nor did his family. Though their real leadership had not agreed to the Treaty of New Echota, no self-respecting Indian approved disobedience when an agreement had been made.

For some reason, the soldiers were in a great hurry. They rushed Tsali's party along. At one point on the rough trail, Tsali's wife stumbled. One of the soldiers prodded her with his bayonet to make her move along.

Tsali became very angry. For by Cherokee custom

this was a great insult to his wife and to him. Having already learned that the soldiers did not understand Cherokee, Tsali whispered to Lowney and his sons. At a certain turn in the trail, he would deliberately trip and fall, and complain that he had hurt his ankle. The soldiers would stop. When they did, Lowney and Tsali's sons could leap on them and seize their rifles. Then all could escape and hide in the hills.

At the appointed place, Tsali stumbled, fell, and cried out in pain. One of the soldiers rushed to him. Tsali's son Ridges and Lowney, both shouting loudly, wrestled with the other soldier. At the same time, Tsali tackled the first soldier and brought him down hard. To Tsali's great horror, the soldier's rifle fired as he fell, and the soldier breathed no longer.

Meantime, Lowney had taken the gun of the other soldier away from him but the soldier wiggled free and ran into the woods.

Now Tsali and his little group faced a dreadful moment. He was old; he had grown up observing the ancient law on many matters, especially prohibitions on the shedding of blood. Murder was unpardonable.

But for now Tsali's main thoughts were of his family's safety, so he led them to a cave he knew about in massive Clingmans Dome, a 6,642-foot-high mountain in the Great Smokies.

Summer came, then fall. The Tsali family kept alive by gathering products of the forest, snaring small game, and taking birds when they could.

For the other Cherokees, the approaching deadline of their forced removal must have been agonizing. Although John Ross and some fifteen thousand of them had signed a petition declaring the Treaty of New Echota fraudulent, the U.S. Congress had approved the treaty, and soldiers were there to enforce it. To fight would have meant great loss of life, but there was resistance. The army stockades for hundreds of the Cherokees weren't escape proof. Others jumped out of army wagons and escaped. Still others simply disappeared when guards weren't looking.

Gen. Winfield Scott, who was in command of the Removal, later wrote in his *Memoirs* that rounding up the Cherokees, many of them more civilized than the whites that pressed upon them, was a distasteful duty for him. The general knew about the Tsali incident and that there were other Cherokee fugitives. The War Department was nagging him to conclude the Removal with utmost dispatch, lest it, too, develop into an embarrassment like the Seminole War in process at that very moment.

General Scott's staff contacted William Holland Thomas, a politician, trader, attorney, and adopted son of Yonagusta, who was the most powerful leader of the Cherokee band on the Oconaluftee River in western North Carolina. Anthropologist James Mooney was told in the 1890's by Cherokees there that Will Thomas, who had excellent relationships with the Cherokee nation, became an intermediary between Tsali and the Army.

Tsali must give himself up, for he had been involved in the death of a soldier. If he would surrender, the Army would make no effort to round up the Cherokees who had either escaped or had not been captured.

Tsali and his family surrendered and a military court sentenced Tsali and Ridges and Lowney to death by a firing squad. It is said that execution was at Bushnell and the sparkling waters of Fontana Lake cover the graves of the three men.

The refugees under ancient Indian law were given sanctuary by the North Carolina Cherokees to whom they went for the most natural, human reasons. Later they became part of what today is the Qualla Boundary in North Carolina. Descendants of Tsali live there yet on small farms along the Oconaluftee River and in the city of Cherokee.

There was a Tsali; there was a Will H. Thomas; there were refugees from the Army.

Will Thomas

Carl G. Lambert, Sr., official historian for the Eastern Band of Cherokee Indians, writing in a documented series of articles in the *Cherokee One Feather* in 1970 and 1971, has clarified the several roles of Will H. Thomas and explained about Qualla Boundary.

Will Thomas was born at Qualla Town, near present-day Cherokee, North Carolina in 1805, son of a white trader who died when Will was quite young. Chief Yonagusta adopted the boy as a son, which impressed even the most independent-minded of the North Carolina Cherokees with Will Thomas. For these people had followed Yonagusta, even to the forsaking of Cherokee citizenship and separation from their kinsmen.

The old chief advised the Mountain Cherokees to stay in North Carolina after he was gone, saying it was "a State better and more friendly disposed to the Red Man than any other."[2] A law had been passed in North

Carolina in 1836 letting these associated families buy land, as they had been doing since 1819.

The adopted white son of Yonagusta prepared for the law by self-study and in 1838 was given power of attorney by the Quallas, as the Cherokees on the Oconaluftee were sometimes called. He retained the office for the next twenty-seven years, until the end of the Civil War. The Quallas also followed Yonagusta's recommendation that Thomas be their business manager. He was sent by the North Carolina Cherokees to Washington in the 1840s to confer with the War Department concerning the New Echota Treaty of 1835, since some were saying that all individuals of Cherokee descent were eligible for monetary benefits under the treaty. Government records show that Thomas obtained a total of $18,759.11 for thirty-three families, including his fee of $265.62.

In many instances, at the request of Cherokees the money was invested by Thomas in land in the vicinity.

In 1848 when Thomas was elected to the North Carolina Senate the Cherokees on the Oconaluftee numbered more than nine hundred, having received some returnees from the West including Junaluska, who had saved Andrew Jackson's life at the Battle of Horseshoe Bend.

In 1848, Congress ordered settlement of the Treaty of New Echota, and State Senator Thomas obtained $38,282.96 for the Cherokees he represented as attorney and business manager. These included: the original Mountain Cherokees, the never-tallied Trail of Tears refugees, and unnumbered returnees from Indian Territory. Most of the Cherokees continued to let Thomas invest their share of the award in land. Senator Thomas became a Confederate colonel in the Civil War, leading two hundred of the Qualla. These Cherokees did guard duty in mountain passes between Gatlinburg, Tennessee, and Cherokee, North Carolina.

Thomas came out of the war broken in health and heavily indebted because of huge personal land speculations. Suits brought against Thomas finally reached the federal circuit court for western North Carolina in 1874. After long hearings and investigations Thomas' own land matters were separated from those in which he had represented the Indians. The court found that the Cherokees in and around Qualla had "variously acquired" some 67,000 acres, mostly nonsurveyed, less than a third of which could be farmed.

Survey was made by federal court order. Then the court placed the land under the trusteeship of the Commissioner of Indian Affairs in Washington, D.C., designating the Indian owners as the Eastern Band of Cherokee Indians. The ancient name "Qualla" for the Oconaluftee area was retained for the new entity.

North Carolina Cherokees emphasize that the Eastern Band of Cherokees is *not* a tribe but is an organization of individual stockholders of a corporation. A few Cherokees in North Carolina, though they don't live on Qualla Boundary, are members of the corporation. Other Cherokees in the state are not members.

In 1886 the U.S. Supreme Court heard a case brought by the government seeking to establish the legal identities of the Eastern Band Cherokees and those in Indian Territory. This was necessary for administering Indian services. The court held that the two peoples were separate and distinct entities. The old Mountain Cherokee contingent, it was noted, preferred associating as individuals in contrast to the tribal organization of the western group.

Three years later the Eastern Band of Cherokees applied for and was granted incorporation under the laws of North Carolina. A business committee drawn from the council supervises the various business endeavors of the corporation.

When lawyer Will Thomas died on the Qualla Boundary in 1893 the Cherokees honored him as a founding father. He was the agent in piecing together a land base that would implement Yonagusta's words to the boundary forefathers: "We wanted to become children of North Carolina, and she has received us as such, and passed

Mrs. Roxie Stamper weaves on a loom at Qualla Boundary.

Handicrafts of all kinds are available. in this Qualla arts and crafts booth.

The shop of the Qualla Arts and Crafts Mutual, Inc., at Cherokee, North Carolina

a law [letting them buy land] for our protection, and we know they will never oppress us." [3]

Others in the Southeast

By the advent of the Civil War years, possibly no more than one hundred fifty Seminoles and Miccosukees remained in all of Florida. These had been forced to retreat to the hammocks of the Everglades where they found of utmost value their knowledge of how to make swamp cabbage from the hearts of the palmetto.

Although by the 1850s most of Louisiana's Choctaw families had drifted to the southern part of the Choctaw nation in Indian Territory, a few families maintained their old ways on Bayou Lacomb on the north shore of Lake Pontchartrain and gathered occasionally to dance the seven dances they remembered. They made cane baskets and sold them in the markets of New Orleans. They made and used drums and mortars of timeless design. And now and then Ahochiobi and other Choctaw men made elbow pipes of clay and spoons of cow's horn.

Caddos of Louisiana—the Adais and Natchitoches—joined their relatives of the Kadohadacho Confederacy in northeastern Texas and southwestern Arkansas and Hasinai Confederacy in northeastern Texas. The small Tunican group had been reduced to thirty by about 1800.

Anthropologist John R. Swanton noted that such groups as the Avoyels were extinct as definite, indentifiable tribes by the 1850s, and the Chitimachan group was reduced to a population of less than one hundred living near Charenton. In and around the Grand Lake area of Louisiana, fragments of once distinct tribes such as Atakapa, Chitimacha, Taensa, and Alabama intermarried. Small numbers of Koasatis, or Coushattas as they prefer to be called, lived in what is now Allen Parish, Tunica near Marksville, and Houma in Terrebonne

Parish. Formerly members of the Creek Confederacy, the Coushattas also live on the Alabama-Coushatta Reservation near Livingston in Polk County, Texas.

Swanton estimated that in the 1850s there were less than one thousand Indians in the state of Louisiana identifiable on a tribal basis in a dozen or more fragments of tribes.

In general, they pieced out a living by farming poor land that no white man wanted. They gathered Spanish moss for cushion and furniture stuffing, trapped, fished, and just got by, few retaining their old Indian languages.

So, few in number and already west of the Mississippi River (supposed to divide forever the white man and the red man), Louisiana's Indians were spared forced removal by government order. In a relative sense they were free to live in their pockets of oblivion in bayou country or on coasts frequented by savage hurricanes and were almost classic examples of "out of sight, out of mind" to government as the great events of American history hurried onward.

Some historians contend that the Lumbees of North and South Carolina may descend from the intermarried Hatteras Indians of coastal North Carolina and Sir Walter Raleigh's fabled Lost Colony of 1587. Others say they may descend from the Eastern Sioux, who once numbered at least twenty-five identifiable tribes, or from Algonkin tribes of the North Carolina area or from Iroquian-Tuscarora elements.

According to Lumbee tradition, the ill-fated Raleigh colonists intermarried with the Hatteras and the group migrated south, joining with some of the Eastern Sioux. In time the Lumbee peoples were "discovered" in their present location. Living along the Lumber River, which rises near the boundary between Montgomery and Moore counties in central North Carolina and flows southeast across the South Carolina border, the Lumbees included many who were speaking English and who had brown hair and blue eyes. They were called Lumbees because of

CHRIS SEGURA

Left, Chitimacha girl

Right, Lumbee girl

the name of the river. Prof. Adolph Dial of Pembroke, who is preparing a book on the Lumbees, reports that today there are less than one hundred surnames among the approximately forty thousand Lumbees, many of them surnames of Raleigh's colonists.

As early as the 1700s, the Lumbees were landholders in lower North Carolina living a settled, free existence. As freemen, they fought in both the Revolutionary War and the War of 1812.

Without a tribal organization and tribal lands, somewhat blended into the surrounding white culture, the Lumbees were untouched by the Removal. But in reaction to abolitionist activity and fear of slave uprisings, North Carolina, in the state constitutional convention of 1835, deprived all non-whites of their political privileges and protections. Designated "free persons of color," the Lumbees, as others, could not vote or even send their children to school. Until the arrival of the federal troops in 1864 in the closing years of the Civil War, the Lumbees were discriminated against and, during the war, even conscripted as slave labor for Confederate war projects. In resistance to harsh persecution in the war years, some Lumbees took to guerrilla activities against the guilty southern whites.

At the Reconstruction their rights were restored by the new amendments to the U.S. Constitution, and the Lumbees in their warm southern land looked to the future.

Like the Lumbees, the nearly 100 Catawbas of South Carolina fought to retain their identity throughout the years preceding, during, and after the Civil War. As the war closed they faced a special dilemma described by Dr. Charles Hudson in his monograph, *The Catawaba Nation*: were they to be a race or a nation? Only by sharecropping outside the tiny reservation could they hope to make a bare living. Some of the Catawba women made pottery and traded it for flour or corn or peddled it in the countryside with the help of their young children. According to Prof. George L. Hicks pottery sales were a major source of income for the tribe.

Catawba Chief Sam F. Blue and his family at home in about 1918

As the necessity for eking out a livelihood carried the Catawbas more and more away from the reservation, they continued to lose elements of their native culture and to don the trappings of another way of life. By 1900 less than a dozen could speak their own language.

Catawba girls in 1918

A Catawba woman of today makes pottery following the age-old Catawba method.

224

The Long Eclipse

The real strides that the former southeastern tribes were making in a land the removing Choctaws called *Oklahoma*, caused many of them to make missions to the old country inviting their brothers to journey west.

Some speculate today that but for the terrific eruption of the American Civil War and the long years of reconstruction afterwards, this west-of-the-Mississippi reunion might well have occurred.

But, the paradise in Indian Territory was short-lived according to University of Oklahoma historian Edwin C. McReynolds, who says that the greatest of misfortunes for the Five Civilized Tribes was the war between North and South and the settling up that followed.

John Ross and many others preached neutrality, but due to the threatening presence of the armies and supporters of the North in neighboring Kansas and of the South in neighboring Arkansas and Texas, this was hard. Another neutralist, the Creek Opothleyoholo, who had many Seminole contacts, called for a great talk near present-day Holdenville and read to three hundred Creeks and Seminoles his letter from a friend, Abraham Lincoln. Opthleyoholo vigorously agreed with President Lincoln that this was a white man's dispute which the Indian, if wise, would avoid.

Neutrality was not to be, however. The Chickasaws and

Choctaws were wooed and won by the Confederacy, as were eventually the governments of the Cherokee, Creek, and Seminole. The federal agents who previously had served as the Indians' contact with the government in Washington had gone over to the Southern side and worked to convince the former Southeasterners to do so too. The newly appointed replacement federal agents were hesitant to leave Kansas. Pressed all around by the Confederacy, their annuities cut off by the United States, the five Indian governments yielded to overwhelming pressures and joined in the war on the side of the Confederacy of Southern States.

Professor McReynolds finds that loss of life among the Cherokees, Creeks, and Seminoles in Indian Territory was heavier in percentage of total population than the losses of any southern or northern state. In each of these nations there were strong groups of supportors for the North, for the South, and for neutrality. Most of those who died were refugees, displaced by these different factions. For instance, in August, 1862, a refugee camp on the Verdigris River contained nearly eight thousand Cherokees, Creeks, and Seminoles. Several hundred, including the venerable neutralist Ophthleyoholo died. Causes included disease, exposure, and starvation.[1]

From the Cherokees in Indian Territory came two Confederate regiments, one led by Stand Watie, a brigadier general in the Confederate army. The Creeks provided one Confederate regiment, and with the Seminoles, a second. Choctaws-Chickasaws added three regiments. In Kansas Unionist elements from the Five Civilized Tribes formed the First Regiment of Indian Home Guards. Some of the Seminole blacks joined the First Colored Infantry which helped capture the Confederate army supply depot at Honey Springs in 1863.

After the Civil War, the factions of the tribes reunited and in 1866 made treaties of peace with the United States in which the western half of their lands was given up for settlement by other Indians. The Five Civilized

Stand Watie

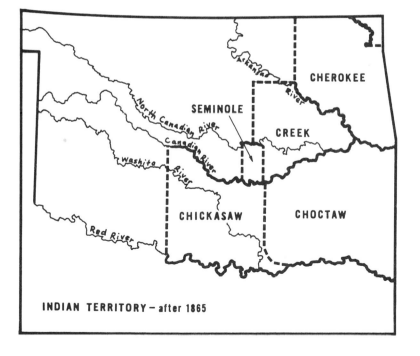

SEMINOLE

CHEROKEE

CREEK

CHICKASAW

CHOCTAW

Arkansas River

North Canadian River

Canadian River

Washita River

Red River

INDIAN TERRITORY — after 1865

Tribes, as they were called, also had to agree to the construction of two railroads through their lands—one going east-west, the other north-south.

According to their treaties, the Cherokees, Creeks, and Seminoles adopted freedmen into their tribes and gave them property rights. The Chickasaws and Choctaws elected the alternative given them of yielding the money they were to receive for their western lands to the government, which would then move and settle elsewhere the Negroes in their territories. The government did not abide by its part of this treaty, so the freedmen stayed but with no recognizable status. Although the Choctaws eventually adopted those in their territory, the Chickasaws never did.

In 1881 Helen Hunt Jackson's book *A Century of Dishonor* raised interest in Indian cultural identity. Urged by humanitarians, who felt the Indian could progress better on his own apart from the tribal organization, and by those who simply wanted his land, Congress in 1887 passed the Dawes General Allotment Act. It sought to terminate tribal relationships by requiring surrender of

Chickasaws at the Cheadle Ranch in Chickasaw Territory

OKLAHOMA HISTORICAL SOCIETY

reservations for division into 160-acre farms that the government would allot to each Indian and then hold in trust for twenty-five years. Land left over would be "surplus" and would be offered for sale to white settlers. Some authorities cite this as the real reason for passage of the legislation.

Although it did affect the tribes which had been moved to what is now western Oklahoma, the Dawes Act did not apply to the Five Civilized Tribes, because they held their land under patented titles. In 1897, however, Congress passed a bill extending federal law to the citizens of the Five Tribes and requiring presidential approval of the acts of their councils. Contrary to the treaties of the United States with the Five Civilized Tribes, the next year, Congress passed the Curtis Act which authorized the termination of their governments, the allotment of the tribal lands, and the division of other property. By 1905 their lands had been allotted or sold.

Sequoyah

Oklahoma historian Dr. Angie Debo points out that gas and oil fields were being opened by white promoters and operators in Muskogee as early as 1904. Concerned, representatives of the Five Tribes, joined by others, attempted to secure congressional recognition for an all-Indian state between the Arkansas line and what is now Oklahoma City to be named Sequoyah, in honor of the man who produced the Cherokee syllabary. Had there been a state of Sequoyah, oil and gas promoters and operators might have had difficulty obtaining valid land titles. They lobbied effectively, for Congress refused the Sequoyah state in 1906.

The state of Oklahoma—a fusion of Indian Territory and of Oklahoma Territory, the former western lands of the Five Civilized Tribes—entered the Union the next year. This new forty-sixth state had a population of 1,414,177, of which only 5.3 percent were Indian.

The Great Seal of Oklahoma has in the center a large five-pointed star. Within the points of the star are the symbols of the seals of the Five Civilized Tribes.

229

OKLAHOMA HISTORICAL SOCIETY

Seminole stickball players in early Oklahoma The Chickasaw nation, never large, numbered some six thousand in 1906, of whom fifteen hundred were full bloods, forty-one hundred mixed bloods, and six hundred intermarried whites. There were some forty-six hundred Negroes in the nation, many having come from the South during troubled times that followed the Civil War. In 1906 Dr. John R. Swanton found that the earlier culture of the Chickasaw "is now so completely discarded" that "practically all the younger people know nothing about it, and even the older ones can furnish only fragmentary information on the subject." University of Oklahoma historian Arrell M. Gibson uses the term "ethnic erasure" to describe what happened to the Chickasaws after removal from their Mississippi lands.

Their lands often taken by fraud and graft, many of the former southeastern Indians in Oklahoma lived long in conditions lacking educational, health, and job opportunities comparable to those of the whites around

230

them. By the first World War issues of alcoholism, poverty, and government paternalism were raised that as yet are not fully resolved. In terms of reasonable quality of living, many of these former Southeasterners were hardly more advanced than their brothers in the old Southeast.

Although the Republicans promised much to non-whites during Reconstruction, results were disappointing. For the Indian peoples still in the Southeast, decades of bare survival accompanied by what later generations call "the culture of poverty" was the rule and not the exception. In Mississippi, for example, groups of Choctaws, a few hundred each, lived in squalor on abandoned, worn-out lands. Some of the women wove traditional cane baskets to barter with local white housewives for food for their children. A few of the older women of the once populous Catawbas made pottery for sale or barter in South Carolina. Fragments of Creek tribes in Alabama picked up work when they could in saw milling or turpentine operations.

Catawba pottery

In North Carolina from the end of the Civil War to 1885, when the General Assembly gave them legal status as Indians, the Lumbees, as others, continued to be treated as second-class citizens and to experience discrimination.

Then in 1887, the General Assembly authorized establishment of a normal school for Indians in Robeson County. Five hundred dollars would be appropriated if the Indians provided a building within two years. Through local subscription of the money the trustees purchased one acre of land west of Pembroke, and residents contributed lumber and labor to build a two-story structure.

The new school opened that fall with fifteen pupils, and two years later the appropriation from the General Assembly was increased to one thousand dollars. In 1912 appropriate ceremony marked the first graduation of a

The home of George M. Murrell near Tahlequah, Oklahoma, a cultural center in Cherokee territory before the Civil War

Students and teachers at the Park Hill Cherokee School

*Members of the
Chickasaw House
and Senate in front
of the second
Chickasaw Council
House at
Tishomingo in 1890*

*J. M. Perryman, George W. Hill, and Johnson
Tiger, members of the Creek School Board*

*Students at a boarding school in the Creek nation
which was begun about 1848*

high school student. College classes were added in the 1930s and the first college degree conferred in June 1940. Only Robeson County Indians attended the school until 1945, when the North Carolina legislature authorized admission of other Indians. In 1953 white students "approved by the Board of Trustees" were admitted. Then, with the public school desegregation decision of 1954, Pembroke was opened to qualified applicants whatever their race, national origin, or religion.

Lumbees rally before "Old Main," historic building on the Pembroke campus, in their successful effort to save it from destruction.

Teachers trained at Pembroke over the years have served in Lumbee schools in Robeson County. One sociologist finds that these schools were successful because Lumbee teachers taught Lumbee children.

NEW YORK TIMES

Although the greatest concentration of Lumbees has been and is in Robeson County, there are many in Bladen, Columbus, Cumberland, Harnett, Sampson, and Scotland counties in North Carolina, and in Marlboro, Dillon, York, Sumter, and Orangeburg counties in South Carolina.

One difficulty of these Indian people had been that they had no specific name, being designated by such general terms as "people of color." The legislation of the North Carolina General Assembly in 1885 gave them the name Croatan Indians, after the mysterious word carved on a tree by Raleigh's vanished colonists. In 1911 the legislature referred to them as Robeson County Indians and in 1913 as the Cherokee Indians of Robeson County. Finally, in legislation passed by the General Assembly in 1953 they were designated Lumbee Indians, a name of their own choosing. The U.S. Congress voted in 1956 that they "shall from and after ratification of this Act, be known and designated as the Lumbee Indians of North Carolina." It was a definite name for a definite identity.

When in a 1958 revival, the Ku Klux Klan tried to put the Lumbees in their "place," the Klan was driven out of the Lumbee lands. Gov. Luther Hodges warned the Klan that it was not welcome in North Carolina, and the Robeson County Grand Jury indicted Klan leaders.

By the Civil War the rocky "reservation" of the Catawbas, as other southern Indians, suffered a crisis of identity even before the Civil War. Post Civil War segregation laws did not relieve this condition.

Elders of the Mormon religion, which gives the American Indians a place in the *Book of Mormon,* successfully made contact with Catawbas in 1883 at Fort Mill, South Carolina, and baptized five Catawba converts. Neighbors subsequently mobbed Mormon services on the Rock Hill Reservation, horsewhipping two white Mormon elders. These "vigilantes" were incensed by one phase of Mormon teaching concerning promiscuity and felt it might interfere with their relations with Catawba women. Nor were white bootleggers cheered by Mormon laws of abstinence from stimulants and alcohol.

But the Catawbas who also had Baptist, Methodist, and Presbyterian adherents, built their own Mormon church and their last full-blooded chief, Robert Lee Harris, was converted to the Mormon religion in 1884, becoming both an elder and priest. Always faithful to Mormonism, Chief Harris died at the age of eighty-seven in 1954.

In the 1880s many Catawbas left their old homes on the river so long sacred to them to join with the Choctaws in Indian Territory near Scullyville. Some families migrated to present-day Sanford, Colorado. Reportedly, a few of the Mormon Catawbas settled in Salt Lake City, center of the Mormon Church.

The Catawbas in South Carolina formally terminated their tribal identity on July 1, 1962, severing their relationship with the federal government. The state of South Carolina holds in trust for the Catawbas 630 acres near Rock Hill where a few families still live.

On the eve of American involvement in World War I, a government report on living conditions of the Mississippi Choctaws suggested the life circumstances of many other Indian remnant tribes in the Southeast. The Choctaws, discouraged from attending Mississippi public schools, had no schools of their own. Housing was makeshift for these poorly fed and poorly clothed Indians who were subject to unending racial prejudice and were stereotyped as "dumb, lazy, and slow."

In the era of reform preceding World War I, the Congress in 1918 appropriated funds for an Indian Agency at Philadelphia, Mississippi to work with Choctaws in the state and with the approximately three hundred Chitimacha in St. Mary's Parish, Louisiana. Curiously, other Louisiana Indians, including Choctaws, were not to be included.

Since then some 16,500 acres of abandoned plantation lands have been acquired by the government in the Philadelphia area and are held in trust for persons of one-half or more Choctaw blood. Lands held under federal trust for the Chitimacha in Louisiana total slightly more than 260 acres.

A major step forward for the Eastern Cherokees in North Carolina came in 1881 when they made a contract, subject to review by the federal government, with the Religious Society of Friends (Quakers) of Indiana to establish and operate for ten years a public school. The government approved, and since 1892 Eastern Cherokee schools have been supported with federal funds supplemented by contributions of work and money from the people. Funds contributed by the Eastern Cherokee for education reached eighty thousand dollars in the year 1971. The boarding school system has long been a feature in the Eastern Cherokee educational program with the result that many young southeastern Indians, some youth from the former Southeasterners in Oklahoma, and other young Indians have received their schooling in Cherokee, North Carolina.

Children recite the alphabet in kindergarten class at Cherokee Elementary School.

U.S. DEPARTMENT OF INTERIOR, CHEROKEE AGENCY

Seminole woman and child pose for the camera about the turn of the century.

In 1881 the state of Florida published a report of a legislative committee's investigation of the Seminoles. The theme of the report was, "While the Florida Indians refuse to vote and pay taxes they are politely social, generously hospitable and asking nothing but to be left alone."

In 1936 Gov. Dave Sholtz called his cabinet members to meet with him in an unprecedented conference with the Seminole leadership on the Tamiami Trail, which cuts across the Okeechobee swamps and the Everglades. Governor Sholtz told the Indian leaders that he wished to be of help to their people. They withdrew for conference among themselves. Their spokesman then announced politely but firmly: the governor could run his state, they would run their own affairs.

At the time, there were two federal reservations for Florida's Indians: one of 475 acres at Dania, in Broward County, and Brighton Reservation of some thirty-five thousand acres on Lake Okeechobee. Established since then are Big Cypress Reservation south of Okeechobee of 42,663 acres, the 106,000-acre State Seminole Reservation in the Everglades, and the Miccosukee Reservation, 333 acres in southwestern Florida along the Gulf of Mexico.

The state of Florida in 1955 made a study of its Indian population. The report noted that the Indian people in Florida differed among themselves in color, politics, religion, life-styles. Some preferred to live on reservations. Others objected to government paternalism and lived in independent trading posts along the Tamiami Trial or in the remoteness of the Everglades.

A landmark year came in 1957, when various groups of Seminoles adopted a constitution and bylaws for self-government and then affiliated as the Seminole Tribe of Florida, Incorporated. Four years later the corporate existence of the Miccosukee Tribe of Florida was announced.

The *Declaration of Indian Purpose* adopted by the American Indian Chicago Conference at the University of

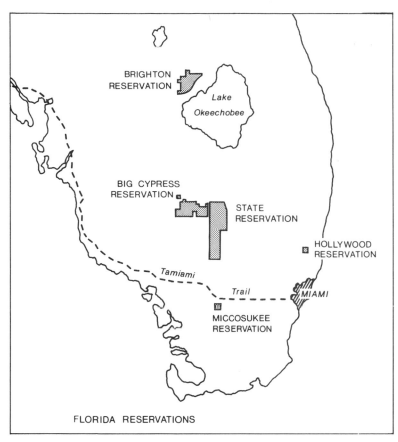

BRIGHTON
RESERVATION

Lake

Okeechobee

BIG CYPRESS
RESERVATION

STATE
RESERVATION

HOLLYWOOD
RESERVATION

Tamiami

Trail MIAMI

MICCOSUKEE
RESERVATION

FLORIDA RESERVATIONS

Chicago, June 13-20, 1961 is considered the definitive
answer to questions about why tribes want tribal lands
and why they are determined to retain tribal lands. Representatives of ninety tribes were at this conference, including the late Chief Calvin McGhee of Atmore, Alabama, whose life's dream was to see the Alabama Creeks
unite; Emmett York of the Mississippi Choctaws; Helen
Maynor (now Scheirbeck) of the North Carolina Lumbees; George Owl of the Eastern Cherokee; representatives of southeastern tribes with Oklahoma descendants;
and others. The Declaration stated:

When our lands are taken for a declared public purpose,
scattering our people and threatening our continued existence, it grieves us to be told that a money payment is the

239

equivalent of all the things we surrender. Our forefathers could be generous when all the continent was theirs. They could cast away whole empires for a handful of trinkets for their children. But in our day, each remaining acre is a promise that we will still be here tomorrow. Were we paid a thousand times the market value of our lost holdings, still the payment would not suffice. Money never mothered the Indian people as the land has mothered them, nor have any people become more closely attached to the land, religiously and traditionally. We insist again that this is not special pleading. We ask only that the United States be true to its own traditions and set an example to the world in fair dealing. . . .

When Indians speak of the continent they yielded, they are not referring only to the loss of some millions of acres in real estate. They have in mind that the land supported a universe of things they knew, valued, and loved.

With that continent gone, except for the few poor parcels they still retain, the basis of life is precariously held, but they mean to hold the scraps and parcels as earnestly as any small nation or ethnic group was ever determined to hold to identity and survival.

A Great Day Coming

While serving as chairman of the Mississippi Band of Choctaw Indians the late Emmett York would sometimes say to white friends, "Everybody *knows* Columbus discovered America. Indian children are taught that. . . ."

Inaccurate though that statement is, since the Indians had been in the Americas for centuries, Indian children and their young white and black friends are asked to learn it as truth.

In another way York summed up the situation that many Indians are experiencing. He said, "It's BIA, BIA, BIA [Bureau of Indian Affairs]. Indians are always being trained. You know, one training program after another. Always meetings in Washington, Oklahoma. . . . Programs prepared, then administration changes. More programs."

Chairman York, of course, was referring to Indians on reservations. Training programs, often complicated and expensive, have too frequently been ends in themselves and led the Indian nowhere. Typically trainees find themselves skilled in jobs that exist nowhere near their reservation homes. They frequently view retraining programs as disguised efforts to continue Indian removal.

Indians on reservations involve themselves in training and retraining programs because they offer a possible new hope for economic betterment. Some say they have participated so often in these programs they feel they are "career trainees." Others say that "program" is an empty word wafted before the Indian as "big magic."

Indian boys are trained as auto mechanics on models of cars that haven't been on the market for fifteen or twenty years or even longer.

Girls in many instances are trained in programs in which they encounter for the first time an electric stove, a telephone, a kitchen sink with running water.

"Many Choctaw youths attain maturity, grow old and die of old age without having had the experience of eating in restaurants, visiting barber shops, eating a banana split at a drugstore, or attending a movie," Superintendent John Gordon of the Choctaw Reservation, Neshoba County, Mississippi, explains.

Mississippi Choctaws move ahead.

"While segregation and discrimination are decreasing, we are faced with a situation where Indian people refuse to participate or interact unless they are positive of their welcome," Superintendent Gordon added.

JIMMY MOORE

The Office of Economic Opportunity in 1970 reported that families with average annual income of less than three thousand dollars constituted 71 percent of the Eastern Cherokees, 55 percent of the Mississippi Choctaws, 84 percent of the Florida Miccosukees, and 68 percent of the Florida Seminoles. Many of the North Carolina Lumbees have had incomes sharply reduced because of the technological revolution in agriculture. Such data on other Indians in the Southeast today have not been compiled, but Chief Joseph Pierite of the Tunica-Biloxi and others, Marksville, Louisiana, indicates that many of the Indians of Louisiana, whose situation he knows intimately, have no life experience but poverty.

Emmett York's wry witticism about Columbus results because BIA schools often are conducted by whites. As in other Indian educational programs in this country, the Mississippi Choctaws, for example, have not had Choctaw language, history, or Choctaw cultural studies.

Columbus is said to have discovered America. That the Indian was here before him is simple fact. But much of the American history the Indian youngster is expected to learn and appreciate and relate to his life is thus European-influenced. All too often the viewpoint of historical accounts is from the European outlook: Europeans came to America, journeyed westward across the continent with the Indian the tricky war opponent.

An Indian educator says of his people, "The root and home of their culture is here and not in Europe or elsewhere, and they fought against great odds to keep intruders out. Their resistance to assimilation into the larger American culture cannot be compared with that of others who have left the mainstream of their own cultures and freely chosen to live in a different one."

For some years, Mississippi Choctaws have had schools of their own, but the BIA estimates that the dropout rate for those not finishing high school may remain at about 50 percent for some years to come.

Calvin J. Isaac, a career teacher who is one of two

Mississippi Choctaws ever to earn a master's degree, points out that many of those dropping out of school do so because of the language barrier. About 90 percent of Choctaw elementary school children must learn English in the first grade.

However, the Indians should benefit from improved methods in teaching English just now beginning to have impact on elementary schools in the general population along with the kindergarten program now beginning to reach the South. As Calvin Isaac says, the government has tried, and is trying, to cope with the language problem.

In addition, a number of major publishers are re-examining their lines of general books and textbooks and are either revising these materials to eliminate the European viewpoint or, as one big publisher said in September, 1971, are having new books written to keep "emphasis on the Indians as peoples with distinctive cultures."

Even so, many recent reports and field studies from North Carolina to Florida to Mississippi to Oklahoma indicate a wide gulf between the school lives and the real lives of young Indians. They may have to study, for example, about the role of inventions in American life without ever having once used the telephone.

But great value is placed on education. In 1970 Cherokee High School, Cherokee, North Carolina had forty-eight seniors graduating compared to less than a dozen twenty years earlier. That same year forty-five graduated from Choctaw Central High School, Philadelphia, Mississippi. There were no graduates in 1950. Nine of the Seminoles were in college. The Atmore, Alabama community of Creeks had at least three young representatives in college programs in 1971. In 1972 Pembroke State University in North Carolina had more than two hundred Lumbee students.

Mississippi Choctaw Frank Henry was graduated from the University of Southern Mississippi and is now working in community health education with his people. Frank's hopes for a B.S. degree began after his service in World

War II, when he worked his way through high school in Chilocco, Oklahoma. He says, "If I at my age can further my education, then the Choctaws can too. The future of our people depends on this vital matter and this is what I eventually want to instill into the young Indian people."

Chairman of the Florida Miccosukee Council, Buffalo Tiger, pointed out in 1968, "For many hundreds of years the Miccosukee people have lived in the Everglades and continue to do so. Most of the time was spent hunting and fishing. They lived on hammocks. Their bare living was based on sales of handmade crafts. Until 1962, they fought against any government or outside help. . . . The government pointed out that customs would not be changed or religious beliefs taken away, but rather, a better way of life added." Thus the Miccosukees were willing to entrust their children to a school. There were nineteen pupils in 1962, and the number increased to forty-five in 1968.

When the Miccosukee child reaches the fourth or fifth grade, he may transfer to the public schools, but this hasn't worked out too well. Conflicting backgrounds cause many Miccosukee youngsters to drop out. Also, for some of them it's seventy miles round trip to the closest high school. The tribe is working towards obtaining a junior high school on its land. In 1972 the Miccosukees were empowered to control their own schools.

Many Indians think that if a greater day is to come for them, another pressing need is proper treatment of their alcoholics, a major problem for Indian communities as well as for the United States as a whole.

Beer and whiskey cannot be sold on federal reservations, but within a few steps of the boundaries honky-tonks operated by non-Indians freely set up shop in the fashion of similar establishments found just over the line when a "wet" county borders a "dry" county.

Noting that these places offer enticement to young Indian males, one middle-aged Indian said recently, "I'd like to see all these roadhouses dynamited." He added, "They sell alcohol to minors and might be raided and fined too, but at the most fifty dollars, and they'll just open up next day. . . ."

A seventh grade Indian youth declared that he and every other boy in his grade had drunk whiskey. Also, substitutes such as antiseptic, hair tonic, camphor, and shoe polish strained through bread were used.

According to the sheriff of Neshoba County, Mississippi the offenses of almost all Choctaws arrested there are alcohol-related.

A leading authority in this field, Edward P. Dozier, says that the stereotype of the Indian's "inherent racial susceptibility to alcohol" is inaccurate.[1] The cause of Indian problem drinking is historical, social, and cultural. For example, the young Indian typically has every chance to experience uninvited emotional upset and frustration and disappointment. Alcoholism, it must be emphasized, is a major problem among all Americans. Indians are not unique in this respect, and they are attempting to cope with the problem.

Established in 1970 the Indian Health Service Task Force on Alcoholism declares, "The Indian Health Service considers alcoholism to be one of the most significant and urgent health problems facing Indians today."

Although alcoholism may be the most urgent health problem that exists, others cry for attention. Southeastern Indians suffer infant mortality three and one-half times the national average; diabetes, four times. The percentage of death caused by pneumonia twice exceeds the national average. Indians can expect to live forty-four years, compared with seventy-one for whites. Death by suicide among teens is ten times the national average.

Mrs. Betty Mae Tiger Jumper, first woman to be elected chairman of the Seminole tribal council, long ago gave herself to advancing her people's welfare especially in the area of health.

When she was five, her family moved to Hollywood

Indian Reservation, now surrounded on three sides by Miami. In an article in *Chahta Anumpa* she wrote:

> As I grew older, I picked up a little of the English language. I knew that if I learned to use the right words for names of things I could interpret for the Indians at the doctor's, or at times when interpretation was necessary. When I was ten years old other people of my Tribe would come from miles around to have me talk for them. When I was twelve years old, people from the Missionary Indian Church started visiting us. They would take a few Indians back to Oklahoma with them to attend church meetings.
>
> In the summer of 1936, my mother took my brother, Howard, and me to Oklahoma with the missionaries to attend the church meetings. While visiting Oklahoma, I discovered funny books (comics) and decided that, more than anything else, I wanted to learn to read. A girl named Juanita Tiger told me that if I went to school I could learn.
>
> When we returned home to the Reservation I asked Mr. Scott, the Superintendent of the Seminole Agency at that time, to help me go to school. He tried to place me and some others in public school, but had no luck. I was determined and kept pestering him about school. Then on January 1, he asked me if I could be ready to go to school within a week.
>
> My grandmother, who lived to be over 100 years old, was against all schools and put her foot down and told me, "no"—I could not go! My mother knew how badly I wanted to go so she signed for me and without my grandmother's permission I went to school. I talked my cousin, Mary, into going with me. My brother cried to go too, so the three of us went off to school.

They attended the Cherokee Indian Boarding School in Cherokee, North Carolina, about one thousand miles from Miami. Mrs. Jumper remembers, "School opened a whole new world for me. I learned to wear white man's clothes. At first they seemed too tight and too short—not at all like the traditional Seminole costume. But before too long I felt right at home with them."

There were over seven hundred young Indians in the school, drawn from scores and scores of places. Since their native languages differed, the only way they could communicate was English, which they had to learn.

Betty Mae was graduated from high school when she was twenty-two. She and another cousin of hers, Agnes, were the first Seminoles from Florida to earn a high school education. Since that time, more than twenty Seminole boys and girls have gone to school in Cherokee, and many have graduated. There now are Seminole college graduates.

After high school, Betty Mae completed one year of nurse's training at the Kiowa Indian Hospital in Oklahoma. "Many of my people who were very much against school claimed that I had broken Tribal law by attending white man's school," she comments. "My grandmother, who saw me graduate from high school and nurse's training, still did not approve of school. I would like to have gone on in the nursing school, but I felt that my duty to my people called me back to the Reservation in Florida."

Her days were full as she worked with the public-health nurse covering three reservations over one hundred miles apart, and with the Miccosukee on the Tamiami Trail. At first, the nurses were not welcome; they seemed to represent the white man, but "we went back time after time and eventually things changed and help was accepted."

In August, 1970, Betty Mae Jumper was elected health director of the newly-formed North American Indian Women's Association at its first meeting. That same year she was appointed to Pres. Richard M. Nixon's Council on Indian Opportunity.

She says of her tribe's progress toward organization:

Not many years ago—in fact in the late 1930's—my people in the State of Florida came out of their shells and began to meet people halfway in the outside world.

Even when we started to school in the 1940's, dirt was thrown at us, and we were told that we were breaking the rules of the Tribe.

In the past, my Tribe had been told so many lies that they cannot change overnight. They must be given time. . . .

In the early 1950's, people began to talk about organizing and in 1957 the Tribe took steps to pick leaders and become organized. This was the beginning of a new future for us, and the road looked a little brighter.

Amid the beauty of western North Carolina's mountains on October 4, 1968, something important happened.

The Declaration of Unity was officially signed by elected representatives of the United Southeastern Tribes of American Indians, Incorporated (USET): Cherokees, Choctaws, Miccosukees, Seminoles. While Richard Crowe, noted Cherokee singer, chanted a specially composed "Chief's Song," Betty Mae Jumper signed for the Seminoles, Buffalo Tiger for the Miccosukees, Walter S. Jackson for the Eastern Cherokees, and Emmett York for the Mississippi Choctaws.

Seminole delegate Joe Dan Osceola addressed the audience, and then the four signers smoked a traditional four-stemmed pipe, the stems symbolizing Indian unity.

States the Declaration of Unity:

Because there is strength in unity, We, the Cherokees of North Carolina, the Choctaws of Mississippi, and the Seminoles and Miccosukees of Florida, being numbered among the Native Peoples of the Southeastern United States, and desiring to establish an organization to represent our united interest and promote our common welfare and benefit, do, of our own free will in Council assembled, affirm our membership in the organization to be known from this day forward as the United Southeastern Tribes, and proclaim the following objectives and declare our purposes to be:

To promote Indian leadership in order to move toward

Buffalo Tiger addresses a session of the
United Southeastern Tribes.

Emmett York

Betty Mae Jumper

the ultimate, desirable goal of complete Indian involvement and increasing responsibility at all levels in Indian affairs;

To lift the bitter yoke of poverty from our peoples through cooperative effort;

To promote better understanding between Indians and other Americans;

To negotiate for more effective use of existing local, state and federal resources;

To provide a forum for exchange of ideas;

To combine our four voices so our one strong voice can be heard clearly;

To dedicate ourselves to improvement of health;

To obtain for ourselves and our descendants the highest level of education;

To reaffirm the committment of We Four Tribes to the treaties and agreements heretofore entered into with the Federal Government, the spirit of which were restated on March 6, 1968, by the President of the United States;

Therefore, we the undersigned representatives of the four Southeastern Tribes, do witness and publicly subscribe to this *Declaration of Unity* of the United Southeastern Tribes.

"Practical, just practical, that's all," the late Choctaw chairman Emmett York evaluated the new group. "Elected officials will be much more mindful of their Indian constituents, though USET is not a lobbying group," he explained.

USET will make for some continuity for Indian efforts for a change. One Indian organization, where there had been none, could better work with the welter of public and private group with programs that could be beneficial to the Indian.

The USET leadership has been working closely with the Multi-Purpose Training Center of Atlanta in developing the Indian Community Action Project geared at lessening poverty.

A 1969 position paper by USET, presented to various federal agencies, and to congressional delegations, stated:

> Indeed, all Indian tribes are not alike. . . .
>
> We have reason to doubt that the non-Indian State governments will, in the foreseeable future, respect our right to be Indian.
>
> Indian-Americans have proved their patriotism to the United States in every one of our modern wars. We want to make it plain that we wish to be the kind of American we are, not some other kind of American. We wish to be Cherokee, Choctaw, Miccosukee, and Seminole—all Americans but also Indians. We wish to be good Americans, but Indians. This is the spirit in which we ask your support.

United Southeastern Tribes seeks to be accepted by the United States. Perhaps that is underway, for in September 1970, an old problem was eliminated when the Cherokee, Choctaw, Miccosukee, and Seminole tribes of the Southeast were brought under the Washington office of the Bureau of Indian Affairs.

Earlier they had been under the Muskogee Area Office, Muskogee, Oklahoma, though that city for nearly all the southeastern Indians is farther away than Washington, D.C. Acting BIA Commissioner, Harold D. Cox, noted that the new organizational setup improves communications between the four southeastern tribes and the government. It also ended their having to send in two sets of reports, one for Muskogee and one for Washington.

Now a tribal council can telephone directly to the BIA in Washington without having to call Muskogee first for permission.

Even though a tribe can be a non-voting member without paying dues, USET's bylaws require each voting tribe to pay yearly dues of one hundred dollars. At a meeting in Atlanta, following the signing of the Declaration of Unity, this was discussed in depth, for all realized one hundred dollars is a lot of money to an Indian tribe. Too, paying dues is a new idea for many Indians.

One hundred dollars, Buffalo Tiger pointed out, was more than any man within his knowledge in the tribe had ever had at one time. If his Miccosukee Council turned down payment of the dues, he did not feel they could consent in all honor to non-voting status.

As one representative said, "We know that unity means strength. We know that by uniting, we can stand much stronger than by going it alone," and the payment of dues was not opposed.

Today there are an estimated five thousand Indians in scattered communities in Louisiana: Natchez, Tunicas, Choctaws, Chitimachas, Avoyels, Houmas, Atakapas, and others as yet "unorganized," in the formal terminology of the government. Most retain but few elements of their former cultures.

In August 1970, Louisiana's Indians met in Baton Rouge for the first meeting of its kind in their long and often heroic history. Planned to develop intertribal communication, the meeting had as guest speakers Emmett York and Key Wolf, Chickasaw, of the U.S. Public Health Service.

Louisiana's Indian leaders such as Thomas Dion, a Houma from Houma, Ernest Sickey, a Coushatta from Elton, Mrs. Matilde Johnson, a Choctaw from Lacombe, and Chief Joseph A. Pierite, Tunica-Biloxi-Ofo-Avoyel-Choctaw from Marksville hope that the Baton Rouge gathering has ended tribal isolation and will stimulate completion of the tribal rolls required by government agencies. More and more Biloxi, Tunica, and Houma act not just as Indians, but by tribe.

*A Chitimacha boy
dresses a deer skin.*

*An Alabama-Coushatta preserves the ancient
method of flaking flint to make arrowheads.*

*In Texas,
an Alabama-Coushatta
follows traditional designs
in her beadwork.*

There are better communications today between the Coushattas, sometimes called Koasatis, of Louisiana and their kindred on the Alabama-Coushatta Reservation in Polk County, east Texas.

Most of Louisiana's Coushattas live in Elton, a mainly agricultural community in which some two hundred own their own lands. The Elton Coushattas are served by a mission church from St. Peter Congregational Church of Reeves, Louisiana.

Commenting on what the Coushattas have had to do, the Rev. Donald K. Johnson says, "They all work to support themselves when they can find jobs. Some of the men have two jobs to keep their full-blooded Indian families together."

A kindergarten operated by the mission gives instruction in English since some of the Coushattas children come from homes in which mostly the Muskogean language is spoken.

At the Chitimacha Reservation near Charenton, beautiful handmade cane baskets may be purchased by the visitor. A good eight days of careful work are needed just to prepare the strips of cane for the natural dyes made from black walnuts and various roots. Louisiana Indian crafts are sold at Louisiana State University, Baton Rouge, and in quality gift shops in New Orleans. There is a fine collection of Chitimacha basketry in the Louisiana State Museum, 523 South Ann Street, New Orleans.

In late 1969 the Indian Claims Commission made Creeks in Oklahoma and Alabama recipients of four million dollars for 8.9 million acres of lands in south Georgia and Alabama that were ceded to the U.S. government in 1814, but had never been paid for. Proof of direct Creek lineage is required of all applying for payment. But records of those who have been extremely poor tend to be short and simple, often going back hardly farther than a generation, much less some one hundred sixty years.

Ernest Sickey, chairman of the Tribal Council of the Louisiana Coushatta, plays with his two sons and their kitten

Solomon Battise, manager of the Coushatta Indian Trading Post, shows one of the beaded baskets woven by tribal women.

*Young Louisiana
Coushattas at play*

*Mrs. Rosabel Sylestine weaves
a basket from pine needles.
Small baskets can be completed
in one day, large ones
take nearly a week.*

*Mrs. Maggie Langley holds one of
her woven baskets. A difficult
craft, this particular style
of basketry is disappearing.*

There is a relatively new American Indian Society of Alabama. C. D. Brown, the president, is calling attention to the fact "that there are many more people of Indian descent in this area than is generally recognized." Alabama's Creeks have found employment in lumbering, pulp mills and other industries, and farming. Some operate their own businesses, such as bait and fish supply shops, and motels. It is reported that in November, 1971, one industry in the Birmingham area employed over three hundred persons of Indian descent but some were so acculturated they weren't sure from which Indians they descended. The largest community of self-identified Indians in Alabama is made up of approximately one thousand Creeks in the vicinity of Atmore. These, some believe, may persevere and win federal recognition after they compile their tribal roll according to specifications.

In 1970, twenty years after their claim was made, the Seminoles in Oklahoma and Florida were awarded twelve million dollars for 29.7 million acres in Florida taken without compensation to the tribe after the treaties of 1823 and 1832.

Seminoles and Miccosukees have been described by the *National Geographic* as "emerging people" who are adapting to the twentieth century yet preserving their Indianness. They have been leaders in making Florida a national center for fine cattle production. Seminole youths are excellent cowboys, and some are studying animal husbandry looking toward cattle ranch management. Others are learning the promising new science of aquaculture being developed by various state and federal agencies in Florida in cooperation with private sources. During the tourist season Seminole youths present alligator wrestling shows, work as Everglades guides, and, in some instances, sell crafts to visitors.

The Miccosukees, often regarded as one of the most conservative of American Indian tribes, are willing to adopt modern methods of health care, sanitation, and transportation. They now use airboats instead of canoes and have been among the developers of this exciting transportation.

Miccosukee people and the Seminoles appreciate the role of such modern appliances as an air-conditioning unit. Many attend government-sponsored classes telling of modern medicine and nutritional science. To cope with the problem of obesity suffered by so many Americans many Seminole and Miccosukee women are willing to diet if necessary for good health. Planned parenthood also is engaging interest with the attractive mimeographed *Alligator Times* of the Seminole publicizing "birth and girth control." However, the Seminoles so far have been unwilling to accept a large sum of money from a major pharmaceutical manufacturer for their secret, traditional medication for nervousness.

Today there are some three thousand Seminoles and Miccosukees in Florida, speaking their own languages, and proudly conserving their heritage as people who would not be conquered.

As the Asheville, North Carolina *Citizen-Times* said in a series of articles early in 1971, the Eastern Cherokee, and perhaps other Indians of the Southeast, tend to be conservative. Buffalo Tiger of the Miccosukees says with a great deal of pungent force, "White men need to learn the simple things from Indians, such as how to live in harmony with what God has given them."

The Lumbee Indians living along the eastern boundary between North and South Carolina are thought to be one of few Indian peoples with a solid middle class. Never having signed a treaty with the United States, the Lumbees have never been under the jurisdiction of the Bureau of Indian Affairs and so have been able to possess individually their own land and to conduct their own business.

Writer Frye Gaillard points out about the Lumbees, "They speak no Indian language, practice no pre-Christian religions, wear no feathers, do not live in tepees, . . .

and they have not done these things for centuries." Although their way of life shows a strong Anglo-Saxon influence, they are still Indian.

Explains Herbert Locklear, Lumbee director of Baltimore's American Indian Study Center, "Being an Indian is not tangible. It is a philosophy, a spiritual attitude—a feeling of reverence and respect for human beings, for other living things and for the universe as a whole. When we are in Robeson County, we are able to feel at one with ourselves and with all other things."

Although the standard of living has been steadily rising in Robeson County, recent reports indicate that 60 percent of the county's inhabitants—red, white, and black—live below the poverty line. Because many have found it necessary to move elsewhere for jobs and income, Detroit and Baltimore, as well as Greensboro, Highpoint, and Charlotte, North Carolina have sizable Lumbee populations. But home is still the Lumber River country, and many families return often.

In 1972 Lumbees in Pembroke opened what the American Indian Press Association said was "the only bank owned by a group of Native Americans in the heartland of their age-old community." The bank, which did not enlist federal aid in getting started, had capital assets of $670,000.

In various roles Lumbees are working in local, regional, and federal programs. Robeson County has more than 350 Lumbee teachers. As a staff member of the Senate Subcommittee on Constitutional Rights, Mrs. Helen Maynor Scheirbeck of Pembroke developed hearings throughout the country on the rights of Indians. This work culminated in passage of the Indian Bill of Rights, a part of the Civil Rights Act of 1968. She later became director of the Education for American Indians Office of the Department of Health, Education, and Welfare in Washington. Brantley Blue serves on the U.S. Indian Claims Commission. Thomas Oxendine is Director of Communications, the Bureau of Indian Affairs.

Submerged in the surrounding culture, other Indians live in the northeast coastal counties, on the northern border and in Bolton, Clinton, and Hollister in North Carolina and around Columbia and along the coast of South Carolina.

Among the Southeasterners and southeastern descendants in Oklahoma the effort to add necessary living income takes several forms but gets much attention.

Perhaps the Eastern Cherokees with their tourist attraction complex at Cherokee, North Carolina lead the southeastern Indians in keeping step with tourism. The outdoor drama *Unto These Hills,* Oconaluftee Indian Village, and the Cherokee Historical Society are examples.

In addition, the Eastern Cherokees have a credit union enrolling some two hundred who work in Indian crafts, a Boys Club, and a reservation planning office, establishments that Choctaws soon may have. Annual fairs featuring crafts and stickball games bring needed revenue to Choctaws and Cherokees, as does the powwow to the Seminoles. The Miccosukees have a restaurant and plans for a craft shop. Reports from Louisiana indicate that Chitimachan crafts enjoy good sales. In recent years Louisiana Chitimachas and Choctaws have attended the Mississippi Choctaw Fair at Philadelphia, some bringing native products to sell.

Indians of southeastern descent have participated in organizing the Indian Trade Fair, which opened in 1970 with a highly successful three-day exhibition at Oklahoma City. Indian craftsmen work either through some eighteen cooperatives, such as the large one at Anadarko, or have their own individual enterprises.

One of the founders of the fair, Dode McIntosh of Tulsa, chief of the Creeks, said afterwards, "It exceeded our expectations by 50 percent. We're not happy, we're overjoyed."

Traditional beadwork done by Choctaws at Idabel, Oklahoma, was sold on order and large advance orders were placed by fair customers from New York. Equally popular were the traditional Seminole patchwork shirts for men, sold at fifty dollars each.

Oklahoma's Cherokees have a hit in their yearly outdoor drama, "Trail of Tears," at Tsa-La-Gi, south of their old national capital of Tahlequah.

All these events and the enterprise and imagination they show may well be indications of better days to come for the southeastern Indian.

In July, 1970 President Nixon described the American

INDIANS OF THE SOUTHEAST TODAY

Indian as "the most deprived and isolated minority group in our nation. On virtually every scale of measurement— employment, income, education, health—the condition of the Indian people ranks at the bottom."

But that was 1970 and hopefully things are changing for the Indians in the Southeast and throughout the United States.

It's Happening with
Southeastern Indian Youth

President Nixon had to be right about the life chances of the Indian in the past, but in the Southeast and in Oklahoma the younger Indians aren't prone to looking back.

As one southeastern Indian youth said, "About all those treaties. . . . I never saw a treaty; and I don't know any person who did. I never signed one. I'm here. Now."

Many Indian youths, like many black and white youths, apparently fret very little about the deficiencies of formal history.

Representative of many, Nellie Littlejohn, an Eastern Cherokee and a fifth grader with wonderful precision and economy wrote, "Columbus didn't know it but he discovered us. . . . He never really got to America at all, and our country was named for the man who later wrote some letters about 'the New World.' "

In a casual conversation with a white man in a Muskogee, Oklahoma, shopping center a nineteen-year-old Seminole-Creek said that history had its place but so far as he was concerned, "Keeping up the payments on my fire-engine red Ford Bronco is where it's happening. The Bronco lets me get to my week job okay and lets me do my truck gardening with a lot less trouble than a four-footed weed burner." He was concerned about *now*.

Indian youth are busy with the interesting present and

the challenging future. They aren't clinging to any bitter memories of the past. Choctaw, Miccosukee, Seminole, Cherokee youth enjoy their tribal gatherings with the offerings of traditional dances and music, but they also like to make the night resound with amplified electric guitar music.

In affirmation of their Indianness, Lumbee young people, too, dress in native American costumes, let their hair grow long, wear headbands, and learn Indian dances.

The whole point about Indian youth of today, the weekly paper *Cherokee One Feather* has said, is that they are alive and aware, and that regardless of their age, "Indians don't necessarily want to be dark-skinned white people."

Lumbee young people

There are reports of drinking among some southeastern Indian youth and some use of marijuana, but others are practicing either moderation or total abstinence like young Mormons among the North Carolina Cherokees who do not smoke or drink coffee, tea, or alcoholic beverages.

Still other youths, like those among the Mississippi Choctaws and the Seminoles, are volunteers in Youth Rehab (rehabilitation) working with youthful heavy drinkers.

Among Alabama Creeks, so long isolated, the young people are increasingly interested in being part of the world about them.

Many young Indians in all parts of the country, as the *Cherokee One Feather* has said, are "helping to change the picture of the stereotyped Indian as has been so poorly portrayed these many years."

Education is important. For example, the Seminoles in the school year beginning September, 1971, sent fifty-five of their youth to boarding schools mainly in Oklahoma, a record number. The Eastern Cherokees also established a record in September, 1971, with thirty-two of their youth enrolled in Haskell Indian Junior College in Lawrence, Kansas.

The long individualistic Miccosukees who don't always agree among themselves, under the leadership of Buffalo Tiger accepted full responsibility in 1971 for directing Head Start, Youth Neighborhood Corps, Youth Rehab, Career Development, Community Action Program (CAP), and counseling after it was offered them by the BIA.

Billy Smith, Mississippi Choctaw, a recent graduate of the University of Southern Mississippi, is now teaching first grade at Conehatta, Mississippi Choctaw Elementary School where he began school himself.

DeLaura Ann Henry from Bok Chitto attends Mississippi State University. Dee may have one of the longest names of any coed there, *Na pakanli usi homa* or "Little Rose." Reportedly the first female Choctaw undergraduate to live on campus at M.S.U., Dee says, "I was scared to death when I first came up here." A full-blood Choctaw girl with a most pleasant smile and a gentle sense of humor, Dee notes some still mistake her for an Oriental. A skilled, natural singer, she is studying marketing management and plans to run a crafts shop, a promising field for prepared Indian youth.

John Julius Wiltnoy who lives in Cherokee, North Carolina along the Oconaluftee River, is a self-taught

U.S. DEPARTMENT OF THE INTERIOR, INDIAN ARTS AND CRAFTS BOARD

John Julius Wiltnoy and a piece of his stone sculpture

Cherokee sculptor, working mostly in stone. Several leading institutions, including the Smithsonian in Washington, have bought his work for their permanent collections. His larger works bring him several thousand dollars each. Mr. Wiltnoy says, "When I was twenty years old there was no way for me to make a living for myself and for my family. Things were pretty dark. One day I did my praying about finding a way to make a living. When I finished, something drew me to some little pieces of pipestone." With his pocketknife he carved some animals and faces, and friends who sold Indian crafts in Cherokee sold them for him. Of the works in his one-man show in June, 1971, in the Qualla Arts and Crafts Museum in Cherokee the *Christian Science Monitor* said, they show "reverence for living things, an appreciation of the beauty of the universe, an exaltation of the human spirit, a delight in being alive. He makes love visible."

Joe Dan Osceola is Indian Health Service director for the state of Florida working with the Seminoles and Miccosukees. The first Florida Seminole to graduate from a Florida public high school, he attended Georgetown College in Kentucky. A full-blood Seminole and former president of the tribe, Mr. Osceola (many Seminole families took the name of the patriot Osceola) says:

> Different tribes have been getting together—this should make for better relationships. Where we used to fight each other, we are now fighting for our rights and legislation for the betterment of our people. At the same time the relationship between and understanding of the First American by the general public is improving. I know some day we will overcome the theories or misunderstandings of the American Indian with which the television and movies have branded our people.

Just on the threshold of her career, Diana Stouff is the 1971 Miss Indian Princess of Louisiana, selected by vote in an Indian meeting in Baton Rouge. From one of the noted Louisiana families of Chitimacha Indians, she is studying English education at Southeastern Louisiana University with plans to teach.

Miss Oklahoma 1971, was a full-blood Creek girl named Susan Supernaw. A Phillips University student from Tulsa, she performs the traditional Creek gourd dance and other Indian dances as well as modern jazz and gymnastic ballet. Her Indian name is *Ella Ponna,* or "Dancing Feet." A Merit Scholar, majoring in anthropology, she has serious plans for advanced study in that field.

To sum up, Indian youth are enjoying a fairer opportunity to achieve in many, many realms of national life. The *Alligator Times,* of the Seminole Tribe of Florida, says so much has happened that today's youth sometimes criticize the existing council for not having done "more,

BOB MCCORMACK

Susan Supernaw

Joe Dan Osceola

JIMMY MOORE

DeLaura Ann Henry

more, more." An unidentified poet's "Seminole Council Oak" explained,

> In tribute to these tribal lands, their ancient
> oak now lonely stands,
> Its rustling leaves whisper of the golden past,
> of feasts and love and war,
> of hunting meets and victory feats and not
> too oft a sad defeat.
> The Council Oak, its vigil keeps, hour in, day
> out, and week by week,
> Old councils die and fade away, the young spring
> up to have their say . . .

Charles Denson of Choctaw Central High School, Philadelphia, Mississippi, voicing the thoughts of many young Indians, says, "As I grew older, my knowledge was broadened by schooling. And because of this, I grew doubtful about becoming what I wanted to be. I was doubtful because I thought I would not stand a chance against the white race. It wasn't that I hated them—no. It was because of a feeling I had—a feeling of fear. This feeling of fear was brought on by the thought that whites were superior and my people were inferior. But in a way it was—back then!"

"Now I have no fear," Charles continued. "What's most important is that I have an ambition. And having an ambition is about as close to being what you want to be as being it."

Gwen Owle says in the *Cherokee One Feather,* "Things are beginning to happen." Mrs. John Bradshaw of Ensley. Alabama, has worked for years with Alabama Creeks, so long submerged as a people they are little known by the general public. She reports a growth of confidence among many Creek youth.

These and other southeastern Indian youths are overcoming that insidious crippler, discouragement. An initial trip to a supermarket may take some heart and resolve, and in social interaction with whites and blacks one may

smile until one's jaws ache to indicate friendliness. "But there now are opportunities to smile," says one young Indian.

In words applicable to all Indian youth, the *Alligator Times* writes, "In any other time of history it would be impossible for Seminole youth to overcome our fate of being the victim of two societies. However, we see hope that we are engaged in the most exciting time in our history as Americans."

In the rich tapestry of American life, that blending of varied cultures—black, Anglo-Saxon, Chinese-American, Spanish-American, Italian-American, and the many more —the southeastern Indian and his brothers everywhere see their own special and beautiful heritage. They are Americans who happen to be Indians and are proud of it.

Appendixes

Notes

Chapter II
(pp. 23-34)

1. Paul Du Ru, *Journal, Feb. 1–May 8, 1700* (Chicago: Caxton Club, 1934), p. 34.
2. *Ibid.,* p. 29.

Chapter IV
(pp. 48-62)

1. John Gilmary Shea, *Discovery and Exploration of the Mississippi Valley* (New York: Redfield, 1852), p. 43.
2. Mary R. Haas, "Men and Women's Speech in Koasati," *Language,* 20 (1944), 145.
3. Gravier as quoted in *Tennessee Historical Quarterly,* 21 (1962), 119.
4. Jean-Bernard Bossu, *Travels in the Interior of North America, 1751-1762,* ed. and tr. Seymour Feiler (Norman: University of Oklahoma Press, 1962), p. 77.

Chapter V
(pp. 63-74)

1. James Adair, a Scot, was born in Ireland about 1709. He worked out of Charleston as an English trader, and probably had at least one Indian wife. A later editor, S. C. Williams, finds Adair in the Southeast in 1735, or earlier, and in 1768, or later, with probable trips to England. Williams, *Adair's History of the American Indian* (Johnson City, Tenn.: Watauga Press, 1930). Quotations are from original edition (London, 1775), hereinafter, Adair.
2. John R. Swanton, *Religious Beliefs and Medical Practices of the Creek Indians,* Forty-second Annual Report, BAE (Washington, D.C., 1928), p. 653.
3. James Mooney, *Myths of the Cherokees,* Nineteenth Annual Report, BAE (Washington, D.C., 1900), p. 435.
4. Swanton, *Creek Indians,* p. 643.
5. *Ibid.,* pp. 612-13.
6. Adair, p. 368.
7. Bossu, *Travels,* pp. 165-66.

Chapter VI
(pp. 75-83)

1. Romans as quoted by Swanton, *Indians of the Southeastern United States,* Bulletin No. 137, BAE (Washington, D.C., 1946), p. 285.
2. Le Page Du Pratz, *The History of*

Louisiana (London: Du Pratz, 1774), p. 349.
3. Adair, p. 409.
4. John Lawson, *A New Voyage to Carolina,* ed. Hugh T. Lefler (1714; reprint ed., Chapel Hill: University of North Carolina Press, 1967), pp. 230-31.
5. Adair, p. 407.
6. *Ibid.,* p. 404.
7. Lawson, *Voyage to Carolina,* p. 184.
8. *Ibid.,* p. 217.

Chapter VII
(pp. 84-95)

1. Laudonnière as quoted in *Hakluyt's Voyages,* Vol. XIII (Edinburgh, 1889), p. 413.
2. George Catlin, *Letters and Notes on the Manners, Customs, and Condition of the North American Indians* (1841; facsimile ed., Minneapolis: Ross & Haines), p. 142.
3. *Ibid.,* p. 143.
4. *Ibid.,* p. 143.
5. *Ibid.,* p. 140.
6. Bossu, *Travels,* p. 170.
7. *Discoveries of John Lederer* (London, 1672), p. 18.
8. Lawson, *Voyage to Carolina,* p. 27.
9. Du Pratz, *Louisiana,* p. 347.

Chapter VIII
(pp. 96-105)

1. Lawson, *Voyage to Carolina,* p. 177.
2. William Bartram, *Travels Through North and South Carolina, Georgia, East and West Florida,* ed. Mark Van Doren (1791; reprint ed., New York: Dover publications, 1959), p. 396.
3. *Ibid.,* p. 398.
4. Frances Densmore, "Choctaw Music," BAE Bulletin No. 136, Anthropological Papers, No. 28.
5. Bossu, *Travels,* p. 63.
6. Frances Densmore, "Seminole Music," BAE Bulletin No. 161, Songs 199 and 200, recorded by Billie Bowlegs.
7. *Ibid.,* p. 54.

Chapter IX
(pp. 106-11)

1. Adair, p. 430.

Chapter X
(pp. 112-17)

1. Quotations of Roullet are from *Mississippi Provincial Archives, 1729-1740,* Vol. I., ed. and tr. Dunbar Rowland, and are used through courtesy of the Mississippi Department of Archives and History, Jackson, 1927), pp. 17-54.
2. *Ibid.,* p. 27.
3. *Ibid.,* pp. 17, 31.
4. Adair, p. 424.
5. William Byrd, *Histories of the Dividing Line Betwixt Virginia and North Carolina,* ed. William K. Boyd (1841: reprint ed., Raleigh: North Carolina Historical Commission, 1928), p. 116.

Chapter XI
(pp. 118-24)

1. Lawson, *Voyage to Carolina,* pp. 17, 34.
2. Quoted in Swanton, *Early History of the Creek Indians and Their Neighbors,* BAE Bulletin No. 73, p. 33.
3. *Ibid.,* p. 123.
4. *Ibid.,* pp. 340-41.

274

Chapter XIII

(pp. 140-58)

1. Brown, *The Catawba Indians: The People of the River* (Columbia: University of South Carolina Press, 1966), p. 231.
2. In William L. Saunders, ed., *The Colonial Records of North Carolina*, Vol. V, 1752-59 (Raleigh, N. C.: Secretary of State's Office, 1887), p. 143.
3. The poetic form here is from Douglas S. Brown, *The Catawba Indians: The People of the River*, facing p. 216. Copyright © University of South Carolina Press, 1966; used by permission. Saunders, ed., *Colonial Records*, was original source.
4. *Tennessee Historical Quarterly*, 21 (1962), 354.
5. John W. Caughey, *McGillivray of the Creeks* (Norman: University of Oklahoma Press, 1938), p. 74.
6. *Ibid.*, p. 23.
7. *Ibid.*, p. 22.
8. *Ibid.*, p. 13.
9. *Ibid.*, p. 24.
10. *Ibid.*, p. 56.
11. *Ibid.*, p. 26.
12. Arrell M. Gibson, *The Chickasaws* (Norman: University of Oklahoma Press, 1971), p. 65.
13. William McKee Evans, *To Die Game: The Story of the Lowry Band, Indian Guerrillas of Reconstruction* (Baton Rouge: Louisiana State University Press, 1971), pp. 195-97.

Chapter XV

(pp. 165-92)

1. Folsom as quoted in Arthur H. De Rosier, Jr., *The Removal of the Choctaw Indians* (Knoxville: University of Tennessee Press, 1970), p. 128.
2. Pitchlynn as quoted in Angie Debo, *The Rise and Fall of the Choctaw Republic* (Norman: University of Oklahoma Press, 1934), p. 56.
3. Brochure from state park at Indian Springs, Ga.
4. *Ibid.*
5. Thomas Bryan Underwood, *Cherokee Legends and the Trail of Tears* (Cherokee, N. C.: Underwood, 1956), p. 23. Burnett's story is in several other places.
6. Edwin C. McReynolds, *The Seminoles* (Norman: University of Oklahoma Press, 1957), p. 209.

Chapter XVI

(pp. 209-24)

1. Quoted in Debo, *Choctaw Republic*, p. 70.
2. Fred B. Bauer, *The Land of the North Carolina Cherokees* (Brevard, N. C.: Bauer, 1970), p. 11.
3. Ibid., p. 7.

Chapter XVII

(pp. 225-40)

1. McReynolds, *The Seminoles*, p. 307.

Chapter XVIII

(pp. 241-63)

1. Quoted in S. Bobo Dean, *Law and Order Among the First Mississippians*, Report for Association of American Indian Affairs (Washington, D.C., 1970).

Places to See and Experience

There are so many places and things bearing on the past and present life of Indians in the Southeast that the following list is far from complete. This region even now is discovering its own archaeological treasures. More attention is being given to "new" sites, and restorations will follow careful and systematic excavations.

Users of this section are advised to check the current hours and days when each attraction is open. Since many of these sites are reached by secondary roads, updated maps are essential.

Most southeastern states have departments devoted to conservation and tourist promotion to which inquiries may be addressed. Be specific. For example, instead of asking for information about Indians, ask where you can learn about the Cherokees.

It makes an interesting hobby to collect the brochures and leaflets available at most of these museums and sites.

To avoid contracting "museumitis" in larger museums, study introductory materials available gratis after entrance. Select carefully what you wish to see. Give adequate time to this, and wear comfortable shoes.

I.   Sites, Prehistoric and Historic

Alabama

> Childersburg: *Kymulga Onyx Cave—prehistoric Indian burial ground.

> Florence: Ceremonial Indian Mound, South Court St.—a 42-foot prehistoric structure, one of the most imposing ceremonial mounds in Tennessee Valley; *museum.

> Horseshoe Bend National Military Park—traces career of Chief Menewa and the Creek nation through March 27, 1814; Indian relics in museum.

* Indicates admission charge.

276

Moundville: *Moundville State Monument and Museum—forty earth mounds; temple restoration on 58-foot mound.

Russell Cave National Monument—310 acres donated to public by National Geographic Society; thirteen displays of pottery, other artifacts, and agricultural methods from Archaic through Woodland period, 7000 B.C to A.D. 1000.

Wetumpka: Fort Toulouse State Monument—site of important 1717 French fort surrendered 1763 to British, believed birthplace of Sehoy Marchand, mother of Alexander McGillivray, Creek statesman.

Arkansas

Fort Smith: National Historic Site, Rogers Ave. between 2nd and 3rd Sts.—old U.S. District Court for Western Arkansas and Indian Territory; *commissary (Old Fort Museum), 100 N. 1st St.—Indian relics.

Florida

Marco Island, southwest tip of Florida—under excavation by private enterprise in cooperation with Florida Bureau of Historic Sites, Calusa Indians (predecessors of Seminoles).

Georgia

Calhoun: New Echota—last capital of Cherokee nation, restored and reconstructed print shop (*Cherokee Phoenix*), Worcester House, courthouse, Vann's Tavern.

Cartersville: Etowah Mounds Archeological Area—museum with artifacts from about A.D. 900.

Dahlonega: Chehaw Indian Monument—memorial to Indian town befriending whites.

Indian Springs State Park: William McIntosh executed here by Creek Indians for treason, May 1, 1825.

Kolomoki Mounds State Park, near Blakely off U.S. 27—site Indian-occupied about A.D. 800; museum.

Macon: *Ocmulgee National Monument—one of the most elaborate archaeological projects (683 acres) in Southeast open to general public; the site of six different cultures from 8000 B.C. to A.D. 1717; three large temple mounds; museum.

Spring Place: Vann House.

Louisiana

*Marksville Prehistoric Indian Park State Monument—40 acres, on bluff overlooking Old River; burial grounds; natural history museum.

Mississippi

> Greenville: *Winterville Mounds State Park and Museum, 5 mi. north on State 1—restoration of ceremonial gathering place of Lower Mississippi Valley Indians; prehistoric Indian artifacts, jewelry, pottery, utensils, art.

> Natchez Trace Parkway: Tupelo Headquarters, National Park Service—"Path of Empire" film covers history of Old Natchez Trace; Emerald Mound, 11 mi. northeast of Natchez—one of largest in U.S.; Chickasaw Village Site, northwest of Tupelo between U.S. 78 and State 6—early historic.

Missouri

> East Prairie: Towosahgy State Park—Mississippian Indian village site, year-round archaeological program.

North Carolina

> Cherokee: See below, under II and III.

> Mount Gilead: Town Creek Indian Mound.

Oklahoma

> Miami: Quapaw Tribal Community.

> Millerton: Wheelock Church and Academy—constructed by Choctaw nation soon after arrival in Indian Territory in 1832.

> Muskogee: Bascone Indian Museum; Five Civilized Tribes Agency, Federal Building, serving more than 60,000 Indians; *Five Civilized Tribes Museum.

> Okmulgee (Old Creek capital): Old House of Warriors—meetings of present-day Creek Indian Council held here on fourth Saturday in January, April, July, October. Open to the public.

> Park Hill: Cherokee Female Academy Ruins—Cherokee village and amphitheater to be built soon on site.

> Sallisaw: Sequoyah's home.

> Tahlequah (seat of old Cherokee Nation): Murrell Mansion—Museum of Cherokee history; Old Cherokee capitol; Old Cherokee supreme court building; Indian weavers.

> Tishomingo: Old Chickasaw Capitol (building now used as county courthouse).

> Tuskahoma (old Choctaw capital): Choctaw Festival, Labor Day weekends.

> Wewoka: Landmarks of early Seminole culture.

Tennessee

> Jackson: Pinson Mounds State Archaeological Park

278

Memphis: *Chucalissa Indian Village (restored, dating approximately A.D. 900-1600)—shelters, ceremonial plaza, temple mound, burial exhibits.

Nashville: Mound Bottom—recently purchased by the state.

II   Artifact Collections

Alabama

Birmingham: Birmingham Museum of Art, Oscar Wells Memorial Bldg., 2000 8th Ave., N.—Creek art and artifacts.

Montgomery: Museum of Fine Arts, Lawrence and Highland Aves.—two Indian rooms with interesting murals.

Arkansas

Fayetteville: University of Arkansas Museum—displays bearing on Caddoan tribes.

Florida

Marathon: *Florida Keys Southeast Museum of the North American Indians —artifacts and handcrafts.

Illinois

Chicago: Field Museum of Natural History; Grant Park at Roosevelt Rd. and Lake Shore Dr.

East Saint Louis: Cahokia Mounds State Park—twenty-five Indian mounds; museum.

Elgin: Audubon Museum—natural history, historical, and Indian exhibits.

Urbana: University of Illinois, Natural History Building—exhibits of animals, plants, American Indian and Eskimo culture.

Mississippi

Philadelphia: Choctaw Indian Agency (jurisdiction over Chitimachas of Louisiana)—beadwork, baskets, blowguns, sticks and balls, and other handmade articles are available at Choctaw Indian Arts and Crafts. The Choctaw Indian Fair is held in July.

New York

New York City: The Heye Foundation; Museum of the American Indian; American Museum of Natural History.

North Carolina

Chapel Hill: University of North Carolina Anthropological Museum, Person Hall—prehistoric period.

Cherokee: Frontierland: Museum of the Cherokee Indian; Oconoaluftee Indian Village; and *Unto These Hills* outdoor pageant. (Lodging reservations must be confirmed well in advance of busy summer season.)

Lawrinburg: The Indian Museum, St. Andrew's College.

Ohio

Columbus: Ohio Historical Society, North High St. at 15th Ave.—collections include famous Adena pipe, one of finest examples of prehistoric Indian art, and thousands of prehistoric Indian artifacts and skeletal remains, one of the great depositories. (Write for free list of Ohio state memorials and museums administered by the Ohio Historical Society, Columbus, Ohio 43210.)

Oklahoma

Oklahoma City: Oklahoma Historical Society—one of the most complete displays of Indian relics and documents.

Tulsa: Thomas Gilcrease Art Museum; Philbrook Art Center

Tennessee

Knoxville: University of Tennessee. McClung Museum—Indian artifacts
Nashville: Vanderbilt University, Kirkland Hall—Thruston Prehistoric Indian Artifacts collection; Children's Museum—exhibits; Traveller's Rest—prehistoric Indians museum.

Texas

Livingston: *Alabame-Coushatta (Alabama-Koasati), 17 miles east on U.S. 190—Museum Arts & Crafts Shop, traditional dances, reptile garden, Living Indian Village, tours.

Washington, D. C.

U.S. Dept. of Interior Museum; U.S. National Museum; Smithsonian Institution.

III   Indian Dancing

Cherokee

North Carolina: Cherokee Harvest Fair (usually October)—write Cherokee Tribal Office, Cherokee, N. C.

Oklahoma: Tsa-La-Gi, south of Tahlèquah—traditional dances featured in *Trail of Tears* outdoor drama, usually late June through August.

Choctaw

Bok Chitto: Choctaws perform traditional tribal dances during annual Choctaw Indian Fair. Pearl River community near Philadelphia, Miss. Write Choctaw Fair Committee, Route 7, Box 21, Philadelphia, Miss.

Seminole

Hollywood, Fla.: Traditional dances can be seen daily during the Seminole Powwow, held in recent years during February. Write Seminole Tribe, Stirling Road, Hollywood, Fla.

Pan-Indian

Usually at each of the above festivals a troupe of dancers is brought in from the Plains area to perform the popular "feather dancing."

IV   Indian Stickball

Three varieties of the fast-moving Indian stickball game may be observed by visiting the Cherokee, Choctaw, and Seminole gatherings mentioned above. Visitors to Cherokee, N.C. may also find games scheduled on week nights during the summer.

V   Handicrafts for Sale

Places mentioned above usually offer handicrafts for sale. For more information write Arts & Crafts Department, Bureau of Indian Affairs, at Cherokee, Choctaw, and Seminole addresses given. For information about some other Indian crafts write Alabama-Coushatta Arts and Crafts Shop, Route 3, Box 170, Livingston, Texas.

A wide variety of articles are available at sales offices on each reservation, usually open every day. These offices are located in Philadelphia, Miss.; Cherokee, N.C.; Stirling Road, Highway 441 Intersection, Hollywood, Fla.; and Alabama-Coushatta Indian Reservation, U.S. 190, Livingston, Tex.

Crafts Centers in Everglades National Park, Florida:

Seminole Indian Village and Crafts Center, 6073 Stirling Rd., Hollywood 33020 (tribal enterprise).

Alice Este Cate Craft Shop, Star Route 1, Box 671, Okeechobee 33472 (U.S. 27 at Moore Haven), Alice Snow and Samaria Leader (Seminole-Creek).

Pete Osceola Indian Village, Box 65, Miccosukee Village, Ochopee 33943 (U.S. 41, 38 mi. west of Miami), Pete Osceola Family (Miccosukee).

John Poole Indian Village, Box 30, Ochopee 33943 (U.S. 41, 41 mi. west of Miami), John Poole (Miccosukee).

Tiger's Miccosukee Indian Village, Box 44021, Tamiami Station, Miami 33144 (U.S. 41, 38 mi. west of Miami), Jimmy Tiger (Miccosukee).

Willie Jim's Camp, Box 19, Ochopee, Collier County 33943 (U.S. 41, 25 mi. east of Ochopee on Tamiami Trail), Willie Jim (Miccosukee).

Typical products: Seminole and Miccosukee skirts, Seminole and Miccosukee patchwork dolls, patchwork shirts, beadwork jewelry. Tours of open-sided, thatched-roofed traditional *chickee* dwellings. Craft demonstrations of patchworking.

Glossary

ACCULTURATION.   The process of cultural borrowing, especially the alteration of a culture through prolonged contact with an advanced society.

ALABAMA.   A state once included in Mississippi Territory 1798; created a territory 1817; admitted to Union, 1819; named after a Creek tribe.

ALGONKIN (also Algonquian).   Indian linguistic family widely distributed in Canada and United States, central and eastern portions. Includes Delawares and Shawnees.

AMERICAN BOARD OF COMMISSIONERS FOR FOREIGN MISSIONS.   Headquarters or administrative base for world evangelization from America, begun about 1810 Boston, Mass. Outreach included Cherokees and then Choctaws before their removal.

ARKANSAS.   A state in the territory visited by de Soto 1541; Louisiana Purchase 1803; Arkansas Territory 1819; admitted to Union, 1836. Named for the Algonkin word for Quapaw Indians.

ARKANSAS RIVER.   A stream approximately 1,450 miles long, rising in central Colorado; flows east through Kansas and southeast across the northeast corner of Oklahoma, bisects Arkansas and empties into Mississippi River.

BISON.   The North American ruminant (cud-chewing) quadruped, *Bison bison,* often called the buffalo. Once present in southeastern United States. Plains Indian tribes relied upon the animal to provide food, shelter, clothing, and tools.

BUSK.   A festival of Creek Indians particularly noted and described by early visitors;

282

included ritual fasting, ceremonial dances, and formal forgiveness of many crimes and injuries. In the Creek language *puskita* means a "fast."

CADDOAN. Linguistic family embracing many Indian tribes in the West, including the Caddo, Wichita, Arikara, and Pawnee.

CALUMET. A sacred object, frequently a decorated pipe, presented before an assembly as a symbol of the earnest intent of the bearer and his party, as in peace or amity. The calumet was one of the most profoundly sacred objects known to the Indians of North America.

CANADIAN RIVER. A stream approximately 906 miles long, flowing from northern New Mexico, eastward across northwest Texas and through central Oklahoma to discharge into Arkansas River in Muskogee County of eastern Oklahoma.

CHATTAHOOCHEE RIVER. A stream approximately 410 miles long, rises northeast Georgia; forms section Alabama-Georgia boundary, section Georgia-Florida boundary.

CHEROKEE STRIP (also *Cherokee Outlet*) A narrow strip of land about 12,000 sq. mi. along southern border of Kansas; ceded to Cherokee nation in treaties of 1828 and 1833; held by Cherokee nation until U.S. purchase in 1891; became part of Oklahoma Territory.

CLAN. A social group comprising a number of households which claim a descent from a common ancestor.

CORN (*Zea mays or maize*). The great food plant developed by agricultural American Indians, which now provides a high percentage of the world's food supply.

CREEK CONFEDERACY. A confederation of more than fifty Indian towns (or tribes), mostly in Alabama and Georgia; mostly Muskogean linguistic stock; advanced agriculture; joined Cherokees, Chickasaws, Choctaws, and Seminoles in Five Civilized Tribes in Oklahoma.

FLORIDA. State in territory first explored by Spanish 1513; St. Augustine founded 1565; ceded to England 1763; retroceded to Spain 1783; purchased by United States 1819; organized as U.S. territory 1822; admitted to Union 1845.

GEORGIA. State in territory first explored by Spanish; last of original thirteen colonies (settled 1733) fourth to become a state; relinquished claims to western lands in 1802, including present-day Alabama and Mississippi.

GORGET. An ornament, such as a modern necklace, worn at or near the throat.

Southeastern Indians in prehistoric times often fashioned gorgets from shells which were engraved with pleasing designs.

HAMMOCKS. Islands of dense tropical undergrowth in the Everglades.

INDIAN TERRITORY. Much of present-day Oklahoma was once formally designated on maps and in literature as Indian Territory because many tribes had been moved there.

IROQUOIAN. North American Indian linguistic family in New York, Pennsylvania, Eastern Canada, and in Southern United States. Tuscaroras, Cherokees.

IROQUOIS CONFEDERACY (also Iroquois League or Iroquoian League). Confederation of Mohawk, Oneida, Onondaga, Cayuga, and Seneca tribes; formed about 1570; generally allies of British (excepting Oneidas).

LOUISIANA. Name of state, originally applied to entire Mississippi River basin claimed for France by LaSalle 1682; first settlement Biloxi (in present-day Mississippi) 1699; New Orleans founded 1718; region east of Mississippi River ceded to Great Britain 1763, excepting West Florida; to United States by British 1783; region west of Mississippi sold by France to United States 1803 as Louisiana Purchase; admitted to the Union, 1812.

LOUISIANA PURCHASE. The purchase of approximately 885,000 sq. mi. of territory, April 30, 1803, by Jefferson Administration, from France for $15 million. Extended from the Mississippi River to Rocky Mountains and from Gulf of Mexico to British America; out of it four states formed (Arkansas, Iowa, Missouri, Nebraska); parts of nine others (Louisiana, Minnesota, Oklahoma, Kansas, Colorado, Wyoming, Montana, North Dakota, South Dakota).

MATRILINEAL DESCENT. Social practice of reckoning descent through the mother's side of the family rather than the father's.

MISSISSIPPI TERRITORY. Southern half present-day states of Mississippi and Alabama; organized as territory in 1798; enlarged 1804, 1813 to include all of present states of Alabama and Mississippi; western part of this territory admitted to Union as state of Mississippi 1817.

MUSKOGEAN. Linguistic family of North American Indians prevalent in southeastern United States, including Natchez, Alabama, Choctaw, Chickasaw, Creek, Seminole, Miccosukee.

MYTH. A traditional story concerning supernatural events and gods, closely associated with religion or tribal history.

284

NATCHEZ TRACE. Road over five hundred miles long from Nashville, Tennessee to Natchez, Mississippi. Colbert Dynasty of Chickasaw Indians had inns and ferries along it. Part of the Trace is now a national parkway.

NORTH CAROLINA. A state, originally part of Carolina grant by Charles II, 1663; royal province 1729; twelfth of the thirteen colonies to join federal Union 1789; 1790 gave up claims to western lands under royal grant from which state of Tennessee was created 1796.

OBSIDIAN. Volcanic glass that is generally black and can be chipped like flint.

OKLAHOMA. A state established on land which was part of Louisiana Purchase from France 1803 (except for the panhandle); settled by Indians as unorganized Indian Territory, 1820-40; part opened to white settlement 1889; western part organized as Oklahoma Territory 1890; Oklahoma Territory and Indian Territory fused and Oklahoma admitted to Union in 1907.

PADDLE-STAMPED DESIGN. Pattern pressed onto surface of pliable clay vessels with curved or flat paddles on which a design has been carved or around which cords have been wrapped. The embossed pots are then fired. Method used by North Carolina Cherokees today in decorating their pottery.

PAN-INDIAN. Having to do with all Indians. Pan-Indian is often applied to activities popular among all tribes such as Plains-style dancing. It also refers to the idea that all Indians shall cooperate to achieve common goals.

PANTHER. North American *Felis cougar,* also called cougar, mountain lion, puma.

PERSIMMON. A tree, sometimes called possum-wood, which bears a small round fruit resembling a yellow plum which ripens after a frost. Virginia Indians dried the fruits on mats spread upon frames. Some tribes made persimmon bread.

POLYGAMY. A term for a marriage in which either sex has more than one spouse at the same time.

POMPION. A pumpkin.

POTTERY. Vessels of fired clay. In America pots were either coiled or molded into form. Most southeastern pottery was coiled, that is, built by coiling together slender "worms" of clay. The vessels were fired, when completely dry, in hot fires protected from the wind. The potter's wheel was unknown in the Americas.

POWHATAN CONFEDERACY. Algonkin-speaking group of about thirty tribes extending along coast and up rivers of Tidewater Virginia. Disappeared after 1722. Remnants of about ten bands survive in eastern Virginia, some intermixed with blacks.

PUBERTY CEREMONIAL. A ceremony to mark the passage of a young person from childhood into womanhood or manhood. After the rites of puberty, the initiate was formally recognized as an adult member of society.

RED RIVER. A stream approximately 1,018 mi. long, from southwestern Oklahoma flows eastward, forming Oklahoma-Texas boundary and section of Arkansas-Texas boundary; flows southeast across Louisiana and into Mississippi River.

RITUAL. Established form of a ceremony (usually religious), customarily repeated acts or series of acts.

SIOUAN. Indian linguistic family of North America; one of most widely distributed of American Indian stocks; includes languages spoken from Gulf of Mexico to Saskatchewan, mainly on Great Plains and western prairie; Eastern Sioux were on Carolina coasts.

SOUTH CAROLINA. A state established on territory first reached by Spanish 1521; Carolina grant by Charles II, 1663; Charleston founded 1680 and long was eastern approach to southeastern Indians for British traders; royal province 1729; ceded western land claims to United States 1787; eighth of the original thirteen colonies to join federal Union 1788.

TABOO. A prohibited act. It is believed that violation will result in certain penalty, usually inflicted by supernatural powers, as interpreted by a people's religious beliefs.

TALLAPOOSA RIVER. A stream approximately 268 mi. long rising in northwest Georgia, flows west to join Coosa River in central Alabama and form Alabama River.

TENNESSEE. A state, originally part of French Louisiana claim; included in charter of Carolina 1663; claim to region ceded by France to Great Britain 1763; North Carolina relinquished claims 1790; admitted to Union 1796; Chickasaws held the land between the Tennessee and Mississippi rivers until 1818; Cherokee nation's Tennessee holdings not taken completely until 1835.

TERRITORY. In U.S. history, an organized and defined portion of national domain given limited self-government, usually in preparation for statehood.

TREATY. Contract or agreement negotiated between two or more political authorities, as between the United States and Indian nations. Under U.S. Constitution, part of the law of the land when ratified by the U.S. Senate (which may reject treaties as well).

TRIBE. Aggregate of peoples sharing common descent, territory, culture. Members may intermarry, with certain prohibitions.

VENISON. Deer meat.

WESTERN LANDS. In early United States history, the name for any territory west of the Appalachian Mountains. There were some very troublesome "western land claims" which grew out of the way in which the charters of the English colonies had been written describing their western borders as extending as far in that direction as possible. This made for many conflicting claims and counterclaims as the nature and extent of the continent unfolded.

Selected Bibliography

In the preparation of this book the authors have used many documents, journals, and books perhaps too technical to benefit the general reader or most young people, and some materials not generally accessible. The list below includes non-specialist items which should be useful in pursuing further the history of the southeastern Indian.

For readers desiring more specialized information, the bibliographies listed below will point the way. Most state and local historical societies are treasuries of information. Valuable bulletins and reports are available from:

Bureau of Indian Affairs, Department of Interior, Washington, D. C.
U. S. Public Health Service, Washington, D. C.
Commissioner of Indian Affairs, Washington, D. C.
Indian Affairs, Association on American Indian Affairs, New York.
Indian Voices, University of Chicago, Chicago, Ill.
Indian Truth, Indian Rights Association, Inc., Philadelphia, Pa.
NCAI Sentinel, National Congress of American Indians, Washington, D. C.
Smithsonian Institution, Bureau of American Ethnology, Washington D. C.
Southern Indian Studies, Archaeological Society of North Carolina, Chapel Hill, N. C.

Bibliographies:

Dawdy, Doris Ostrander. *Annotated Bibliography of American Indian Painting.* New York: Heye Foundation, 1968.

Hirschfelder, Arlene B. *American Indian Authors: A Representative Bibliography.* New York: Association of American Indian Affairs, 1970.

Klein, Bernard, and Icolari, Daniel. *Reference Encyclopedia of the American Indian.* 2nd rev. ed. New York: Klein, 1971.

Library Services Institute for Minnesota Indians. *American Indians: An Annotated*

Bibliography of Selected Library Resources. Minneapolis: University of Minnesota Press, 1970.

Reference Works and Atlases:

Adams, James Truslow, and Coleman, R. V., eds. *Atlas of American History.* New York: Charles Scribner's Sons, 1943. For grades seven and up. Especially useful on Georgia's western lands, Indian cessions, Oklahoma Indian Territory; maps.

Kagan, Hilde Heun, ed. *The American Heritage Pictorial Atlas of United States History.* New York: American Heritage Press, 1966. Survey of Indian history, including prehistoric times; maps and illustrations, many in color.

Library of Congress. *Folklore of the North American Indians.* Publication No. S/N 3001-0005. Washington: U.S. Government Printing Office, 1968. Excellent source materials in this inexpensive, illustrated book.

Terrell, John. *American Indian Almanac.* New York: World Publishers. One of the best syntheses of archaeological discoveries with early historical accounts; chronology; population information. Good reference for amateur archaeologist.

Periodicals:

Newspapers:

Alligator Times. Monthly of the Community Action Program of the Seminole Tribe, Hollywood, Florida.

Chahta Anumpa. Published in Nashville, Tenn., 1968-71; now published by Choctaw Tribe, Philadelphia, Miss., who also publish *Choctaw Community News.*

Cherokee One Feather. Published weekly by Tribal Council of Eastern Band of Cherokee, Cherokee, N.C. This is widely circulated southeastern Indian newspaper, about 16,000. It covers national, regional, and local news of concern to Indians, along with social news, special material, poetry, and letters to the editor.

Christian Science Monitor. Consistently reports developments affecting Indian life, and presents many features tracing various aspects of that life today.

New York Times Index. This annual provides a guide to locating news of Indian affairs.

Journals:

Agogino, George A. "Man's Antiquity in the Western Hemisphere." *Indian Historian,* 3 (Spring, 1970), 49-52.

American Indian Issue. *Mankind Magazine,* 2 (September, 1970). Fine account of Cherokee "Trail of Tears."

Braden, Guy B. "The Colberts and the Chickasaw Nation." *Tennessee Historical Quarterly* (hereinafter *THQ*), 17 (September, 1958), 222-49, 318-35.

Capron, Louis. "Florida's Emerging Seminoles." *National Geographic,* 136 (November, 1969), 716-34.

Deloria, Vine, Jr. "This Country Was a Lot Better Off When the Indians Were Running It." *New York Magazine,* 8 March 1970; "The War Between the Redskins and the Fed." *Ibid.,* 7 December 1969.

Dietz, Angel De Cora. "Native American Art." *Indian Historian,* 3 (Winter, 1970), 27-30.

Franklin, W. Neil. "Virginia and the Cherokee Indian Trade, 1673-1752." *East Tennessee Historical Society Publications,* 4 (1932), 3-21.

Haas, Mary R. "Creek Inter-Town Relations." *American Anthropologist,* 40 (1940), 479-89.

———. "Men and Women's Speech in Koasati." *Language,* 20 (1944), 142-49.

Hoffman, W. S. "Andrew Jackson, State Rightist: The Case of the Georgia Indians." *THQ,* 11 (December, 1952), 329-45.

Jack, Marvin. "Indians in Agriculture." *Indian Historian,* 3 (Winter, 1970), 24-27.

Jennings, Jesse D., ed. "Nutt's Diary." *Journal of Mississippi History,* 9 (January, 1947), 34-61.

Lincecum, Gideon. "Life of Apushmataha." *Mississippi Historical Society,* 9 (1905-1906), 415-85.

McClary, Ben Harris. "Nancy Ward: The Last Beloved Woman of the Cherokees." *THQ,* 21 (December, 1962), 352-64.

Nash, Charles H., and Gates, Rodney, Jr. "Chucalissa Indian Town." *THQ,* 21 (June, 1962), 103-21.

Phelps, Dawson A. "The Chickasaw, the English, and the French, 1699-1744." *THQ,* 16 (June, 1957), 117-33.

Sloan, Thomas L. "The Indian Reservation System." *Indian Historian,* 3 (Winter, 1970), 30-34.

White, Douglas R.; Murdock, George P.; and Scaglion, Richard. "Natchez Class and Rank Reconsidered." *Ethnology,* 10 (October, 1971), 369-89.

Books:

Bartram, William. *Travels.* Mark Van Doren, ed. New York: Dover Publications, 1955. A classic, often charming and touching; at times the romanticism is misleading.

Bauer, Fred B. *Land of the North Carolina Cherokees.* Brevard, N. C.: Bauer, 1970. Product of thorough research into the fragmentary written records. Reworks James Mooney's interpretation of Will H. Thomas and his role in genesis of Qualla Boundary.

Bell, Corydon. *John Rattling-Gourd of Big Cove.* New York: The Macmillan Co., 1955. An illustrated collection of Cherokee legends.

Benson, Henry C. *Life Among the Choctaw Indians.* Cincinnati: Swormstedt and Poe, 1860. A Methodist minister's account of his life among the Choctaws in Indian Territory. A wonderfully calm statement of high character qualities found among Choctaws and other Indians.

Beverley, Robert. *History of Virginia.* Louis B. Wright, ed. Reprint of 1722 ed.

Chapel Hill: University of North Carolina (hereinafter UNC), 1947. A primary source on Indians in Virginia in the seventeenth century. A classic for all interested readers.

Bourne, Edward Gaylord, ed. *Narratives of the Career of Hernando De Soto.* 2 vols. New York: 1904. The journals of the Gentleman of Elvas and Rodrigo Ranjel (through Oviedo) are often dry, sparse, and ultra restrained.

Bossu, Jean-Bernard. *Travels in the Interior of North America, 1751-1762.* Tr. and ed. Seymour Feiler. Norman: University of Oklahoma Press (hereinafter UOK), 1962. Influenced by Rousseau's "noble savage" idea, full of observations both practical and speculative. Sometimes humorous.

Brown, Mrs. Douglas S. *The Catawba Indians: The People of the River.* Columbia: University of South Carolina Press, 1966. Readable, careful historical scholarship, maps.

Brown, John P. *Old Frontiers.* Kingsport, Tenn.: Southern Publishers, 1938. Story of the Cherokees from early times until the Removal; maps.

Byrd, William. *History of the Dividing Line.* 2 vols. Richmond: 1866. A famous book, available in many editions. Shows how the whites of Virginia, who set the pace for the South, seem always to have been certain they were "right."

Cahn, Edgar S., ed. *Our Brother's Keeper: The Indian in White America.* New York: Community Press, 1969. Contemporary viewpoints on Indian problems.

Caruso, John A. *The Appalachian Frontier.* Indianapolis: Bobbs-Merrill, 1959. Story of first westward movement by Europeans; maps. Dr. Caruso has other titles in this series, including *The Southern Frontier,* 1963.

Caughey, John Walton. *McGillivray of the Creeks.* UOK, 1938. A collation of McGillivray's letters with a valuable introductory essay. Good source material; maps.

Catlin, George. *Episodes from Life Among the Indians and Last Rambles.* Marvin C. Ross, ed. UOK, 1959. Scenes and portraits by this famous artist.

————. *North American Indians.* Reprint, 2 vols. Minneapolis: Ross and Haines, 1965. Observations of customs and conditions among Indians he visited 1832-39. Excellent reading for any serious student above grades five or six; illustrated.

Collier, John. *Indians of the Americas.* New York: E. P. Dutton, 1947. Overall treatment by Pres. Franklin D. Roosevelt's Commissioner of Indian Affairs; absorbing style.

Corkran, David H. *The Cherokee Frontier: Conflict and Survival, 1740-1762.* Reprint. UOK, 1966. Excellent scholarly study.

————. *The Creek Frontier, 1540-1783.* UOK, 1967. Excellent scholarly study.

Corn, James Franklin. *Red Clay and Rattlesnake Springs.* Cleveland, Tenn.: Corn, 1959. History of the Cherokees in Bradley County, Tenn. Gives picture of physical and psychological environment.

Costo, Rupert, ed. *Textbooks and the American Indian.* San Francisco: Indian Historian Press, 1970. Examines presentation of the Indian in textbooks. Fine for bright grade school readers.

Cotterill, R. S. *The Southern Indians.* UOK, 1954. History of civilized tribes before the Removal. Much political and economic data; maps. Style suitable to upper secondary students.

Crane, Verner W. *The Southern Frontier, 1670-1732.* Ann Arbor: University of Michigan, 1956. Valuable work by a historian. Considered a classic, though done before anthropology and archaeology were much applied to history.

Cushman, Horatio B. *History of the Choctaw, Chickasaw, and Natchez Indians.* Greeneville, Texas: Headlight Printing House, 1899. Similar to Benson book, written by a religious man who served the Indians. Sometimes rambling, but very moving. (No longer in print, but in many libraries.)

Davis, Russell G., and Ashabranner, Brent K. *The Choctaw Code.* New York: Whittlesey House, 1961. A well-researched book especially for young readers.

Debo, Angie. *The Rise and Fall of the Choctaw Republic.* UOK, 1934. An outstanding study, rich content suitable for all readers; maps.

————. *The Road to Disappearance.* UOK, 1941. Excellent study for all serious students; maps.

Deloria, Vine, Jr. *Custer Died for Your Sins.* New York: The Macmillan Co., 1969. An Indian manifesto. Young readers should know this author.

————. *We Talk, You Listen.* New York: The Macmillan Co., 1970. A major contemporary Indian voice.

Densmore, Frances. *American Indians and Their Music.* New York: Woman's Press, 1936. A great authority on the subject. Readable style.

DeRosier, Arthur H., Jr. *The Removal of the Choctaw Indians.* Knoxville: University of Tennessee Press (hereinafter UTP), 1970. Clear, concise, lively. Suitable for any serious student, grade six or above.

Driver, Harold E. *Indians of North America.* Chicago: University of Chicago Press, 1961. A comprehensive and scholarly work; maps.

Du Ru, Paul. *Journal, Feb. 1–May 8, 1700.* Ruth Lapham Butler, ed. Chicago: Caxton Club, 1934. This little gem by a French Jesuit missionary from Canada, written during momentous times, deserves to be much better known.

Evans, W. McKee. *To Die Game: The Story of the Lowry Band, Indian Guerrillas of Reconstruction.* Baton Rouge: Louisiana State University Press, 1971. One of the few historical works bearing on the North Carolina Lumbee Indians. Readable.

Farb, Peter. *Man's Rise to Civilization as Shown by the Indians of North America.* New York: E. P. Dutton, 1968. Popular book, though some experts challenge his treatment of the Natchez; pp. 153-64, 248-55.

Faulkner, Charles H. *The Old Stone Fort.* UTP, 1968. Exploration of an archaeological mystery in Tennessee.

Foreman, Grant. *Advancing the Frontier, 1830-60.* UOK, 1933. Excellent scholarly study; maps.

————. *The Five Civilized Tribes.* UOK, 1934. Excellent study with introduction by John R. Swanton.

————. *Indian Removal.* Reprint of 1932 ed. UOK, 1953. Scholarly account of emigration of Five Civilized Tribes; maps.

292

————. *Sequoyah*. UOK, 1938. Excellent. One of the early front-ranking historians of the southeastern tribes. A tireless researcher not tangled in academic and scholarly apparatus. Gives many major insights.

Foreman, Carolyn. *Indian Women Chiefs*. Muskogee, Okla.: Foreman, 1938. Good idea, but light on facts.

Fundaburk, Emma Lila, and Foreman, Mary Douglas. *Sun Circles and Human Hands*. Luverne, Ala.: Fundaburk, 1957. Story of art and industry among southeastern Indians; many illustrations and maps.

————. *Southeastern Indians: Life Portraits: A Catalogue of Pictures, 1564-1860*. Luverne, Ala.: Fundaburk, 1958. Extremely useful, with text mostly quotations from authorities.

Gabriel, Ralph Henry. *Elias Boudinot*. UOK, 1941. Story of this famous Cherokee and his America.

Garraty, John A. *The American Nation: A History of the United States*. New York: Harper & Row, 1968. A good reference work, well illustrated and devoid of the European bias; color photos and pictures.

Gibson, Arrell M. *The Chickasaws*. UOK, 1971. Excellent on Colbert Dynasty and the role of Negroes; a vivid account which makes the people real. Recommended for serious students from junior high up.

Griffin, J. B., ed. *Archaeology of the Eastern United States*. Chicago: University of Chicago Press, 1952. Indispensable. Sharp-minded students of all ages ought to encounter this work.

Halbert, H. S., and Ball, T. H. *The Creek War of 1813 and 1814*. Frank L. Owsley, Jr., ed. Tuscaloosa: University of Alabama Press, 1969. First published, 1895. Contains tradition, oral testimony, and printed sources.

Hall, William. *Early History of the South-West. Indian Battles and Murders— Narratives of General Hall*. Gallatin, Tenn.: Edward Ward Carmack Sumner County Public Library, 1968. First published by The South-Western Monthly, 1852. Written from the white man's viewpoint, but clearly shows the ferocity of wars between settlers and Indians. Vivid picture of wild game resources.

Hofsinde, Robert. *Indians at Home*. New York: William Morrow & Co., 1964. For young readers grades four to six, includes information on Seminole house architecture; illustrated.

Hudson, Charles M. *The Catawba Nation*. Athens: University of Georgia Press (hereinafter UGP), 1970. Very enjoyable example of social anthropology without the harness of technical jargon. For advanced students.

Hudson, Charles M., ed. *Red, White, and Black*. Symposium on Indians in the Old South. Proceedings of Southern Anthropological Society, No. 5. UGP, 1971. Gives new insights into position of blacks with relation to Indians.

Hunter, Kermit. *Unto These Hills*. UNC, 1954. Famous dramatization of Cherokee Trail of Tears. Might qualify as class play.

Hyde, George E. *Indians of the Woodlands, from Prehistoric Times to 1725*. UOK, 1962. Clearly written and comprehensive; shows interplay of tribal ambitions.

Jackson, Helen Hunt. *A Century of Dishonor*. New York: Harper Torchbooks, 1965. Junior highs might be stirred by this classic by the author of *Ramona*, who was horrified to discover the plight of the Indians long after the slaves had been freed. First published, 1881.

Jacobs, Wilbur R., ed. *The Appalachian Indian Frontier: The Edmond Atkin Report and Plan of 1755*. Reprint. Lincoln: University of Nebraska Press, 1967. Atkin was British Indian superintendent for the South in the 1750s. Data on Catawbas and others earlier than Adair. For all readers who enjoy "you are there" documents.

James, Marquis. *The Life of Andrew Jackson*. Indianapolis: Bobbs-Merrill, 1938. High-level popular history. Jackson's role is undergoing reinterpretation as the final agent in a long process. Much reliable information on Indians.

Jefferson, Thomas. *Notes on the State of Virginia*. William Peden, ed. UNC, 1955. Deceptive title for one of the first accounts of the natural history of America with bearing on the Indians. The style is very Jeffersonian, i.e. graceful but oblique. What did he really think about the Indian?

Josephy, Alvin M., Jr., ed. *The American Heritage Book of Indians*. New York: Simon & Schuster, 1961. See below.

_____. *The Indian Heritage of America*. New York: Alfred A. Knopf, 1968. Both are handsome books, though the maps are disappointing. Some students may object to the "heritage" approach. The Creeks, as so often happens, are featured and we hardly know about the others. The now-questioned interpretation of Natchez society is passed along.

Kilpatrick, Jack, and Kilpatrick, Anna Gritts, eds. and trs. *Shadow of Sequoyah. Social Documents of the Cherokees, 1862-1964*. UOK, 1965. Documents bearing on daily life and attitudes after removal to Oklahoma.

LaFarge, Oliver. *A Pictorial History of the American Indian*. New York: Crown Publishers, 1956. Text is sometimes jovial, but illustrations are comprehensive.

Lawson, John. *A New Voyage to Carolina*. Hugh Talmage Lefler, ed. Reprint of *History of Carolina,* London, 1714. UNC, 1967. A marvellous book by a young man who seems to have had medical training coupled with unlimited energy and curiosity. Fills in the common gap of understanding of the Atlantic Seaboard Siouan tribes. Fine documentation, useful to teachers. Gripping style, attractive to young readers.

Lewis, Anna. *Chief Pushmataha, American Patriot*. New York: Exposition Press, 1959. An old-fashioned but admirable synthesis of the greatest Choctaw culture hero.

Lewis, Thomas M. N., and Kneberg, Madeline. *Eva, An Archaic Site*. UTP, 1961. See below.

_____. *Hiwassee Island*. UTP, 1946. This and the foregoing title are rather technical reports with illustrations and maps.

_____. *Tribes that Slumber*. UTP, 1958. Story of Indian times in Tennessee; archaeological emphasis; illustrations.

Loomis, Augustus Ward. *Scenes in the Indian Country*. Philadelphia: Presbyterian Board of Publication, 1859. Old-fashioned and moralistic in tone, but good description.

McKenney, Thomas L. *Memoirs.* New York: Paine & Burgess, 1846. By a man who knew the southeastern Indians. His high sense of humor comes through the fine English style.

McKenney, Thomas L., and Hall, James. *History of the Indian Tribes of North America.* 3 vols. Philadelphia: E. C. Biddle, 1836-44. An excellent firsthand account by sensitive observers.

McNitt, Frank. *The Indian Traders.* UOK, 1962. Scholarly but not dull.

McReynolds, Edwin C. *The Seminoles.* UOK, 1957. Good, but rather conventional history. Young readers should read with benefit and enjoyment.

Malone, James Henry. *The Chickasaw Nation.* Louisville: Morton, 1922. One of the first overall accounts of the Chickasaws and valuable despite its deficiencies.

Milfort, Leclerc. *Memoirs, or a Quick Glance at My Various Travels and My Sojourn in the Creek Nation.* Ben C. McCary, tr. Kennesaw, Ga.: Continental Book Company, 1959. A dramatic adventure story with many fabrications but an enthusiastic tone that encourages young readers.

Milling, Chapman J. *Red Carolinians.* 2nd ed. UNC, 1940. A useful study and readable.

Mooney, James. *The Aboriginal Population of America North of Mexico.* Vol. 80. Washington: Smithsonian Miscellaneous Collection, 1928. Authoritative but technical.

Parsons, Elsie Clews, ed. *American Indian Life.* Lincoln: University of Nebraska Press, 1967. A unique book of popular writings by some of America's greatest anthropologists of a few decades past. See "Tokulki of Tulsa" by John R. Swanton, pp. 127-45.

Pope, John. *A Tour Through the Southern and Western Territories of the United States.* Richmond: J. Dixon, 1792. Readable travel account, a classic source of often-repeated data on the Creeks.

Pound, Merritt B. *Benjamin Hawkins—Indian Agent.* UGP, 1951. Hawkins was an Indian agent in the South about 1796 to 1814. Interesting data on Cherokees, Choctaws, Chickasaws, and Creeks.

Rights, Douglas L. *The American Indian in North Carolina.* 2nd ed. Winston-Salem, N.C.: John F. Blair, Publisher, 1971. Information appealing to both general reader and scholar.

Romans, Bernard. *A Concise Natural History of East and West Florida.* Vol. 1. New York: Romans, 1775. If Romans did in fact print a second volume of his firsthand observations, it has not been found.

Rowland, Dunbar. *Mississippi Provincial Archives.* Vol. 1. Jackson: Mississippi Department of Archives and History, 1927. A basic book but with inadequate index.

Shea, John Gilmary, ed. *Discovery and Exploration of the Mississippi Valley.* New

York: Redfield, 1852. Translations of the narratives of Marquette, Hennepin, Membre, and others.

Sherman, William T. *Memoirs*. Bloomington: University of Indiana Press, 1957. Sherman rambles on about many things, but he did have many contacts with the Indians and makes interesting observations.

Speck, Frank G., and Broom, Leonard. *Cherokee Dance and Drama*. Los Angeles: University of California Press, 1951. Uses Cherokee oral traditions; somewhat technical.

Spencer, R. F., Jennings, J. D., *et al. The Native Americans*. New York: Harper & Row, 1951. A beautiful textbook blending of anthropology, archaeology, geography, and history.

Starkey, Marion L. *The Cherokee Nation*. New York: Alfred A. Knopf, 1946. Well-written study and political emphasis.

Swanton, John R. *The Indian Tribes of North American*. Washington: Smithsonian Institution Press, 1952. See below.

————. *Early History of the Creek Indians and Their Neighbors*. Reprint of 1922 ed. Washington: Bureau of American Ethnology (hereafter BAE), Bulletin 73, 1971. See below.

————. *Indian Tribes of the Lower Mississippi Valley and Adjacent Coast of the Gulf of Mexico*. Reprint of 1911 ed. BAE, Bulletin 43, 1970. See below.

————. *Indians of the Southeastern United States*. Reprint of 1946 ed. Bulletin 137. BAE, 1968. See below.

————. *Social Organization and Social Usages of the Indians of the Creek Confederacy; Religious Beliefs and Medical Practices of the Creek Indians*. Forty-second Annual Report. BAE, 1928. All the Swanton titles are fundamental studies. Accurate and comprehensive, though sometimes technical.

Timberlake, Henry. *Memoirs, 1756-1765*. Facsimile reprint of 1927 ed. Samuel C. Williams, ed. Marietta, Ga.: Continental Book Company, 1948. Readable account by a young man full of daring, also a fair observer.

Turner, Frederick Jackson. *The Frontier in American History*. New York: Holt, 1921. Collection of essays by the father of the "frontier school" of historians. Rather difficult style.

Tuttle, Sarah. *Conversations on the Choctaw Mission*. 2 vols. Boston: Massachusetts Sunday School Union, 1830. Slanted for Sunday school use, but full of interesting information about school children and the details of daily life. A reprint is expected soon.

Underwood, Tom, and Sandlin, Moselle. *Legends of the Cherokee*. Asheville, N. C.: Stephens Press, 1956. Has an authentic feel. Good for general reader.

Van Every, Dale. *Disinherited: The Lost Birthright of the American Indian*. New York: William Morrow & Co., 1968. Splendid account of the Removal.

Wardell, Morris. *A Political History of the Cherokee Nation, 1838-1907*. UOK, 1938. Very readable and useful; maps.

Washburn, Wilcomb E. *The Indian and the White Man*. Garden City, N. Y.:

Doubleday Anchor Books, 1964. Somewhat technical with anthropological emphasis.

Wilkins, Thurman. *Cherokee Tragedy. The Story of the Ridge Family and the Decimation of a People.* New York: The Macmillan Co., 1970. Very good popular history. Sequoyah, Trail of Tears, and the difficult adjustment in present-day Oklahoma. Fifty pages of good maps and bibliography. Good readers junior high and above should enjoy.

Williams, Samuel Cole, ed. *Adair's History of the American Indian.* Johnson City, Tenn.: Watauga Press, 1930. One of the primary sources on Indians of the Southeast. Somewhat subjective, but Adair was there; maps.

Woodward Thomas S. *Reminiscences of the Creek or Muscogee Indians.* Reprint of 1859 ed. Birmingham, Ala.: Southern University Press, 1970. Interesting personal account.

Wright, James Leitch, Jr. *William Augustus Bowles, Director General of the Creek Nation.* UGP, 1967. Lucid account of a spectacular adventurer. Should appeal to all readers.

Young, Mary Elizabeth. *Redskins, Ruffleshirts and Rednecks: Indian Allotments in Alabama and Mississippi, 1830-1860.* UOK, 1961. The tensions and realities arc indicated in the subtitle; somewhat technical treatment.

Index

The page numbers for illustrations are printed in **boldface** type

Acolapissas, 36, 44, **51,** 53, 76

Adair, James, 57, 62, 63, 64, 73, 75, 76, 79, 80, 82, 109, 115, 121

Adena culture, 25, **25,** 26, **27,** 28

Agriculture, 16, 17, 18, 28, 29, 37, 48, **49, 51,** 54, 56, 78, **78,** 80, 82, 108, 128, 132, 136, 149, 160, 162, 163, 221-24, 255, 258, 264

Alabama, 18, 23, 27, 29, 35, 41, 171. *See also* Creek Confederacy; Creeks; Mobile

Alabama-Coushattas, 221, **254,** 255

Alabamas, 36, 52, 57, 73, 108, 129, 220

Alcohol, 119, 121, 137, 140, 141, 146, 174, 177, 211, 231, 236, 245, 246, 265

Algonkin (Algonquian): language, 35, 36, 37, 41, 45, 68; people, 15, 35, 36, 143, 221

Alligator, 26, 59-60, 76, 258

Alligator Times, 259, 268, 271

Apalachees, 20, 43, 48, 121, 128

Appalachian Mountains, 19, 20, 28, 37, **38,** 39, 53, 125, 126. *See also* Great Smoky Mountains

Archaeological sites: Cahokia (Ill.), 29, **29;** Copena (Ala.), 27; Crystal River (Fla.), 27; Etowah (Ga.), 29; Eva (Tenn.), 24; Kolmoki (Ga.), 29; Mandeville (Ga.), 27; Marksville (La.), 27; Mound Bottom (Tenn.), 29; Moundville (Ala.) 29; Okmulgee (Ga.), 29; Russell Cave (Ala.), 23; Spiro, (Okla.), 29. Also see maps pp. 27, 30; Places to See and Experience, 277-82.

Arkansas Indians. *See* Quapaws

Arkansas, state of, 44, 169, 172, 178, 179, 180, 183, 220, 225, 229

Arpeika, Chief, 153, 154

Atakapas, 36, 38, 44, 76, 129, 220, 253

Attakullakulla, **126,** 144

Avoyels, 36, 44, 129, 220, 253

Baptists, 163, 166, 236

Bartram, William, 55, 96-99

Basketry, 25, 53, **54,** 62, 116, **200, 212,** 220, 231, 255, **256, 257**

Battise, Solomon, **256**

Bayogoulas, 36, 44, 62, 76, 93, 111

Bear, 28, 53, 65, 68, 75, 78, 79, 107, 110, 112, 116, 125

Beaver, 23, 79, 112, 116, 163

Biloxis, 36, 43, 61, 129, 243, 253

Bison, 16, 44, 53, 56, 65, 75, 76, **76,** 110, 116, 117, 125, 163

Black Drink, 65, 68, 69, **69,** 101

Blue, Brantley, 260

Body paint. *See* Paint, body

Bone pickers, 62, 102

Bossu, John Bernard, 5, 56, 73, 92, 99, 109, 124

Bureau of Indian Affairs (BIA), 241, 243, 252

Busk, 59, 68, 69-72, 96, 103, 105

Caddoan: language, 36, 44; people, 79, 80, **81,** 107, 111, 220

Calhoun, John C., 160, 166

Calumet, 32, 55, **55, 100,** 114. *See also* Tobacco: pipes

Calusas, 36, 43, 73, 80, 123, 128

Cane, uses of, 49, 53, 93, 94, 98, 107, **200, 212,** 220, 231, 255

Canoes, 55, **55,** 101, 157, 259

Carolinas, 80, 96, 101, 107, 112, 119, 120, 126. *See also* North Carolina; South Carolina

Catawbas, 25, 36, 43, 53, 63, 72, 86, 107, 111, 120, 121, 140-43, 223, 224, **224, 225,** 231, **231,** 235, 236

Catlin, George, 80, 87-91, 152; paintings by, **81, 85, 90, 127, 131, 133, 139, 151, 169, 176, 177, 180, 187, 189**

Chahta Anumpa, 247

Charleston, South Carolina, 113, 116, 118, 120, 121, 128, 144, 189

Cherokee Indians of Robeson County. *See* Lumbees

Cherokee One Feather, 216, 265, 266, 270

Cherokee Phoenix, 160, **161**

Cherokees, 21, 22, 35, 36, 45, **47,** 63, 66, 72, 75, 93, 94, 99, 119, 143, 144, 159-61, **198, 229;** in Arkansas, 133, **133,** 179, 180, **180;** crafts of, 25, 53, 54, 55, **98, 200, 204,** 261, 266, 267, **267;** customs of, 57, 67, 86, 106; Eastern Band of, **205,** 211-20, **216, 219,** 237, 239, 243, 247, 249, 259, 261, **262,** 264-67; and other Indian peoples, 41, 46, 80, 124, 141, 236;

in Indian Territory, 180-83, 191, **191,** 192, 217, 218, 220, 225-31, **227, 232,** 236, 262; Mountain, 37, 38, 47, 64, 181, 213; removal of, **170,** 179-87, **183, 184, 196,** 209; and whites, 112, 125, 126, **126,** 130, 132, 133

Chickasaws, 34, 36, **41, 47,** 60, 63, 72, **128,** 131, 132, 147-50, **149, 150,** 161, 162; customs of, 57, 80, 106, 107; and other Indian peoples, 22, 41, 45, 53, 124, 135, 136, 179; in Indian Territory, 148-50, **172,** 191, **191,** 192, 225-31, **227, 228, 233;** removal of, 170-72, **170;** and whites, 62, 112, 115, 125, 128, 133

Chickee, 52, **52**

Chitimachas, 36, 44, 52, 61, 79, 80, 129, 220, 222, 253, 254, 268; crafts of, 53, 54, **54,** 255, 261; customs of, 62, 101, **101,** 102; reservation of, 236, 237

Choctaws, 34, 36, 40, 41, **47,** 63, 65, 73, 79, 81, 108, **108, 109,** 110, 131, 132, **138, 262;** customs of, 52, 53, 56, 62, 107; games of, **85,** 87-91, **89, 90,** 92, **92,** 93, 94, **203;** and other Indian peoples, 22, 45, 135; in Indian Territory, 87, 171, 191, **191,** 225-31, **227;** in Louisiana, 129, 209, 220, 236, 253, 261; in Mississippi (1838-1918), 209-12, **212,** 231, 236; music of, 96, **98,** 99; removal of, 165-69, **168, 169, 170;** reservation of, 236, 237, 242, 243, 244; today, **199, 202, 242,** 245, 246, 249, **250,** 261, 266, **269,** 270; and whites, 112-15, 123, 128, 133, 137

Chunkey, 92, **92,** 93, **93,** 108

Civil War. *See* War, Civil

Clans, 57-61, 66, 71, 73, 107, 110, 144, 145, 163

Clothing, 15, 24, 30, **31, 32,** 53, 55, 87, 115, 116, 132, 142, **199, 202, 205, 208,** 247, 262

Coacoochee, 151-55, **153**

Cobb, 210, 211

Cofitachequi, Lady of, 46-47
Colbert family, 136, 147-50, **149, 150,** 162, 171
Congarees, 36, 68, 78, 94, 101
Cooking, 51, 52, 53, 54, 67, 75-83, **77,** 82, 83
Corn, development of, 17, **17,** 18, **71,** 79; importance of, 26, 28, 37, 43, 44, 48, **50,** 64, 75; preparation of, 54, 77, 78, 82, 83, 94; as trade item, 119, 162; other uses of, 93. *See also* Busk
Coushattas, 128, 220, 221, 253, 255, **256-57.** *See also* Alabama-Coushattas; Koasatis
Cradle boards, 107, **107**
Creek-American War. *See* War, Red Stick
Creek Confederacy, 36, 39-41, 61, 72, 112, 134, 144-47, 174, 221. *See also* Creeks; War, Red Stick
Creeks, **127, 173, 175, 176, 177, 197;** in Alabama today, 179, 231, 239, 244, 255, 258, **262,** 266, 270; customs of, 34, 57, 58, 60, 68, 93, **93,** 106, 107, **111;** and de Soto, 46, 47, 79; food of, 75, 77; and other Indian peoples, 96-98, 121, 122, 144, 148; in Indian Territory, 59, 94-95, 154, 155, 190-92, **191,** 225-31, **227, 233,** 264, 268, **269;** religion of, 63, 64, 65, 66, 99 (*see also* Busk); removal of, **170,** 173-79, **194;** and Seminoles, 41, 128, 154-55, 177, 187, 190, **198;** tribes who joined, 22, 45, 124, **131.** *See also* Alabama-Coushattas; Alabamas; Creek Confederacy; Coushattas; Koasatis; War, Red Stick
Croatans. *See* Lumbees
Curtis Act, 229
Cusabos, 36, 118, 120
Dances, 56, 57, **70,** 87-89, **90,** 94, 96-105, **97, 202,** 220, 265. *See also* Busk
Dawes General Allotment Act, 228, 229
Death, 22, 24, **26,** 33, 61, 62, **62,** 66,

74, 101, 102, 210. *See also* Mounds, burial
Debo, Angie, 60, 229
Declaration of Indian Purpose, 238-39
Deer, 53, 56, 59, 65, 66, 75, 79, **79,** 85, 98, 112, 116, 119, 125, 144, **254**
Delawares, 21, 41, 43
Densmore, Frances, 104
de Soto, 45-48, **46,** 51, 79, 112
Dial, Adolph, 222
Dion, Thomas, 253
Disease, 34, 66, 68, 118, 119, 121, 146, 168, 179, 183, 226
Du Pratz, 75, 94, 108; art of, **21, 31, 32, 70, 76, 100**
Durant, Sophia McGillivray, 146
Du Roullet, Regis, 113-15
Du Ru, Paul, 31, 33, 76

Eastern Band of Cherokees. *See* Cherokees; Eastern Band of; Mountain
Education, 107-11, 136, 148, 150, 160-62, 163, 213, 230, 231, **232-33,** 234, **234,** 236, 237, **237,** 241-45, 247-49, 263, 266, 268, 270
Ee-mat-la, 151-54, **151**
Elvas, Gentleman of, 51
Eneah Emathala, 176-78
Enos, 36, 68, 78, 93

Fire, 21, 28, 29, 38, 51, 52, 71, 72, 74, 102, 103, 142, 210
Fish, 33, 59, 76, 78, 79, 86, 103, 108, 109, 142, 258
Fishing, 24, 43, 44, 56, 76, 77, 79, 80, 107, 221, 245
Florida, 18, 26, 27, 38, **46, 47, 170, 239, 262;** British in, 121, 125, 128, 139; French in, 84, 122; Spanish in, 45, 48, 80, 112, 122, 123, 131, 134, 135, 136, 138, 139, 146; state of, 238. *See also* Apalachees; Seminoles; Timucuas; War: Seminole; Yamasees
Folsom, David, 162, 167, **168**

Gaillard, Frye, 260

Gentleman of Elvas. *See* Elvas, Gentleman of

Georgia, 18, 27, 29, 34; colony of, 118, 126, 145; de Soto in, 45-47; state of, 134, 135, 138, 147, 152, 154, 166, 173-77, 181, 182, 188. *See also* Cherokees; Creek Confederacy; Creeks; Timucuas; War, Red Stick

Gibson, Arrell, 230

Great Smoky Mountains, 181, 213, 214, 249. *See also* Appalachian Mountains

Green Corn Ceremonial. *See* Busk

Gulf of Mexico, 18, 19, 24, 26, 28, 29, 37, 51, 76, 79, 80, 112, 178, 238

Haas, Mary R., 36, 53, 94

Hagler, Chief, 140-43

Harris, Robert Lee, 236

Haskell Indian Junior College, 266

Ha-tchoo-tuc-knee. *See* Peter Pitchlynn

Henry, DeLaura (Na pakanli usi homa), 266, **269**

Henry, Frank, 244

Hopewell culture, **20,** 26, **26,** 27, **27,** 28, **28**

Hopothleycholo. *See* Opothleyoholo

Horseshoe Bend, 137, 138, 173, 187, 217

Houmas, 36, 44, 123, 124, 129, 221, 253

Houses, 32, 49-51, **50, 51,** 57

Hudson, Charles, 223

Hunting, 17, **76,** 107, 126, 221, 245, 270; ceremonies of, 65, 66, 68; as reason for war, 41, 45, 73, 131; tools for, **23,** 28, 44, **108, 109,** 116, **129**

Ilex vomitoria. See Black Drink

Illinois (Indians), 26, 27, 28, 29, 62, 183

Indian Bill of Rights, 260

Indian Line, 160, **160,** 166

Indian Removal Bill, 165, 171, 173, 181

Indian Territory, 132, 133, 160, 166-92,

191, 225-31, **227,** 236. *See also* Cherokees; Chickasaws; Choctaws; Creeks; Oklahoma; Seminoles

Iroquoian: language, 35, 36, 37, 41, 45; people, 22, 42, 121, 221

Isaac, Calvin, 244

Jackson, Andrew: administration of, 166, 182; as general, 60, 137, 138, 148, 152, 159, 160, 170, 171, 173, 187, 217; as president, 165, 176, 177, 181

Jackson, Helen Hunt, 228

Jackson, Walter, 249

Jefferson, Thomas, 61, 132, 133, 134, 160, 167

Jesup, Gen. T. S. 152, 153

Jewelry, 24, 25, 27, **28,** 43, 46, 71, 110, **110, 199.**

John Jolly, Chief, 179, 180, **180**

Jumper, Betty Mae Tiger, 246-49, **250**

Kentucky, 41, 131, 160, 171, 183, 268

King Phillip. *See* Ee-mat-la

Kneberg, Madeline, 106, 128

Koasatis, 36, 50, 52, 178. *See also* Coushattas

Koroas, 36, 44, 79

Ku Klux Klan, 157, 235

Lambert, Carl G. S. Sr., 216

Lawson, John, 78, 82, 94, 96, 98, 99, 101, 118, 119

Le Moyne, Jacques, art of, **26, 42, 49, 69, 78, 85**

Lewis, Thomas M. N., 106

Littlejohn, Nellie, 264

Locklear, Herbert, 260

Louisiana, 18, 39, 44, 45, 84; colony of, 31, 57, 62, 75, 109, 113, 114, 123, 125, 131, 133; prehistoric, 26, 27, 29. *See also* Atakapas; Caddos; Chitimachas; Coushattas

Lowney, 213-15

Lowry, Henry Berry, 155-58

Lumbees, 155-58, 221-23, **222**, 231-35, **234**, 239, 243, 244, 259, 260, 265, **265**

McGhee, Calvin, 239
McGillivray, Alexander (Hoboi-hili-miko), 60, 134, 344-47
McIntosh, Dode, 261
McIntosh, William, 173-75, **173**
McReynolds, Edwin C., 225, 226
Maize. *See* Corn
Marriage, 56-58, 61, 66
Marshall, John, 181
Medicine, 56, 66, **67**, 211, 259
Medicine man. *See* Priesthood.
Men, duties of, 53-56, 82, 107, 108, 110
Menewa, 137, 138, 174, 175, **175**
Methodists, 150, 163, 166, 236
Miccosukees, 36, 139, 187, 220; reservation of, 238, 250; in Seminole wars, 153-55, 187-90; today, 107, 243, 248, 249, 253, 258, 259, 261, 265, 266, 268
Mississippi River: east of, 18, 35, 39, 125, 130, 145, 166, 171, 173; as waterway, 28, 52, 112, 133, 178, 179, 190; west of, 44, 45, 129, 132, 221, 225
Mississippi, state of, 18, 45, 246. *See also* Chickasaws; Choctaws; Natchez
Mississippian tradition, 28-34, **29, 30,** 37, 54
Mobile, Alabama, 81, 96, 112, 113, 121, 138, 178
Mooney, James, 64, 86, 183, 215
Mormons, 235-36
Mounds: burial, 19, 24, **24,** 26, 27, 28, 29, 102; effigy, 25, **25,** 26; temple, 28, 29, **29,** 32-34, 38
Music. *See* Song
Muskogean language, 22, 35, 36, 40, 41, 43, 44, 52, 122, 255
Myths, 22, 59-60, 64

Natchez, 21, **21,** 31-33, **31, 32,** 36, 41, **70, 76,** 78, 81, 253; customs of, 93, 94, 102, 108, 111; and the French, 123-24
Natchitoches (Indians), 36, 44, 123, 129, 220
Neuse River, 41
Nixon, Richard M., 248, 263, 264
North Carolina, 18, 93, 107, 119, 140-42, 249. *See also* Carolinas; Cherokees; Lumbees; Tuscaroras

Office of Indian Affairs, 209-11
Ofos, 44, 129, 253
Oglethorpe, James, 118
Ohio River, 18, 24, 27, 37, 45, 130
Ohio, state of, 25, 26, 28, 125, 131
Oklahoma, 28, 29, 105, 124, 229, 239, 241, 245, 247, 248, 252, 255, 258, 261, 262, 264, 266, 268; Great Seal of, 229, **229.** *See also* Indian Territory
Old Brim, Chief, 127
Opothleyoholo, 174, **197,** 225, 226
Osages, 44, 45, 172, 209
Osceola, 138, 152, 154, 188, 189, **189**
Osceola, Joe Dan, 249, 268, **269**
Ouachitas, 79
Outachepas, 57
Owl, George, 239
Owle, Gwen, 270
Oxendine, Thomas, 260

Paint, body, 92, 99-101, 110, 115
Palmetto, **39,** 51, 52, 80, 188, 220
Pascagoulas, 36, 43, 61, 129
Patterson, Caleb Perry, 42
Peace towns, 39, 94
Pembroke State University, 231-34, **234,** 244
Persimmon, 80, 81, 93
Pierite, Joseph, 243, 253
Pitchlynn, Peter, 162, 167, **169**
Pocahontas, 45
Poskita. *See* Busk

Pottery, 26, **26**, 53, 56, 71, **77**, 78, 82, 116, 224, **224, 231, 231;** fabric-decorated, **30;** freehand design, 29, **29;** negative painted, 54, **54;** stamped, 25, **25,** 54

Powhatans, 36, 38, 45, 61

Presbyterians, 143, 145, 148, 162, 166, 167, 236

Priesthood, 33, 38, 66, 68, 69, 71, 72, 89, 91, 101, 151. *See also* Medicine

Pumpkins, 17, 18, 28, 48, **50,** 75, 77

Punishment, 21, 57, 58, 59, 61, 109, 143, 163, 174, 215

Pushmataha, 45, 60, 135, **138**

Qualla Boundary. *See* Cherokees: Eastern Band of; Mountain

Quakers, 237

Quapaws, 36, 44, 73, 96

Red Sticks. *See* War, Red Stick

Red towns, 39, 40, 94, 95

Removal, 221, 222; routes of, **170.** *See also individual tribes*

Reservations, 22, 64, 218, 220, 229, 238, **239,** 241, 245, 247, 248, 255, 261. *See also* Choctaws, Reservation of

Revolutionary war. *See* War, Revolutionary

Ridges, 214-15

Robeson County Indians. *See* Lumbees

Roman Catholics, 33, 122, 123, 143

Romans, Bernard, 75; art of, **41, 62**

Ross, John, 60, 159-61, 163, 181-83, **196,** 214, 225

Ross, Quatie, 60, 163, 183

Salt, 78, 79

Scheirbeck, Helen Maynor, 239, 260

Scott, Winfield, 178, 183, 215

Seminoles, 36, 43, **47, 139, 151, 153, 187, 189, 193, 198, 206;** chickee of, 52, **52;** Civil War-1950, 220, 238, **238,** 246, 247, 248; in Indian Territory, 152-55, 225-30, **230;** music of, 99, 103-5; origins of, 22, 41, 123, 128, 135, 138, 177, 209; today, 105, 107, **208,** 225, **239,** 243, 244, 249, 258, 259, 261, **262,** 265. *See also* Coacoochee; Indian Territory; War, Red Stick

Sequoyah, 160, 229, **229**

Serpent Mound. *See* Mounds, effigy

Sevier, John, 130

Sewees, 36, 118-20

Shawnees, 34, 36, 41, 43, 45, 121, **134,** 135, 143

Shells, 19, 27, 53, 69, **69**

Sherman, William Tecumseh, 155, 189

Sickey, Ernest, 253, **256**

Siouan: language, 35, 36, 37, 43, 44, 68, 101, 107, 118, 120, 143; people, 78, 221

Slavery: of blacks, 40, 128, 132, 144, 147, 148, 149, 152, 153, 154, 155, 156, 162, 188, 192, 228; of Indians, 42, 43, 97, 120, 121, 122, 123, 124, 155, 223

Snakes, 25, 33, 55, 65, 109, 174

Song, 56, 64, 72, 89, 96-105, 114, 212; black drink, 69; hunting, 65; medicine, 66; music for, 99, 104, 105; mourning, 97

South Carolina, 18, 46, 119, 124, 261. *See also* Carolinas; Catawbas; Charleston; Lumbees

Southeast, maps of, **18, 46, 47, 262**

Spores, Ronald, 16

Stand Watie, 226, **226**

Stickball, 40, 55, 68, 84-91, **85, 89, 90,** 94, 99, 108, **203,** 211, **230,** 261

Stouff, Diana, 268

Sun, 21, **21,** 22, 33, 38, 63, 64, 72, 91, 103, 107, 167

Supernaw, Susan (Ella Ponna), 268, **269**

Swanton, John R., 44, 45, 46, 58, 59, 60, 64, 66, 69, 72, 98, 102, 106, 107, 187, 220, 221, 229

Taensas, 36, 44, 220

Tahlonteskee, 133

Tallapoosas, 57, 137

Tamiami Trail, 23, **239,** 248

Tecumseh, 45, **134,** 135, 136

Temples, 28, 33, 101. *See also* Mounds, temple

Tennessee River, 130, 144, 148, 170, 172

Tennessee, state of, 18, 24, 29, 45, 106, 120, 126, 132, 137, 147, 166. *See also* Cherokees; Chickasaws

Texas, 29, 38, 44, 129, 150, 220, 221, 225, 255

Thomas, Will H., 215-18, **216**

Tiger, Buffalo, 244, 249, **250, 253,** 259, 266

Timucuans, 36, **42,** 43, **49,** 53, 55, **78, 85,** 122

Tobacco, 75; pipes, 20, **21,** 27, 63, **63,** 72, 82, 89, 114, 154, 220, 249

Totem, 59, **59,** 60

Trade, 56, 133, 177, 211, 231; between tribes, 40, 79, 80, 162; with Europeans, 112-17, 119, 128, 142, 172; extent of, 20, 27, 55

Traders, 110, 133, 136, 141, 144, 146, 147, 216

Trail of Tears, 183, **184, 194,** 217, 262

Treaty, 130, 131, 132, 134, 163, 165, 170, 177, 226, 228, 229, 251; of Dancing Rabbit Creek, 166, 167, 210-12; of 1819, 180; of 1823, 258; of 1826 (Menewa's), 175, 176; of 1828, 180; of 1832, 258; of 1856, 190; of Fort Jackson, 180; of Indian Springs, 173-75; of New Echota, 182, 212-14, 217; of Pontotoc, 171

Tribal lands, desire for, 239-40

Troup, George M., 173-75

Tsali, 213-15

Tunican language, 36, 44

Tunicas, 36, 56, 57, 79, 81, 129, 220, 221, 243, 253

Tuscaroras, 20, 22, 36, 41, 42, 45, 82, 119, 221

Ucheans. *See* Yuchis

United Southeastern Tribes, 249-53, **250**

Vann House, 182, **183**

Vann, Joseph, 182

Virginia, 39, 45, 53, 61, 80, 93, 112, 116, 126, 140, 142

War, 38, 42, 56, 60, 116, 132, 252; between Indian nations, 41, 45, 47, 148; ceremonies of, 62, 68, 69, 96, 99-101; Civil, 150, 155-58, 171, 183, 189, 191, 215, 217, 221-31, 235; French and Indian, 125; Little Brother of, 91; method of, 72, 74, **74;** of 1812, 130, 222; Red Stick, 135-39, **137,** 148, 159, 174, 187, 217; Revolutionary, 130-31, 134, 144-45, 222; Seminole, 138-39, 152-55, 187-90, 215; towns of, 39, 94; weapons of, 28, **31,** 55, 112, 115, 116, **116,** 127, 142; Yamasee, 43, 121

Ward, Nancy, 130, 143-44

Washington, George, 134, 146, 147

Weatherford, William, 136, 138

White, John, art of, **50, 55, 77, 97**

White towns, 39, 40, 72, 94, 95

Wild Cat. *See* Coacoochee

Wiltnoy, John Julius, 265-66, **267**

Wolf, Key, 253

Wolfe, Mrs. Eva, **200**

Women: as barbers, 53; as bone pickers, 62; as brewers of black drink, 68, **69;** duties of, 53, 54, 82, 108, 111, **212;** as leaders, 39, 46-47, 143-44, 147

Yamasees, 36, 43, 121

Yonagusta, 181, 215-20

York, Emmett, 39, 241, 242, 249, **250,** 251, 253

Yuchis, 21, 22, 36, 106, 122, **131**